BIOTECHNOLOGY, AGRO-ECOLOGY AND ENVIRONMENT

ENV BOOKS SERIES

BIOTECHNOLOGY, AGRO-ECOLOGY AND ENVIRONMENT

Editors

Dr. Avnish Chauhan
Associate Professor
Department of Applied Sciences
Phonics Group of Institutions
Roorkee (Uttarakhand) (India)

Dr. Pawan Kumar 'Bharti'
Vice President (Executive)
Society for Environment, Health, Awareness of Nutrition & Toxicology (SEHAT)
1775, Sohan Ganj, Near Clock Tower, Delhi-7, (India)

Associate Editor

Dr. Anubhuti Sharma
Sr. Scientist
Plant Biochemistry Lab
VPKAS (ICAR), Almora (UK), (India)

DPH

DISCOVERY PUBLISHING HOUSE PVT. LTD.
NEW DELHI-110 002

Published by:
Tilak Wasan
DISCOVERY PUBLISHING HOUSE PVT. LTD.
4383/4B, Ansari Road, Darya Ganj
New Delhi-110 002 (India)
Phone : +91-11-23279245, 43596064-65
Fax : +91-11-23253475
E-mail : discoverypublishinghouse@gmail.com
sales@discoverypublishinggroup.com
web : www.discoverypublishinggroup.com

***First Edition:* 2015**

ISBN: 978-93-5056-757-9

Biotechnology, Agro-ecology and Environment

Printed at:
Infinity Imaging Systems
Delhi

ENV Books Series, India

Calls lengthy and error free chapters for further volumes of books on various environmental issues. (Send your manuscripts to envbooks@gmail.com)

Founding Editor **(*Editor-in-Chief*)**

Dr. Pawan Kumar 'Bharti'

Society for Environment, Health, Awareness of Nutrition & Toxicology (SEHAT-India)
1775, Sohanganj, Near Clock Tower, Delhi-7, India
E-mail:*gurupawanbharti@rediffmail.com*

Other Titles by Editor-in-Chief:

1. **Advances in Biotechnology and Ecological Sciences (2013)**
   Bharti, P.K., Chauhan, A. and Ray, J. (eds.)
   (ISBN: 978-93-5056-358-8).
2. **Advances in Agriculture and Ecology (2013)**
   Bharti, P.K.; Chauhan, A. and Ezeaku Peter Ikemefuna (eds.)
   (ISBN: 978-93-5056-362-5).
3. **Agriculture and Environmental Biotechnology (2014)**
   Bharti, P.K. and Chauhan, A. (eds.)
   (ISBN: 978-93-5056-479-0).
4. **Agriculture Ecology and Environment (2014)**
   Bharti, P.K. and Olubukola O. Babalola (eds.)
   (ISBN: 978-93-5056-480-6).
5. **Agro-forestry and Climate Change (2014)**
   Bharti, Pawan K. and Singh, Narayan (eds.)
   (ISBN: 978-93-5056-514-8).
6. **Aquaculture and Fisheries Environment (2014)**
   Gupta, S.K. and Pawan K. Bharti (eds.)
   (ISBN: 978-93-5056-408-0).
7. **Aquatic Biodiversity and Pollution (2013)**
   Bharti, P.K.; Chauhan, A. and Kaoud, H.A.H. (eds.)
   (ISBN: 978-93-5056-359-5).

8. **Aquatic Ecology and Biotechnology (2014)**
Bharti, P.K. and Zaki, M.S.A. (eds.)
(ISBN: 978-93-5056-451-6).
9. **Aquatic Environment and Toxicology (2013)**
Bharti, Pawan K. (ed.)
(ISBN: 978-93-5056-236-9).
10. **Biodiversity, Biotechnology and Environmental Conservation (2015)**
Bharti, P.K. and Bhandari, G. (eds.)
(ISBN: 978-93-5056-750-0).
11. **Biodiversity of Aquatic Ecosystem: *Significance, Threat and Conservation* (2013)**
Bharti, P.K. and Kaoud, H.A.H. (eds.)
(ISBN: 978-93-5056-297-0).
12. **Clean Technologies and Environmental Protection (2015)**
Chauhan, A.; Sharma, S. and Bharti, P.K. (eds.)
(ISBN: 978-93-5056-731-9).
13. **Climate Change and Agriculture (2012)**
Bharti, P.K. and Chauhan, Avnish (eds.)
(ISBN: 978-93-5056-148-5).
14. **Climate Change and Biodiversity (2013)**
Bharti, P.K. and Chauhan, Avnish (eds.)
(ISBN: 978-93-5056-360-1).
15. **Conservation and Cultivation of Medicinal Plants (2015)**
Bharti, P.K. and Singh Narayan (eds.)
(ISBN: 978-93-5056-740-1).
16. **Eco-toxicology and Eco-technology (2013)**
Bharti, P.K. and Zaki, M. (eds.)
(ISBN: 978-93-5056-313-7).
17. **Environmental Biotechnology and Application (2013)**
Bharti, P.K. and Chauhan, Avnish (eds.)
(ISBN: 978-93-5056-262-8).
18. **Environmental Conservation and Biotechnology (2014)**
Chauhan, A. and P.K. Bharti (eds.)
(ISBN: 978-93-5056-512-4).
19. **Environmental Health and Problems (2013)**
Bharti, P.K. and Gajananda, Kh. (eds.)
(ISBN: 978-93-5056-263-5).
20. **Environmental Pollution and Biodiversity (2012)**
Bharti, P.K.; Chauhan, Avnish and Kumar, P. (eds.)
(ISBN: 978-93-5056-149-2).

21. **Fisheries and Toxicology (2014)**
Zaki, M.S.A.; Bharti, P.K. and Chauhan, A. (eds.)
(ISBN: 978-93-5056-452-3).

22. **Fish Habitat and Aquaculture (2015)**
Bharti, P.K.; Gupta Kr. Sanjay (eds.)
(ISBN: 978-93-5056-744-9).

23. **Freshwater Ecosystem and Xenobiotics (2013)**
Bharti, P.K.; Zaki, M. and Chauhan, A. (eds.)
(ISBN: 978-93-5056-299-4).

24. **Limnology and Aquatic Science (2015)**
Sharma, S. and Bharti, P.K. (eds.)
(ISBN: 978-93-5056-735-7).

25. **Medicinal Plants: *Distribution, Utilization and Significance* (2015)**
Sharma, P.; Bharti, P.K. and Narayan Singh (eds.)
(ISBN: 978-93-5056-734-0).

26. **Microbial Applications and Environment (2014)**
Bharti, Pawan K. (ed.)
(ISBN: 978-93-5056-515-5).

27. **Microbial Ecology and Habitat (2014)**
Bharti, Pawan K. (ed.)
(ISBN: 978-93-5056-514-8).

28. **Natural Ecosystem and Climate Change (2015)**
Bharti, P.K., and Kh. Gajananda (ed.)
(ISBN: 978-93-5056-745-6).

29. **Prakriti me Aushadhi (*in Hindi*) (2012)**
Singh, J.R.; Bharti, P.K. and Bharti, B.
(ISBN: 978-93-5056-200-0).

30. **Seed Technology, Plant Growth and Cropping System (2015)**
Tyagi, P.K. and Bharti, P.K. (eds.)
(ISBN: 978-93-5056-738-8).

31. **Soil Contamination and Conservation (2015)**
Ezeaku, P.I. and Bharti, P.K. (eds.)
(ISBN: 978-93-5056-737-1).

32. **Soil Quality and Contamination (2013)**
Bharti, P.K. and Chauhan, Avnish (eds.)
(ISBN: 978-93-5056-361-8).

33. **Waste Disposal and Management (2015)**
Bharti, P.K.; Tabassum, B. and Bajaj, P. (eds.)
(ISBN: 978-93-5056-729-6).

34. **Water Resources and Agriculture (2014)**
Bharti, P.K. and Ezeaku Peter Ikemefuna (eds.)
(ISBN: 978-93-5056-481-3).

Preface

Biotechnology is the use of living systems and organisms to develop or make useful products, or any technological application that uses biological systems, living organisms or derivatives thereof, to make or modify products or processes for specific use (UNCBD). Depending on the tools and applications, it often overlaps with the related fields of bioengineering and biomedical engineering. For thousands of years, humankind has used biotechnology in agriculture, food production, and medicine.

The pollution from petroleum, xenobiotics, organic compounds, heavy metals and other contaminants is a growing environmental concern that harms both terrestrial and aquatic ecosystems. Bioremediation as a cleanup method and through the exploitation of the activities of microorganisms would degrade or attenuate such contaminants. Phytoremediation as one of the developed and implemented technologies of bioremediation is another option for cleaning up environmental pollution, which focuses on the use of living green plants for the removal of contaminants and metals from contaminated ecosystems, although some phytoremediation applications are believed to work through stimulation of rhizosphere bacteria by the growing plant root.

Environmental biotechnology is not an easy subject to cover, but therefore so much the more important that it should be. For years, the environmental technologies had a little too much tail wind because of the overwhelming sympathy for green solutions. This often led to misuse and discredit of the technologies among some end users. In those years, too many studies underestimated the complexity of the task.

This book updates the subject matter, illustrations and problems to incorporate new concepts and issues related to biotechnology, agriculture, ecology and environmental conservation.

Thanks are due to contributors from different institutions and publisher for their interest in this book. We hope this book will provide a multi-disciplinary forum to explore emerging areas in the field of biotechnology, agriculture, ecology and environmental conservation.

There is no doubt that this book will be one of inspiration for all professionals in the field. It is a very good framework to understand the complex nature of processes and technology, and as such it will be useful for researchers, practitioners and other parties who need a working knowledge of this fascinating subject.

–Editors

(envbooks@gmail.com)

Contents

Pages: 1-34

BIOTECHNOLOGY, AGRO-ECOLOGY AND ENVIRONMENT
Edited by: Dr. Avnish Chauhan; Dr. Pawan Kumar 'Bharti'
ISBN: 978-93-5056-757-9
Edition: 2015
Published by: Discovery Publishing House Pvt. Ltd., New Delhi (India)

1

Microbial Biotechnology
Role in Sustainable Agriculture and Environmental Management

Wafaa M. Haggag[1]; Hoballa Essam[2] and Lashin, S.[1]

ABSTRACT

Biotechnology is the rapidly growing segment in biological sciences. It has diversified applications in sustainable agriculture. Of all the life forms occurring in nature within the biodiversity there should be no doubt to realise that microorganisms are the most powerful creatures in existence. Microorganisms are ubiquitous in nature and make up the biodiversity on earth. Micro-organisms have several uses in the environment, and new biotechnology can potentially be used to improve these micro-organisms. They perform several important processes in cycling of nutrients, degradation of various compounds globally. The chapter deals with microorganisms in biotechnology and their diversified applications in agriculture as biofertilizers, bio-pesticides, bio-herbicides, bioinsecticides, fungal based bioinsecticides, viral based bioinsecticides, Utilization and Recycling of Energy and control of pollution and treatment of toxic wastes. One application is the use of soil microbes as bioinoculants for supplying nutrients and/or stimulating plant growth. Some rhizospheric microbes are known to synthesize plant growth-promoters, siderophores and antibiotics,

[1] Plant Pathology Department, National Research Centre, Dokki, Egypt.
[2] Agriculture Microbiology Department, National Research Centre, Dokki, Egypt.

as well as aiding phosphorous uptake. Further, precise descriptions have been made on Microbiology Ecology Biotechnology and Sustainable . The microbial activities that help us to design an excellent new strategy of life leading to sustainable future are presented.

Key words: Biotechnology, Microorganisms; Sustainable Agriculture; Food security; Environmental Management.

INTRODUCTION

The world's population is estimated to be double by the end of 2033. Food demand in Asia is expected to exceed the need by the end of 2010. This poses a great challenge to agricultural systems. Traditional farming equipment and practices are reaching their limits of effectiveness in increasing agricultural productivity. As countries develop, people are also demanding more and better food. Biotechnology offers an additional method to improve the sustainability of existing system to produce more and better quality of our agricultural products. The potential benefits of plant biotechnology are numerous and include providing resistance to crop pests, increasing crop yield and reducing chemical pesticide usage. The processing of food and food ingredients using biotechnology provides a wide variety of fermented foods and food ingredients that are extensively used (Haggag, Wafaa and Essam Hoballa, 2014). Agricultural technologies that ensured a 'green revolution' in the middle of 20th century, causing now high ecological cost and contributing global pollution, unfavourable climate change and loss of biodiversity (Vance, 1998). The broad application of microbes in sustainable agriculture is due to the genetic dependency of plants on the beneficial functions provided by symbiotic cohabitants (Noble and Ruaysoongnern, 2010). Therefore, microbial biotechnology and its applications in sustainable development of agriculture and environmental health are getting better attention (Haggag, Wafaa and Essam Hoballa, 2014). The purpose of the review is to further prioritize the importance in the scientific community as well as stakeholders.

WHAT IS BIOTECHNOLOGY?

Biotechnology is the branch of biological science, which deals with the manipulation through genetic engineering of living organisms or their components to produce useful products for various applications in biological sciences (Haggag, Wafaa, 2007). Contrary to its name, biotechnology is not a single technology. Rather it is a group of technologies that share two (common) characteristics — working with living cells and their molecules and having a wide range of practice uses that can improve our lives. Biotechnology can be broadly defined as "using organisms or their products for commercial purposes." As such, (traditional) biotechnology has been practices since it beginning of records history (Speeding , 1993, Haggag, Wafaa, 2002b, Haggag, et al., 2005).

WHAT IS AGRICULTURAL BIOTECHNOLOGY ?

Biotechnology can be applied to all classes of organism - from viruses and bacteria to plants and animals - and it is becoming a major feature of modern medicine, agriculture and industry. Modern agricultural biotechnology includes a range of tools that scientists employ to understand and manipulate the genetic make-up of organisms for use in the production or processing of agricultural products (Bonny, 1989). Some applications of biotechnology, such as fermentation and brewing, have been used for millennia. Other applications are newer but also well established. For example, micro-organisms have been used for decades as living factories for the production of life-saving antibiotics including penicillin, from the fungus *Penicillium*, and streptomycin from the bacterium *Streptomyces*. Modern detergents rely on enzymes produced via biotechnology, hard cheese production largely relies on rennet produced by biotech yeast and human insulin for diabetics is now produced using biotechnology (Haggag, Wafaa et al., 2011, 2013, 2014a, b, c).

MICROBES AND BIOTECHNOLOGY

Microbes/micro-organisms are mostly micropsic small creatures are placed in different groups such bacteria, fungi, protozoa, micro-algae and viruses. These organisms live in soil, water, food, animal intestines and other different environments. Various microbial habitats reflect an enormous diversity of biochemical and metabolic traits that have arisen by genetic variation and natural selection in microbial populations.Men used some of microbial diversity in the production of fermented foods such as bread, yogurt, and cheese. Some soil microbes release nitrogen that plants need for growth and emit gases that maintain the critical composition of the Earth's atmosphere. Other microbes challenge the food supply by causing yield-reducing diseases in food-producing plants and animals. In our bodies, different microbes help to digest food, ward off invasive organisms, and engage in skirmishes and pitched battles with the human immune system in the give-and-take of the natural disease process.Microbial biotechnology, enabled by genome studies, will lead to breakthroughs such as improved vaccines and better disease-diagnostic tools, improved microbial agents for biological control of plant and animal pests, modifications of plant and animal pathogens for reduced virulence, development of new industrial catalysts and fermentation organisms, and development of new microbial agents for bioremediation of soil and water contaminated by agricultural runoff. Microbial biotechnology is an important area that promotes for advances in food safety, food security, value-added products, human nutrition and functional foods, plant and animal protection, and overall fundamental research in the agricultural sciences.

MICROBIAL BIOTECHNOLOGY AND ITS APPLICATIONS IN AGRICULTURE

Conceptual design is important in developing new technologies for utilizing beneficial and effective microorganisms for a more sustainable agriculture and environment. The basis of a conceptual design is imply to first conceive an ideal or model and then to devise a strategy and method for achieving the reality. However it is necessary to carefully coordinate the materials, the environment, and the technologies constituting the method. Moreover one should adopt a philosophical attitude in applying microbial technologies to agricultural production and conservation systems.There are many opinions on what an ideal agricultural system is. Many would agree that such an idealized system should produce food on a long-term sustainable basis. Many would also insist that it should maintain and improve human health, be economically and spiritually beneficial to both producers and consumers, actively preserve and protect the environment, be self-contained and regenerative, and produce enough food for an increasing world population (Higa, 1991).

Why use microorganisms in agriculture?

It is ironic that agriculture developed this past century without a focus on microbe management, despite the fact that rhizosphere microorganisms and their activities are essential for soil health (Haggag Wafaa, 2010). They are responsible for basic functions such as decomposition of organic materials and nitrogen (N) fixation and form the basis of above- and belowground food webs (Morrisey *et al*. 2004). In addition, many rhizosphere bacteria and fungi are linked to plants in symbiotic relationships ranging from mutualistic to parasitic. Their interactions with plants, the soil environment, and each other determine what will grow, and how well. Ostensibly, crop rotations were developed to discourage deleterious plant/microbe interactions, namely crop-specific pathogens, but there has been little attempt to manage beneficial microbes. *Rhizobium* spp, a well known and extensively researched symbiotic group of N-fixing bacteria, are an obvious exception.Microbe management, either through selection and inoculation of specific microbial strains or by simply promoting naturally existing microbes, holds great promise for sustainable agriculture. First, microbes are multifunctional, with effects ranging from pathogen protection to improved nutrient uptake. Secondly, microbes can reproduce and may be self-sustaining. Finally, microbe management may promote resilient systems. Current agricultural systems are impoverished in terms of biodiversity, and genetic and functional diversity (Tilman 1999). Such systems are vulnerable to disturbance and changes in the environment (Fig. 1.1).

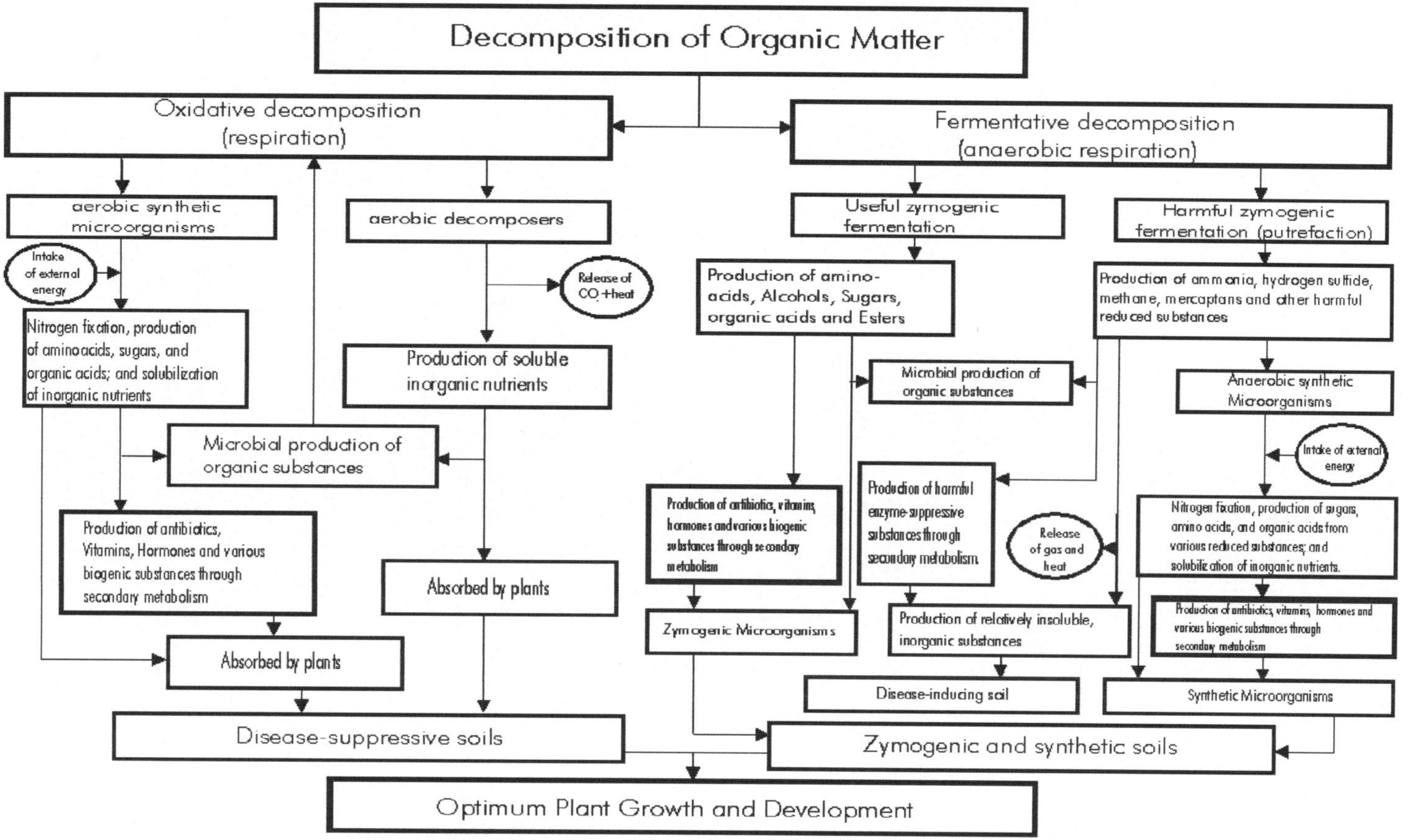

Fig. 1.1: Flow Chart of Organic Matter Transformations by Soil Microorganisms and the Development of Soils that may be disease-including, Zymogenic or Synthetic (Adapted from Prof. Dr. Teruo Higa)

Importance of Soil Microorganisms:

- Involved in nutrient transformation process
- Decomposition of resistant components of plant and animal tissue
- Role in microbial antagonism
- Participate in humus formation
- Predator to nematodes
- Surface blooming reduces erosion losses
- Improves soil structure
- Maintenance of biological equilibrium

Controlling the Soil Microflora for Optimum Crop Production and Protection

The idea of controlling and manipulating the soil microflora through the use of inoculants organic amendments and cultural and management practices to create a more favorable soil microbiological environment for optimum crop production and protection is not new. For almost a century, microbiologists have known that organic wastes and residues, including animal manures, crop residues, green manures, municipal wastes (both raw and composted), contain their own indigenous populations of microorganisms often with broad physiological capabilities.It is also known that when such organic wastes and residues are applied to soils many of these introduced microorganisms can function as biocontrol agents by controlling or suppressing soil-borne plant pathogens through their competitive and antagonistic activities. While this has been the theoretical basis for controlling the soil microflora, in actual practice the results have been unpredictable and inconsistent, and the role of specific microorganisms has not been well-defined.For, many years microbiologists have tried to culture beneficial microorganisms for use as soil inoculants to overcome the harmful effects of phytopathogenic organisms, including bacteria, fungi and nematodes. Such attempts have usually involved single applications of pure cultures of microorganisms which have been largely unsuccessful for several reasons. First, it is necessary to thoroughly understand the individual growth and survival characteristics of each particular beneficial microorganism, including their nutritional and environmental requirements. Second, we must understand their ecological relationships and interactions with other microorganisms, including their ability to coexist in mixed cultures and after application to soils (Higa, 1991; 1994).There are other problems and constraints that have been major obstacles to controlling the microflora of agricultural soils. First and foremost is the large number of types of microorganisms that are present at any one time, their wide range of physiological capabilities, and the dramatic fluctuations in their populations that can result from cultural and management practices applied to a particular farming system. The diversity of the total soil microflora depends on the nature of the soil environment and those factors which affect the growth and activity of each individual organism including temperature, light, aeration, nutrients, organic matter, pH and water.

Chemical-based conventional farming methods are not unlike symptomatic therapy. Examples of this are applying fertilizers when crops show symptoms of nutrient-deficiencies, and applying pesticides whenever crops are attacked by insects and diseases. In efforts to control the soil microflora some scientists feel that the introduction of beneficial microorganisms should follow a symptomatic approach. However, we do not agree. The actual soil conditions that prevail at any point in time may be most unfavorable to the growth and establishment of laboratory-cultured, beneficial microorganisms. To facilitate their establishment, it may require that the farmer make certain changes in his cultural and management practices to induce conditions that will (a) allow the growth and survival of the inoculated microorganisms and (b) suppress the growth and activity of the indigenous plant pathogenic microorganisms (Higa, 1994).

Natural Fermentation

Micro-organisms found in the soil to improve agricultural productivity. Men use naturally occurring organisms to develop biofertilizers and bio-pesticides to assist plant growth and control weeds, pests, and diseases.Micro-organisms that live in the soil actually help plants to absorb more nutrients. Plants and these friendly microbes are involved in "nutrient recycling". The microbes help the plant to "take up" essential energy sources. In return, plants donate their waste by-products for the microbes to use for food. Scientists use these friendly micro-organisms to develop biofertilizers.

Biofertilizers

Phosphate and nitrogen are important for the growth of plants. These compounds exist naturally in the environment but plants have a limited ability to extract them. Phosphate plays an important role in crop stress tolerance, maturity, quality and directly or indirectly, in nitrogen fixation. A fungus, *Penicillium bilaii* helps to unlock phosphate from the soil. It makes an organic acid, which dissolves the phosphate in the soil so that the roots can use it. Biofertilizer made from this organism is applied by either coating seeds with the fungus as inoculation, or putting it directly into the ground. Rhizobium is a bacteria used to make biofertilizers. This bacterium lives on the plant's roots in cell collections called nodules. The nodules are biological factories that can take nitrogen out of the air and convert it into an organic form that the plant can use. This fertilization method has been designed by nature. With a large population of the friendly bacteria on its roots, the legume can use naturally-occurring nitrogen instead of the expensive traditional nitrogen fertilizer.Biofertilizers help plants use all of the food available in the soil and air, thus allowing farmers to reduce the amount of chemical fertilizers they use (Xiang et al., 2012, Fig. 1.2). This helps preserve the environment for the generations to come.*Azotobacter* and *Rhizobium* sp. are nitrogen fixers, *Pseudomonas* spp. are popular for phosphate solubilization and siderophore production but various *Bacillus* sp. are also phosphate solubilizers. *Pseudomonas* and *Bacillus* sp. not only produce auxins, vitamins and growth factors that enhance plant growth but also degrade proteins into amino acids (Haggag, Wafaa and Saber 2000 and Haggag Wafaa 2010).

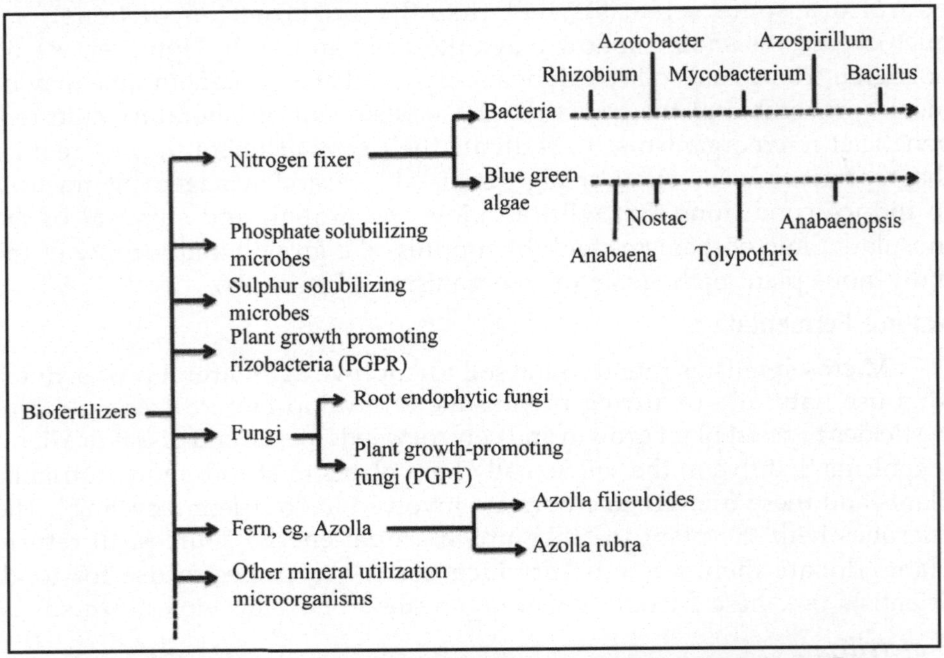

Fig. 1.2: Microorganisms Used for Exploitation for Biofertilizers Up to Date

Siderophores

The term siderophores is derived from Greek word which means iron carriers. These are ferric ion specific chelating agents synthesized by bacteria, actinomycetes, fungi and certain algae growing in low iron stress. Siderophores are iron binding proteins with molecular weight ranging from 400-1500 Da. These compounds play important role in scavenging iron from the environment (Marques *et al.*, 2010). Most of the aerobic and facultative anaerobic microorganism synthesizes at least one siderophore. Siderophores have also found to be associated with virulence mechanisms in pathogenic microorganism of animals and plants. These compounds have applications in clinical, agricultural and environmental fields. Presently 500 siderophores are reported from different microorganisms (Marques *et al.*, 2010). The important groups of siderophores are:

- Hydroxamate siderophores,
- Catecholate (phenolates) siderophores and
- Carboxylate siderophores

Hydroxamate siderophores possess three secondary hydroxamate groups and each hydroxamate groups provide two oxygen molecules that form a bidentate ligand with iron. These are produced by both bacteria and fungi (Tircso *et al.*, 2013). Catecholate siderophores are produced by certain bacteria. The catecholate group provides two oxygen atoms for chelation with iron so that a hexadentate octahedral complex is formed as in the hydroxamate siderophores (Renshaw *et al.*, 2002). The finest example for catecholate siderophore is enterobactin produced by *Escherichia coli*. Carboxylate siderophores are produced by *Rhizobium* and *Staphylococcus* strains and fungi belonging to mucorales, coordinating iron with carboxyl and hydroxyl groups.

Siderophore Producing Microorganisms

Some important siderophore producing bacteria includes *Escherichia coli, Salmonella, Klebsiella pneumoniae, Vibrio cholerae, Vibrio anguillarum, Aeromonas, Aerobacter aerogens, Enterobacter, Yersinia and Mycobacterium* species. *Ustilago sphaerogina, Saccharomyces cerevisiae, Rhodotorula minuta and Debaromyces species* are siderophore producing fungi (Koulman *et al.*, 2002). Siderophore producing actinomycetes includes *Actinomadura madurae, Nocardia asteroids, and Streptomyces griseus*. *Anabaena flos-aquae* and *Anabaena cylindrica* produce siderophores (Harrington *et al.*, 2012).

Microbes as Biocontrol Agents

Pseudomonas and *Bacillus* spp. produce siderophores and enzymes like chitinases and proteinases that in turn help in growth inhibition of various plant pathogenic fungi. The entomopathogenic bacteria, fungi, and viruses are used as bioinsecticides ex: *Bacillus thuringiensis, Beauveria bassiana*, etc. Potentials of microbes are required to be explored to decrease the use of chemical fertilizers and pesticides in agriculture whose adverse effects are well known (Prestes *et al.*, 2012)

Bio-pesticides

Microorganisms found in the soil are all not so friendly to plants. These pathogens can cause disease or damage the plant. As scientists developed biological "tools," which use these disease-causing microbes to control weeds and pests naturally.Pathogenic microorganisms with ability to invade and kill the insect pests were commonly termed as entomopathogens (Zhuang *et al.*, 2011). *Metarrhizium anisopliae*, a muscordine fungus was first documented as pathogenic microorganism that was mass produced and applied as microbial pesticide for crops like sugar beets and grains. In 1940 White and

Dutky (Ishiwata, 1901) introduced bacterium *Bacillus popilliae* spores to control Japanese bettle. *Bacillus thuringiensis* was introduced in 1960-63 as effective bacterial insecticide and today nearly 40 types of products are popular as insecticide. Studies of Balch and Bird (1944) and Thompson and Steinhaus (Zayed, 2012) (1950) succeeded in use of viruses against the insect pests. *Bacillus thuringiensis*: It was detected in dying larva of *Bombyx mori* by Ishiwata in 1901 and Berliner in 1911 from Germany in larva of *Ephestia kuehniella* (Ishiwata, 1901) In 1938 it was first used as microbial insecticide against Lepidopterous larvae with name 'sporeine' and this resulted in the development of several pesticide companies all over the world. It is pathogenic in Lepidopteran larvae and 4 insect orders. Bacterium is transmitted orally, after sporulation bacteria form a toxic crystal and ingestion of these spores causes cessation of feeding. The crystal activity depends on the pH of larval gut (pH 9-10.5) and the action of proteolytic enzymes. The crystal is a protoxin activated by enzymatic hydrolysis. The crystal protein is ecologically safe and successfully tested for controlling insects affecting cotton, cabbage, maize, sunflower, sunflower and pigeon pea (Ishiwata, 1901) It is formulated under trade names such as - Thuricide (Sandoz AG), Bakthane, Dipel (Abbott labs), Biotrol, Karab, Agritol, Bactospeine (Rhone-Poulene) in dust, liquid concentrate, spray concentrate, granules and baits formulations. *Bacillus popilliae*causes milky disease in Japanese beetle *Popillio japonica*. After ingestion, spores germinate and penetrate the alimentary canal and blood appears milky due to spores and then the larva dies. This bacterium is produced commercially by feeding or injecting in the host that multiplies in the body of host. Then it is recovered by grinding the host with talc. This dust is expected to contain 100 million spores/g. when it is ingested by host; the mortality is due to septicemia (Zhuang *et al.*, 2011).

Virus-based Bioinsecticides

Baculoviruses are the common choice among the 1600 viruses to control insect species. The selected viruses were targeted against sawflies in forestry during 1950. Baculoviruses affect insect pests like corn borers, potato beetles, flea beetles and aphids. One particular strain is being used as a control agent for bertha army worms, which attack canola, flax, and vegetable crops. Traditional insecticides do not affect the worm until after it has reached this stage and by then much of the damage has been done. Nuclear polyhedrosis viruses (NPV): Virus is rod in shape and outer envelope with protein crystals called polyhedra. NPV is transmitted by oral ingestion of polyhedra. Ingested polyhedra dissolve, releasing virus rods into the lumen of the insect host midgut, then larval skin darkens, hemolymph becomes turbid and prior to death, infected larva usually climbs to the highest point available and then dies. The disease of *Heliothis armigera* is visible after 2-3 days of ingestion of virus. The cuticle of infected larva in the first instar become milky white in appearance but the later infected instars turn pinkish color. The diseased larva discharges a yellowish grey fluid from their mouth. The death occurs in 3-7 days; the integument became fragile and burst liberating the liquefied body contents. Granulosis viruses (GV): GV particles are surrounded by an envelope similar to NPV envelope. The virion is rod shaped with DNA as genetic material with inclusion body i.e. capsule or granule hence the virus is named Granulosis virus. This virus is active against rice leaf roller *Cnaphalocrocis medinalis*, castor semi looper *Achaea janata*, hairy cater pillar *Pericallia ricini*, cut worm *Agrotis ipsilon*, internode borer *Chilo* spp. and sugarcane shoot borer *C. infuscatellus*. The fat body of Lepidopteran larvae is the primary site of infection. GV are transmitted orally and via the egg. GV infections involving the epidermis cause liquefaction of larvae similar to NPV infections (Berliner, 1911)

Bio-fungicides

Control of fungal pathogens is based on the use of agronomic practices and pesticides, but widespread application of chemicals inundates the agroecosystems with toxic compounds that affect the balance of the natural food chain. Most sustainable and environmentally acceptable control may be achieved using BCAs (Haggag, Wafaa 2002 and Haggag Wafaa, 2010). The commercial development of biofungicides received a significant boost in recent years, primarily because of impressive progress in the isolation and characterization of novel strains of microorganisms that can fulfill the mam characteristics of a biofungicide, which are the consistent suppression of pathogens under field conditions, and easy mass production in standard fermentation facilities. Numerous studies have described the isolation of micro-organisms and demonstrated their potential to antagonize (Table 1.1). Considering that environmental conditions are important, the right selection of BCAs, is equally important since the exact identification of strains to the species level is the first step in utilizing the full potential of BCA in specific applications . In recent years, the induction of the plant defense response by fungi and bacteria that normally colonize living plants without causing visual damage, had received ample attention. Microbial elicitors derived from some fungal endophytes promote biomass and induce terpenoid (artemisinin) biosynthesis and production in plant suspension cells. Many groups of fungi are well known as biocontrol agents. For example, *Trichoderma viride* and *T. harzianum* could produce amylolytic, pectinolytic, proteolytic and cellulolytic enzymes for growth inhibition of *A. flavus* and *Fusarium moniliforme* (Haggag, Wafaa *et al.* 2006 and 2014). Themost important antimicrobial components of all protective mechanismsare proteinaceous compounds. These include enzymessuch asβ 1, 3 glucanases, protease and chitinases, inhibitors of proteases and á amylases and also other proteinsand peptides which have antimicrobial, ant-fungal activities (Valueva and Mosolov, 2004).

Table 1.1: Sample Biofungicides Available for use in California Landscapes

Active Ingredient	Sample Trade Name	Sample Diseases	Types of Plants on Labels	Application Notes
Bacillus subtilis	Serenade, Rhapsody	Powdery mildew, bacterial spot and many foliar fungal and bacterial pathogens	Annual, perennial and woody plants	Foliar application
Streptomyces lydicus	Actinovate Actono-Iron	Turf diseases including Pychium, Rhizoctonia, Fusarium, powdery mildew, grey mold	Turf primarily, although used on vegetables in commercial agriculture	Soil drench or foliar treatment
Trichoderma harzianum	Rootshield Home and Garden Fungicide	Many soil pathogens including Pychium, Rhizoctonia and Fusarium	Many woody or herbaceous plants	Application on seeds or roots prior to planting. Mostly used in nurseries.
Pseudomonas fluorescent A506	BlightBan A506	Fireblight	Apple, pear	Foliar. Used primarily in commercial agriculture. A bactericide.

Chitinolytic showed to be potential agents for the biological control of plant diseases caused by various phyto-pathogenic fungi, (Haggag, Wafaa, 2002a, b). The antifungal potential of extracellular metabolites of *Streptomyces* strains against some fungi was previously reported from different locations of the world. The antagonistic activity of *Streptomyces* to fungal pathogens is usually related to the production of extracellular hydrolytic enzymes (HaggagWafaa *et al.*, 2011 and 2014c). Several *Bacillus* and related species had been tested as potential biological control agents as they produce a range of antibiotics peptide. *Paenibacillus polymyxa* (formerly *Bacillus polymyxa*) is a common bacterium that belongs to the group of plant growth promoting rhizobacteria (PGPR). In the frame of former FORMAS financed project we studied the bacterial antagonism against root rot and crown rot (*Aspergillus niger*) and highlighted importance of biofilms in biocontrol initiation Haggag Wafaa and Timmusk, 2007 Biofilms consist of cells and extracellular matrix which provide an almost infinite range of macromolecules. The molecules usually contribute directly to the properties of biofilms. They interact with polysaccharides and other macromolecules and cells as well with ions and low mol mass solutes providing a multitude of microenvironment within the biofilm. Currently many of these effects could only be speculated. The macromolecules synthesized by microbial cells vary greatly in their composition and hence in their biofilm influencing chemical and physical properties. At the same time, this isolatescapable of suppressing plant diseases andis known to produce an antifungal peptide, the antibiotic polymyxin and oligo and polysaccharide (Haggag, Wafaa and Salme Timmusk, 2007). Recently, an antagonistic yeast strain of *Rhodotorula glutinis* had been reported as an effective biocontrol agent against post-harvest decay of fruits and vegetables (Malisorn and Suntornsuk, 2008). We observed a significant reduction of grey mould of greenhouse sweet pepper grey mould by yeast strain of *Rhodotorula glutinis* and its autoploidy (in vivo) and (in vivo) (Haggag, Wafaa *et al.*, 2005) and against aflatoxin B_1- intoxication in mice (Ghaly *et al.*, 2010).In this respect the role that these secondary metabolites, bio-polyermar could play an efficient role in plant protection (Haggag, *et al.*, 2005). The use of yeast as antagonists against Mycotoxin fungi is a promising approach to manage aflatoxin contamination via biological control.

PGPR may protect plants against pathogens by direct antagonistic interactions between the biocontrol agent and the pathogen, as well as by induction of host resistance(Podile and K Kishore 2007). In recent years, the role of siderophore-producing PGPR in biocontrol of soil-borne plant pathogens has created great interest. Microbiologists have developed techniques for introduction of siderophore producing. PGPR in soil system through seed, soil or root system. PGPR that indirectly enhance plant growth via suppression of phytopathogens do so by a variety of mechanisms (Haggag Wafaa 2007). These include:

- The ability to produce siderophores (as discussed above) that chelate iron, making it unavailable to pathogens.
- The capacity to synthesize anti-fungal metabolites such as antibiotics, fungal cell wall-lysing enzymes, or hydrogen cyanide, which suppress the growth of fungal pathogens.
- The ability to successfully compete with pathogens for nutrients or specific niches on the root; and the ability to induce systemic resistance.

Among the various PGPRs identified, *Pseudomonas fluorescens* is one of themost extensively studied rhizobacteria, because of itsantagonistic action against several plant pathogens (Table 1.1) (Podile and Kishore 2007).

Bio-herbicides

Weeds are the problem for farmers. They not only compete with crops for water, nutrients, sunlight, and space but also harbor insect and disease pests; clog irrigation and drainage systems; undermine crop quality; and deposit weed seeds into crop harvests.Bio-herbicides are another way of controlling weeds without environmental hazards posed by synthetic herbicides. The microbes possess invasive genes that can attack the defence genes of the weeds, thereby killing it.The benefit of using bioherbicides is that it can survive in the environment long enough for the next growing season where there will be more weeds to infect. It is cheaper than synthetic pesticides thus could essentially reduce farming expenses if managed properly. Further, it is not harmful to the environment compared to conventional herbicides and will not affect non-target organisms.

Efficient Utilization and Recycling of Energy

Agricultural production begins with the process of photosynthesis by green plants which requires solar energy, water, and carbon dioxide. It occurs through the plants ability to utilize solar energy in "fixing" atmospheric carbon into carbohydrates. The energy obtained is used for further biosynthesis in the plant, including essential amino acids and proteins. Past studies have shown that photosynthetic efficiency of the chloroplasts of host crop plants cannot be increased much further; this means that their biomass production has reached a maximum level. Therefore, the best opportunity for increasing biomass production is to somehow utilize the visible light, which chloroplasts cannot presently use, and the infrared radiation; together, these comprise about 80% of the total solar energy. Also, we must explore ways of recycling organic energy contained in plant and animal residues through direct utilization of organic molecules by plants (Higa and Wididana, 1991).Thus, it is difficult to exceed the existing limits of crop production unless the efficiency of utilizing solar energy is increased, and the energy contained in existing organic molecules (amino acids, peptides and carbohydrates) is utilized either directly or indirectly by the plant. This approach could help to solve the problems of environmental pollution and degradation caused by the misuse and excessive application of chemical fertilizers and pesticides to soils. Therefore, new technologies that can enhance the economic-viability of farming systems with little or no use of chemical fertilizers and pesticides are urgently needed and should be a high priority of agricultural research both now and in the immediate future (National Academy of Sciences, 1989; 1993).

Due to increased human population, civilization as well as industrial growth, there is increased demand for energy sources because natural non-renewable sources such as petroleum, oil, natural gas, coal are depleting day by day, and a day may come when future generation will have to face dangerous situation. To avoid these consequences, alternative renewable energy sources such as microorganisms can help in production of biofuels, ex: ethanol, hydrogen, and methane.

MICROBIOLOGY ECOLOGY BIOTECHNOLOGY AND SUSTAINABLE AGRICULTURE

Now increasing attention has been paid to the development of sustainable agriculture in which the high productivities of plants and animals are ensured using their natural adaptive potentials, with a minimal disturbance of the environment (Haggag, Wafaa, 2002 a and Noble & Ruaysoongnern, 2010). It is our view that the most promising strategy to reach this goal is to substitute hazardous agrochemicals (mineral fertilizers, pesticides) with environment-friendly preparations of symbiotic microbes, which could improve the nutrition of crops and livestock, as well as their protection from biotic (pathogens, pests) and abiotic (including pollution and climatic change) stresses (Yang et al., 2009). The broad application of microbes in sustainable agriculture is due to the genetic dependency of plants on the beneficial functions provided by symbiotic cohabitants (Noble & Ruaysoongnern, 2010). The agronomic potential of plant–microbial symbioses proceeds from the analysis of their ecological impacts, which have been best studied for N_2 fixing (Franche et al., 2009). This analysis has been based on 'applied co-evolutionary research' (Arnold et al., 2010), addressing the ecological and molecular mechanisms for mutual adaptation and parallel speciation of plant and microbial partners. For plant–fungal interactions, it has been demonstrated that the host genotype represents the leading factor in the biogeographic distribution of mycobionts and for their evolution within the mutualist"!antagonist and specialist"!generalist continua (Peay et al., 2010).The application of nutritional symbionts could be based on plant mixotrophy, e.g. on a simultaneous symbiotrophic and combined N nutrition. This is why the maximal productivity of the majority of crops is reached using an optimal (species- and genotype-specific) combination of both nutritional types because of which a high sustainability of legume production may be achieved. Moreover, the energy costs for N_2 fixation and for assimilation of combined

N differ by less than 10% (Andrews et al., 2010). The balance between symbiotrophic and combined N nutrition may be improved by a rapid removal of N-compounds from the actively N_2-fixing symbioses, as has been suggested for tropical forest ecosystems (Hedin et al., 2009). This approach is most promising in legume–rhizobia symbioses where the strong correlations between the ecological efficiency of mutualism and its genotypic specificity are evident (Provorov & Vorobyov, 2010). At present, a wide spectrum of preparations of diverse microbial species may be used to enhance crop production (Andrews et al., 2010). However, different approaches for improving the nutritional and defensive types of microbial mutualists need to be developed. For the nutritional types, an effective colonisation of plants in a host-specific manner is optimal and the impacts of beneficial symbionts are increased in parallel with their host specificity (Provorov & Vorobyov, 2009). The application of microbial symbiotic signals or their derivatives for remodelling plant developmental or defensive functions may represent a promising field for agricultural biotechnology.The prospects for a future development of agricultural microbiology may involve the construction of novel multipartite endo- and ecto-symbiotic communities based on extended genetic and molecular (metagenomic) analyses. The primary approach for such construction is to create composite inoculants, which simulate the natural plant-associated microbial communities. For balancing the host plant metabolism, a combination of N- and P-providing symbionts would appear promising.

Chemical pesticides pose economic problems like destruction of non-target organisms (beneficial insects, natural predators) along with environmental pollution. Another aspect of chemical pesticides is development of insect resistance. Synthetic fertilizers are made as fossil fuel byproduct and increase in fuel prices also show effect on the fertilizers price. Prolonged use of fertilizers results in the loss of soil quality and possibility of ground water contamination. Hence the conservation of agriculture is identified as best alternative to sustain the soil quality (Hiltner, 1904).In 1904, Hiltner (Hiltner, 1904). introduced the term 'rhizosphere' for the area of soil surrounding the plant root that stimulates the bacterial growth. This zone supports the diverse microbial population colonizing the habitat. Root exudates promote the colonization of roots in rhizosphere. 30% of plant photosynthesis products are found to be released through root exudation by passive and active secretion. Passive transport releases low molecular weight compounds and the active transport secretes the high molecular weight compounds. There are physical and chemical benefits in the plant root exudations such as reduced friction, desiccation, improved soil structural stability and attracting the microorganisms. Some bacteria that inhabit the root zone also elicit exudation like *Pseudomonas aeruginosa* which stimulate the root exudation in rye grass by twenty fold. Plant root colonizing bacteria promote the growth directly or indirectly (Hiltner, 1904). These organisms directly promote the growth by nitrogen fixation, solubilization of minerals (phosphorus), production of siderophores to solubilize the iron and produce plant growth regulators. Indirectly they promote antagonism to avoid the invasion of pathogens, parasitism, competition for nutrients and enhance disease resistance.

Several organisms of this category are capable to produce auxins, gibberellins, cytokinins, ethylene and abscisic acid. *Azospirillum*, *Agrobacterium*, *Pseudomonas* and *Erwinia* induce the auxins, cytokinins and gibberellins as well as lateral root development by root colonization of *Azospirillum*. These organisms act as biocontrol agents against the soil borne pathogens by producing antibiotics, siderophores, increase competition of nutrients for pathogen and various types of enzymes. Fluorescent pseudomonads produce phenazine derivatives as antibiotics in root zone that reduces the disease causing organisms in root zone.

Plant Growth Promoting Rhizobacteria (PGPR) are a group of bacteria that enhances plant growth and yield via various plant growth promoting substances as well as biofertilizers. Given the negative environmental impact of artificial fertilizers and their increasing costs, the use of beneficial soil microorganisms such as PGPR for sustainable and safe agriculture has increased globally during the last couple of decades. PGPR as biofertilizers are well recognized as efficient soil microbes for sustainable agriculture and hold great promise in the improvement of agriculture yields (Podile and Kishore 2007 and Haggag Wafaa , 2010).

Beneficial and Effective Microorganisms for a Sustainable Agriculture Towards Agriculture without Chemicals and with Optimum Yields of High Quality Crops

Agriculture in a broad sense, is not an enterprise which leaves everything to nature without intervention. Rather it is a human activity in which the farmer attempts to integrate certain agroecological factors and production inputs for optimum crop and livestock production. Thus, it is reasonable to assume that farmers should be interested in ways and means of controlling beneficial soil microorganisms as an important component of the agricultural environment. Nevertheless, this idea has often been rejected by naturalists and proponents of nature farming and organic agriculture. They argue that beneficial soil microorganisms will increase naturally when organic amendments are applied to soils as carbon, energy and nutrient sources. This indeed may be true where an abundance of organic materials are readily available for recycling which often occurs in small-scale farming. However, in most cases, soil microorganisms, beneficial or harmful, have often been controlled advantageously when crops in various agroecological zones are grown and cultivated in proper sequence (i.e., crop rotations) and without the use of pesticides. This would explain why scientists have long been interested in the use of beneficial microorganisms as soil and plant inoculants to shift the microbiological equilibrium in a way that enhances soil quality and the yield and quality of crops.Most would agree that a basic rule of agriculture is to ensure that specific crops are grown according to their agroclimatic and agroecological requirements. However, in many cases the agricultural economy is based on market forces that demand a stable supply of food, and thus, it becomes necessary to use farmland to its full productive potential throughout the year.Low agricultural production efficiency is closely related to a poor coordination of energy conversion which, in turn, is influenced by crop physiological factors, the environment, and other biological factors including soil microorganisms. The soil and rhizosphere microflora can accelerate the growth of plants and enhance their resistance to disease and harmful insects by producing bioactive substances. These microorganisms maintain the growth environment of plants, and may have secondary effects on crop quality. A wide range of results are possible depending on their predominance and activities at any one time. Nevertheless, there is a growing consensus that it is possible to attain maximum economic crop yields of high quality, at higher net returns, without the application of chemical fertilizers and pesticides. Until recently, this was not thought to be a very likely possibility using conventional agricultural methods. However, it is important to recognize that the best soil and crop management practices to achieve a more sustainable agriculture will also enhance the growth, numbers and activities of beneficial soil microorganisms that, in turn, can improve the growth, yield and quality of crops (National Academy of Sciences, 1989; Hornick, 1992; Parr *et al.*, 1992).

Classification of Soils based on The Functions of Microorganisms

In most soils, these three functions are going on simultaneously with the rate and extent of each determined by the types and numbers of associated microorganisms that are actively involved at any one time.

Disease-inducing Soils: In this type of soil, plant pathogenic microorganisms such as Fusarium fungi can comprise 5 to 20 percent of the total microflora if fresh organic matter with a high nitrogen content is applied to such a soil, incompletely oxidized products can arise that are malodorous and toxic to growing plants. Such soils tend to cause frequent infestations of disease organisms, and harmful insects. Thus, the application of fresh organic matter to these soils is often harmful to crops. Probably more than 90 percent of the agricultural land devoted to crop production worldwide can be classified as having disease-inducing soil (Haggag Wafaa, 2010). Such soils generally have poor physical properties, and large amounts of energy are lost as “greenhouse” gases, particularly in the case of rice fields. Plant nutrients are also subject to immobilization into unavailable forms.

Disease-Suppressive Soils: The microflora of disease-suppressive soils is usually dominated by antagonistic microorganisms that produce copious amounts of antibiotics. These include fungi of the genera Penicillium, Trichoderma, and Aspergillus, and actinomycetes of the genus Streptomyces. The antibiotics they produce can have biostatic and biocidal effects on soil-borne plant pathogens, including Fusarium which would have an incidence in these soils of less than 5 percent. Crops planted in these soils are rarely affected by diseases or insect pests. Even if fresh organic matter with a high nitrogen content is applied, the production of putrescent substances is very low and the soil has a pleasant earthy odor after the organic matter is decomposed. These soils generally have excellent physical properties; for example, they readily, form water-stable aggregates and they are well-aerated, and have a high permeability to both air and water. Crop yields in the disease-suppressive soils are often slightly lower than those in synthetic soils. Highly acceptable crop yields are obtained whenever a soil has a predominance of both disease-suppressive and synthetic microorganisms.

Zymogenic Soils: These soils are dominated by a microflora that can perform useful kinds of fermentations, i.e., the breakdown of complex organic molecules into simple organic substances and inorganic materials. The organisms can be either obligate or facultative anaerobes. Such fermentation-producing microorganisms often comprise the microflora of various organic materials, i.e., crop residues, animal manures, green manures and municipal wastes including composts. After these amendments are applied to the soil, their number: and fermentative activities can increase dramatically and overwhelm the indigenous soil microflora for an indefinite period. While these microorganisms remain predominant, the soil can be classified as a zymogenic soil which is generally characterized by (a) pleasant, fermentative odors especially after tillage, (b) favorable soil physical properties (e.g., Increased aggregate stability, permeability, aeration and decreased resistance to tillage (c) large amounts of inorganic nutrients, amino acids, carbohydrates, vitamins and other bioactive substances which can directly or indirectly enhance the growth, yield and quality of crops, (d) low occupancy of Fusarium fungi which is usually less than 5 percent, and (e) low production of greenhouse gases (e.g., methane, ammonia, and carbon dioxide) from croplands, even where flooded rice is grown.

Synthetic Soils: These soils contain significant populations of microorganisms which are able to fix atmospheric nitrogen and carbon dioxide into complex molecules such as amino acids, proteins and carbohydrates. Such microorganisms include photosynthetic bacteria which perform incomplete photosynthesis anaerobically, certain Phycomycetes (fungi that resemble algae), and both green algae and blue—green algae which function aerobically. All of these are photosynthetic organisms that fix atmospheric nitrogen. If the water content of these soils is stable, their fertility can be largely maintained by regular additions of only small amounts of organic materials. These soils have a low Fusarium occupancy and they are often of the disease-suppressive type. The production of gases from fields where synthetic soils are present is minimal, even for flooded rice.

AGRICULTURE AND ENVIRONMENTAL BIOTECHNOLOGY

Environmental biotechnology could also imply that one try to harness biological process for commercial uses and exploitation (Harger and Meyer, 1996) The International Society for Environmental Biotechnology defines environmental biotechnology as "the development, use and regulation of biological systems for remediation of contaminated environments (land, air, water), and for environment-friendly processes (green manufacturing technologies and sustainable development)" (Gerben *et al.*, 2005) . Environmental biotechnology can simply be described as "the optimal use of nature, in the form of plants, animals, bacteria, fungi and algae, to produce renewable energy, food and nutrients in a synergistic integrated cycle of profit making processes where the waste of each process becomes the feedstock for another process"(Vidya Sagar *et al.*, 2005). Environmental biotechnology is the used in waste treatment and pollution prevention. Environmental biotechnology can more efficiently clean up many wastes than conventional methods and greatly reduce our dependence on methods for land-based disposal. Every organism ingests nutrients to live and produces by-products as a result. Different organisms need different types of nutrients. Some bacteria thrive on the chemical components of waste products. Environmental engineers use bioremediation, the broadest application of environmental biotechnology, in two basic ways. They introduce nutrients to stimulate the activity of bacteria already present in the soil at a waste site, or add new bacteria to the soil. The bacteria digest the waste at the site and turn it into harmless byproducts. After the bacteria consume the waste materials, they die off or return to their normal population levels in the environment.

Bioremediation. Through application of biotechnical methods, enzyme bioreactors are being developed that will pretreat some industrial waste and food waste components and allow their removal through the sewage system rather than through solid waste disposal mechanisms. Waste can also be converted to biofuel to run generators. Microbes can be induced to produce enzymes needed to convert plant and vegetable materials into building blocks for biodegradable plastics. In some cases, the byproducts of the pollution-fighting microorganisms are themselves useful. For example, methane can be derived from a form of bacteria that degrades sulfur liquor, a waste product of paper manufacturing. This methane can then be used as a fuel or in other industrial processes.

Soil Microorganisms in Biodegradation

Biodegradation is the break down of organic matter by microbes. Bioremediation is an engineered technique applied by people to clean up organic matter by helping microbes with the biodegradation process. One way of doing that is to introduce oxygen into the subsurface to help more aerobic microbes.

Bioremediation is a microorganism mediated transformation or degradation of contaminants into nonhazardous or less-hazardous substances. The employability of various organisms like bacteria, fungi, algae, and plants for efficient bioremediation of pollutants has been reported (Vidali 2001 and Leung 2004). The involvement of plants in the bioremediation of pollutants is called as phytoremediation. The process of phytoremediation is an emerging green technology that facilitates the removal or degradation of the toxic chemicals in soils, sediments, groundwater, surface water, and air (RTDF). Genetically, engineered plants are also in use. For instance arsenic is phytoremediated by genetically modified plants such as Arabidopsis thaliana which expresses two bacterial genes. One of these genes allows the plant to modify arsenate into arsenite and the second one binds the modified arsenite and stores it in the vacuoles (Leung 2004).

The process of bioremediation mainly depends on microorganisms which enzymatically attack the pollutants and convert them to innocuous products. As bioremediation can be effective only where environmental conditions permit microbial growth and activity, its application often involves the manipulation of environmental parameters to allow microbial growth and degradation to proceed at a faster rate. A large number of enzymes from bacteria, fungi, and plants have been reported to be involved in the biodegradation of toxic organic pollutants. Bioremediation is a cost effective and nature friendly biotechnology that is powered by microbial enzymes. The research activity in this area would contribute towards developing advanced bioprocess technology to reduce the toxicity of the pollutants and also to obtain novel useful substances.

Biodegradation of Pesticides in Soil: Pesticides reaching to the soil are acted upon by several physical, chemical, and biological forces. However, physical and chemical forces are acting upon/degrading the pesticides to some extent, microorganism's plays major role in the degradation of pesticides. Many soil microorganisms have the ability to act upon pesticides and convert them into simpler non-toxic compounds. This process of degradation of pesticides and conversion into non-toxic compounds by microorganisms is known as "biodegradation". Not all pesticides reaching to the soil are biodegradable and such chemicals that show complete resistance to biodegradation are called "recalcitrant".

The chemical reactions leading to biodegradation of pesticides fall into several broad categories which are discussed in brief in the following paragraphs.

(a) **Detoxification:** Conversion of the pesticide molecule to a non-toxic compound. Detoxification is not synonymous with degradation. Since a single chance in the side chain of a complex molecule may render the chemical non-toxic.

(b) **Degradation:** The breaking down / transformation of a complex substrate into simpler products leading finally to mineralization. Degradation is often considered to be synonymous with mineralization, e.g. Thirum (fungicide) is degraded by a strain of *Pseudomonas* and the degradation products are dimethlamine, proteins, sulpholipaids, etc.

(c) **Conjugation (complex formation or addition reaction):** In which an organism make the substrate more complex or combines the pesticide with cell metabolites. Conjugation or the formation of addition product is accomplished by those organisms catalyzing the reaction of addition of an amino acid, organic acid or methyl crown to the substrate, for e.g., in the microbial metabolism of sodium dimethly dithiocarbamate, the organism combines the fungicide with an amino acid molecule normally present in the cell and thereby inactivate the pesticides/ chemical.

(d) **Activation:** It is the conversion of non-toxic substrate into a toxic molecule, for eg. Herbicide, 4-butyric acid (2, 4-D B) and the insecticide Phorate are transformed and activated microbiologically in soil to give metabolites that are toxic to weeds and insects.

(e) **Changing the spectrum of toxicity:** Some fungicides/pesticides are designed to control one particular group of organisms/pests, but they are metabolized to yield products inhibitory to entirely dissimilar groups of organisms, for e.g. the fungicide PCNB fungicide is converted in soil to chlorinated benzoic acids that kill plants.

Biodegradation of pesticides/herbicides is greatly influenced by the soil factors like moisture, temperature, PH and organic matter content, in addition to microbial population and pesticide solubility. Optimum temperature, moisture and organic matter in soil provide congenial environment for the break down or retention of any pesticide added in the soil. Most of the organic pesticides degrade within a short period (3-6 months) under tropical conditions. Metabolic activities of bacteria, fungi and actinomycetes have the significant role in the degradation of pesticides.

Criteria for Bioremediation: For successful biodegradation of pesticide in soil, following aspects must be taken into consideration. (i) Organisms must have necessary catabolic activity required for degradation of contaminant at fast rate to bring down the concentration of contaminant,

(ii) the target contaminant must be bioavailability, (iii) soil conditions must be congenial for microbial/plant growth and enzymatic activity and iv) cost of bioremediation must be less than other technologies of removal of contaminants.

Strategies for Bioremediation

Bioremediation: A technology that encourages growth and reproduction of indigenous microorganisms (bacteria and fungi) to enhance biodegradation of organic constituents in the saturated zone. Bioremediation can effectively degrade organic constituents dissolved in groundwater and adsorbed onto the aquifer matrix. Generally requires a mechanism for stimulating and maintaining the activity of the microorganisms, e.g., addition of an electron acceptor (oxygen, nitrate); nutrients (nitrogen, phosphorus); and an energy source (carbon).

For the successful biodegradation/bioremediation of a given contaminant following strategies are needed.

(a) **Passive/intrinsic Bioremediation:** It is the natural bioremediation of contaminant by tile indigenous microorganisms and the rate of degradation is very slow.

(b) **Biostimulation:** Practice of addition of nitrogen and phosphorus to stimulate indigenous microorganisms in soil.

(c) **Bioventing:** Process/way of Biostimulation by which gases stimulants like oxygen and methane are added or forced into soil to stimulate microbial activity.

(d) **Bioaugmentation:** It is the inoculation/introduction of microorganisms in the contaminated site/soil to facilitate biodegradation.

(e) **Composting:** Piles of contaminated soils are constructed and treated with aerobic thermophilic microorganisms to degrade contaminants. Periodic physical mixing and moistening of piles are done to promote microbial activity.

(f) **Phytoremediation:** Can be achieved directly by planting plants which hyperaccumulate heavy metals or indirectly by plants stimulating microorganisms in the rhizosphere.

(g) **Bioremediation:** Process of detoxification of toxic/unwanted chemicals/contaminants in the soil and other environment by using microorganisms.

(h) **Mineralization:** Complete conversion of an organic contaminant to its inorganic constituent by a species or group of microorganisms.

Waste Management and Recycling: Clean and Green Technologies

During the past decades, production systems have been based on the assumption that wastes are an unavoidable part of our daily lives but that ecological and environmental destruction could be avoided because of the planet's vast natural resources. However, ecosystems and renewable resources are being destroyed at an increasingly rapid rate and the problems of pollution and waste disposal are growing. It is thus becoming increasingly evident that new production methods must be devised to fulfil society's basic needs. In order to maintain the vitality of the rural sector and preserve the environment, a system must be devised in which energy, food, animal feed, fuel and fertiliser requirements can all be met from renewable resources used at a sustainable level (Sasson 1990).

The new socio-economic concept is based on the requirement for full exploitation of a harvested renewable resource and the replacement of monoculture/monoproduct farming with a multiproduct system (Doelle & Prasertsan 2003). Because it produces a variety of products, this system will hopefully enjoy a constant and reliable market demand and will be able to secure income for the rural sector as well as for joint venture industries. It also will help to reduce the vast multiplication rates of pests in mono-culture system operations .In order to develop an appropriate biotechnology, resources available together with the social structure of the population are of vital importance. It is often the need and not the economics of the process, which is of importance. Here seems to lie one of the cardinal differences between the thoughts of appropriate technology in developed, from those in developing countries. In this context, a new concept has been developed specifically for rural communities: the so-called *integrated rural biotechnology systems* (Haggag Wafaa and Saber, 2006). The development of these systems depends primarily on the climatic conditions of the regions.

Two of the premises of sustainable development are that economic growth has to be in harmony with the environment and that a rational and sustainable use of natural resources has to be implemented (Olguin 2000). In congruence with such premises, industrial development has to change from the degradative to the sustainable style, which requires the adoption of cleaner production systems.

The United Nations Environment Programme (UNEP) defines the cleaner production concept as 'the continuous application of an integrated preventive environmental strategy to processes, products and services to increase eco-efficiency and reduce risks to humans and the environment' (UNEP 1996). One of its distinctive features is that reduction of the quantity and toxicity of all emissions and wastes is made before they leave the process stream. In the case of services, environmental concerns should be incorporated into design and delivery.Eco-efficiency, on the other hand, involves 'the delivery of competitively priced goods and services that satisfy human needs and bring quality of life while progressively reducing ecological impacts and resource intensity, throughout the life cycle, to a level at least in line with the Earth's estimated capacity' (UNEP 1994). It is becoming very clear that adoption of clean production systems by industries calls for fundamental changes, not only at the technological level but also at the legislative level (Olguin 2000). Cleaner bioprocesses are under intensive research and development following the general guidelines for cleaner production.

Change in living standards contributes increased dependence on chemicals in day to day life. These chemicals are from soaps, detergents, disinfectants, insecticides, like DDT etc., which can pollute receiving water bodies through sewage. Many of these chemicals are harmful to humans and other higher organisms and vegetation. They may be carcinogenic, neurotoxic, teratogenic some of these may persist in the environments for long period and the phenomenon is called recalcitrance. Diverse group of microorganisms can be used for bioremediation of waste water and soil with such recalcitrant and xenobiotic compounds.

Xenobiotic compounds accumulate in huge amount of biodegradable organic waste that creates a big problem. Due to increased consumerism, industrialization, various kind of solid wastes are generated daily and natural rate of biodegradation is very slow as compared to their rate of accumulation. These wastes are now-a-days treated by using inherent biodegradability of microorganisms. Microorganisms have the ability to transform various toxic hazardous wastes (such as heavy metals, radioactive nuclides, colored compound, from various types of industries such as fabric industries, pharmaceutical industries, etc.) into nontoxic one. Above all, these microorganisms play main role in human health by virtue of producing various drugs and antibiotics, vitamins, amino acids and proteins etc. Several microbial activities could help to design a new strategy of life that leads to sustainable future.

Environmental Health and Microbial Biotechnology

In considering all the available technologies together with those under development, the first and basic priority thinking has to be the fact that 'technologies in general do not transfer from developed to developing countries. Rather they need to be built up *in situ* using local knowledge and innovative ability after which, if successful, they are being adopted' . Social aspects of psychology, religion and gender are of paramount importance (Warner 2000).

Health

It is very hard to understand why our International Agencies have failed to eliminate the health problems in developing countries. Biotechnologists and in particular microbial technologists must fail to comprehend why the numerous existing technologies have neither been supported nor implemented. Basic sanitation should be made available as a first priority in human development. It is well known that the handling of human and animal excreta or manure depends on and varies with the social and religious background of a particular society, but the technologies available today caters for all aspects of human society.The basis for socio-economical integrated biosystems, recently referred to also as 'ecological sanitation' (Esrey 2001) has been with us for the last century in form of:

(a) composting toilets wet or dry;

(b) composting together with household waste and other biomass.

(c) anaerobic digestion or biogas digesters.

Neither of these systems requires any handling of excreta or manure, as these can be channelled through pipelines to a cesspit, compost or anaerobic digester. Whereas composting and anaerobic digestion takes care of all pathogens, the cesspit requires the addition of lime or ash to help desiccate the manure and raise the pH, which effectively kills off all pathogens within several months (Esrey 2001). This pathogen-free manure can directly be returned to the soil or, in order to be safe, be added to compost heaps before improving the fertility of soils.Composting reaches a thermophilic range of 50-80° C and anaerobic digestion reduces the redoxpotential to such an extent that pathogens are killed.

In the case of cesspits, compost and anaerobic digestion, the residue can be safely used for soil improvement, replacing chemical fertilisation. Whether this organic fertilisation is used on fields of flower or food crops is dependent on the local society (Kasule 1998) and their religious belief. Technologies are also available to treat and recycle the water [greywater] (Guenther 2001) effectively for reuse.

The best ecological as well as economic sanitation system is undoubtedly the use of anaerobic or biogas digesters. In this case, the families will be able to use the biogas formed for cooking and electricity. These systems are becoming very popular in Bangladesh, Vietnam, Cambodia and China. Biodigesters are also the best socio-economic systems with establishment costs becoming very cheap as has been demonstrated in Vietnam (An *et al* 1997), Bangladesh (Shakti 2000) and Cambodia using polyethylene tubing as construction material . Sizes of these digesters in use at present range from 6-20 m^3 , whereas digesters up to 2000 m^3 require concrete or steel construction.

It is very distressing to realise that many international organisations, eg FAO, do not condemn the use of raw manure for soil improvement, and do not emphasize the absolute need for treatment before use as was shown in one of the latest electronic conferences on 'Area wide integration of crops and livestock production'. If these old and improved biotechnological techniques are fully supported and properly funded in a way the introduction of GMO crops are funded by UNDP, UNEP, UNIDO, FAO, WHO etc, health in developing countries could be quickly raised to the level of developed countries (WHO 2001).

In addition to these disease prevention technologies, International Agencies must also be forced or force corporations to make biotechnological products available to the 2 billion people [one third of the world population], who still have no access to low-cost essential medicines such as penicillin, a technological process developed in the late 1940s (UNDP 2001).

Small amounts of biotechnological products may be taken up by the worker during occupationalhandling. Enzymes, a typical class of biotechnological products, are potent allergens, and there arenumerous reports of work-related allergies, in particular from the food, feed, paper and detergentindustries. Concerns about the potential of other biotechnological products used in medicaltreatment to cause work-related allergies have so far not proven justified. But vigilance is bothneeded and applied."Upstream" production processes must be strictly protected from outside contamination. Thisprotection must also be guaranteed "downstream" because many of the biotechnologicallymanufactured drugs are peptides or proteins, which are typically administered by injection and musttherefore be protected during manufacture. Such operational necessities help prevent exposure ofworkers to these processes and their products.Health surveillance is important to ensure that no adverse health effects occur in the workers or thatthey are detected early if they do. Evaluation of these surveillance data has shown that the protectivemeasures taken at the workplace are effective.One of the most sophisticated groups of commonly used biotechnological medicines is monoclonalantibodies (MAbs). MAbs are very effective drugs, as they are designed and developed to target thediseased organ directly and exclusively. For this reason, often no effects of the drug are expected inhealthy individuals. Side effects in patients are generally mild and predictable. However, there areexamples indicating that serious unexpected effects can occur due to MAb administration. Therefore,Roche handles this class of drugs with all necessary safety measures, as appropriate to any Rocheproduct.

Poverty

The term poverty is very often misinterpreted with starvation. Whereas poverty is flourishing in most developing countries, this is certainly not the case with lack of food causing starvation. However, poverty may cause starvation as the people are not able to buy the available food. Poverty is mainly caused through strong increases in urbanisation, as low income rural farmers stream into the cities to find work and a better income. This depletes very efficient and productive rural agriculture, and reduces the possible maximal agricultural food or crop production. Whereas the green revolution technologies resulted in increased food production in favourable and irrigated environments, they had little impact on the millions of smallholders living in rainfed and marginal areas, where poverty is concentrated in Asia. The reasons for this trend are manyfold, but can mainly be traced to changes in farm management [single crop production] as well as farm mechanisation [big farms] resulting in a severe reduction of small farm holders, and a severe reduction of funding and investment into agriculture. In order to alleviate poverty and make certain that we are able to continue with feeding an ever increasing population, we need a socio-economic biotechnology revolution (Doelle & Prasertsan 2002) realising that we have to learn from the mistakes of the green revolution and secure a proper income to the farmer. One major problem of the green revolution was that the farmers were made to believe in the production for markets, forgetting their own consumption. It is evident that farmers in some developing countries grow crops solely under contract for supplying processing factories, while they have to buy the food for their own consumption. Traditional food was demoted, whereas canned and bottled food was promoted. Local (traditional) wisdom and knowledge in food preservation and medicine were treated as an 'uncivilized way of life' and is disappearing, so the younger generation is not practising it anymore.

Such a new biotechnology revolution has to take into consideration.

1. that farming in developing countries is profoundly different from developed countries with crops like cassava, rice, soybean, sago etc.;
2. that farms are small and should stay small with minimal mechanisation but more intensive and integrated farming;
3. that single crop production must make way to a multi-product farming, including livestocks on the farm;
4. that we use existing biotechnological techniques to develop biotechnological industries using locally grown biomass such as sago palm and cassava;
5. combine the biomass waste, excessive amounts of agro-industrial wastes with human and animal waste treatments for novel product and renewable energy production.

The additional incorporation of aspects of modern biotechnological techniques (DaSilva 2001) will come as soon as society has learned the advantages of the existing technologies. Some biotechnological issues such as pest-resistant plants and organic fertilisation will involve some GMO plants. However, one should always be aware and not forget, that local breeding experience may be a better way to go initially than GMO introduction.

It is very surprising, for example, that agricultural biotechnology development sofar has totally ignored plants such as cassava and the sago palm as a starch resource, as they are hardly known in developed countries. Cassava can yield up to 65 t/ha with a 65% starch content in marginal soils and the sagopalm can easily produce 25 t of starch/ha in swampy areas unsuitable for any other crop. Both crops are ideal for obtaining a variety of bioproducts ranging from biofuel, bioplastics, biodetergents, biolubricants to bio-pharmaceuticals (Bujang *et al.* 2001).The establishment of biorefineries will diversify rural farming, keep people employed in the rural areas and will also increase the income of the individual farmer, helping in the alleviation of poverty.

Starvation

The elimination of starvation in arid zones could become an ideal place for combining 'old' biotechnological concepts of soil fertility improvement with 'new or modern' biotechnological concepts of increasing crop and livestock production. Soil fertility improvement should also go hand in hand with a reduction or elimination of rain and other forest clearings, which in turn would stop the expansion of the arid zone areas. Such a combined concept would create more small holding farms with a proper income, helping to stop the development of further poverty.

Safety

For the commercial production of pharmaceuticals, biotechnological processes use microorganisms or cell lines exclusively from the lowest possible risk group, which includes only agentsthat, by definition, "present no or a low individual and community risk". They are not pathogenic tohumans and animals and have no adverse environmental impact.In research and development, and in certain processes used for the commercial manufacture of diagnostic tests, micro organisms may be used that can cause disease. In handling these agents,Roche strictly complies with the appropriate biosafety standards recognized across the world.

Genetically modified micro organisms and cells are generally classified in the same risk group astheir naturally occurring variants, although they are often dependent on a protected environmentand will die when released. Roche complies with all pertinent regulations and additionally performsindividual process risk assessments based on the precautionary principle.Unlike most classical chemical processes, biotechnological transformation ("upstream") processestake place in an aqueous environment. This eliminates the risk of fire or explosion associated withcertain solvents frequently used in chemical syntheses. The use of toxic chemicals inbiotechnological process steps is limited, as such chemicals could easily have an adverse effect on thecells involved. However, organic solvents still play a role in some "downstream" biotechnologicalprocesses, where they are used to extract certain products from the fermentation broth and to purifythem.

SUMMARY AND CONCLUSION

In summary, it is our view that an increased knowledge of microbe-based symbioses in plants could provide effective ways of developing sustainable agriculture in order to ensure human and animal food production with a minimal disturbance of the environment. The effective management of symbiotic microbial communities is possibleusing molecular approaches based on the continuity of microbial poolswhich are circulating regularly between soil-, plant- and animal-provided niches in natural and agricultural ecosystems. Analysis of this circulation could enable the creation of highly productive microbe-based sustainable agricultural system, whilst addressing the ecological and genetic consequences of the broad applicationof microbes in agricultural practice.Stable or sustainable agricultural production is food production that satisfies the needsof present day generations and at the same time does not endanger the possibility of satisfyingthe needs for food for future generations. It is ecological, ethical and economical.One of ecological and economical aspects in sustainable agriculture is biotechnology.By applying modern biotechnological methods and techniques, constant food productioncan be provided both qualitatively and quantitatively (Haggag Wafaa and Nofal 2006).Our science and profession must follow modern trends in agriculture, because withoutsustainable development and technology we will not be able to keep the pace and secureour position in world food production.

REFERENCES

Andrews M., Hodge S., Raven J.A. (2010). Positive Plant Microbial Interactions. Annals of Applied Biology, 157, 317-320.

Arnold A.E., Mamit L.J., Gehring C.A., Bidartondo M.I., Callahan H. (2010) Interwoven Branches of the Plant and Fungal Trees of Life. New Phytologist, 185, 874-878.

Berliner, E. (1911). Uber de schlaffsucht der Mehlmottenraupe. Zeitschrift fur das. *Gesamstadt.* 252: 3160-3162. [German]

Bonny, S., (1989). Biotechnology and the New Information Technologies in Agriculture, Medit, 9, 1, 3.

Bujang, K.B., Adeni, D.S.A. and P.Jolhery (2001). Potemntials of Sago Starch in the Energy and Lactate Industries in Malaysia. In '*Diversity and Optimum Utilization of Biological Resources in the Torrid and Subtropical Zones.* Sago Intern. Symp., Fukuoka, Japan.

Chandrakant S. Karigar and Shwetha S. Rao (2011). Role of Microbial Enzymes in the Bioremediation of Pollutants: A Review. Enzyme Research Volume 2011 (2011), Article ID 805187, 11 pages.

DaSilva, E.J. (2001) GMOs and Development. *Electronic Journal of Biotechnology* at http://www.ejb.org/content/issues/01/index.html

Dodds, J.H., R.Ortiz, J.H. Crouch, V.Mahalasksmi & K.K. Sharma (2001). Biotechnology, the Gene Revolution, and Proprietary Technology in Agriculture. A Strategic Note for the World Bank. *bio*Developments-International Institute Inc., Ithaka NY.

Doelle, H.W. & P.Prasertsan (2003). Environmental Biotechnology Socio-economic Strategies for Sustainability. In 'Biotechnology' [H.W.Doelle & E.J.DaSilva, eds] *Encyclopedia for Life Support Systems,* EOLSS Publishers, Cambridge, UK.

Doelle, H. 2002 Using a Biorefinery to Recycle Biomass and Control of Pathogens. *Biocycle* 43, 83-86.

Esrey,S.A. (2001). Ecological Sanitation Closing the loop. At http://www.ruaf.org/1-3/35-37.pdf

Franche C., Lindstrom K., Elmerich C. (2009) Nitrogen-fixing Bacteria Associated with Leguminous and Non-leguminous Plants. Plant and Soil, 321, 35-59.

Gerben J Zylstraa and Jerome J Kukor, (2005). *What is Environmental Biotechnology?* Current Opinion in Biotechnology 16(3): 243-245.

Ghaly, S., M.Hassanane, E.S. Ahmed, Haggag Wafaa, S., Nada and I. Farag (2010). Cytogenetic and Biochemical Studies on the Protective Role of *Rhodotorula glutinis* and its Autoploidy Against the Toxic Effect of Aflatoxin B1 in Mic. Nature and Science USA; 8(2): 7-23.

Haggag Wafaa, Enayat A. Omara, Somaia A. Nada, Hamdy Abou Eleid and Hassan A. Amra (2014b). *Rhodotorula glutinis* and Its Two Mutants Ameliorate Hepato-Renal Dysfunction Induced by Ochratoxin A on Rats. *British Microbiology Research Journal 4(12):* 1392-1408*, 2014.*

Haggag Wafaa (2007). Colonization of Exopolysaccharide-producing Paenibacillus Polymyxa on Peanut Roots for Enhancing Resistance Against Crown Rot Disease. African Journal of Biotechnology Vol. 6 (13), pp. 1568-1577.

Haggag Wafaa , F. Abd-El-Kareem and Malaka AE Saleh (2014c). Management of Aflatoxin B1 Producing *Aspergillus flavus* on Walnuts and Pistachio Seeds Research Journal of Pharmaceutical, Biological and Chemical Sciences. RJPBCS 5(4) Page No. 1194-1202.

Haggag Wafaa M (2010). Role of Entophytic Microorganisms in Biocontrol of Plant Diseases. Life Science Journal 7(2): 57-62.

Haggag Wafaa M and M. Nofal (2006). Improving the Biological Control of Botryodiplodia Disease on Some Annona Cultivars Using Single or Multi-bioagents in Egypt. Volume 38, Issue 3, September 2006, Pages 341-349.

Haggag Wafaa M and M.S.M. Saber (2006). Suppression of Early Blight on Tomato and Purple Blight on Onion by Foliar Sprays of Aerated and Non-aerated Compost Teas. Food, Agriculture and Environment (JFAE) Vol. 5, 2, 302-309.

Haggag Wafaa, Enas, M. Mostafa , El Azzazy, A.M. (2011). Optimization and Production of Antifungal Hydrolysis Enzymes by *Streptomyces aureofaciens* Against *Colletotrichum gloeosporioides* of Mango. *Agriculture Science*; USA 2(2): 146-157 http://www.scirp.org/journal/AS/

Haggag, Wafaa , M. (2002a). Sustainable Agriculture Management of Plant Diseases. Online Journal of Biological Science. 2: 280-284.

Haggag, Wafaa and Essam Hoballa (2014). Food, Agriculture and Microbes. International Journal of Agriculture Innovations and Research, Vol. 2 No. 4 pp. 422-425.

Haggag, Wafaa and Salme Timmusk (2007). Colonization of Peanut Roots by Biofilm-forming Paenibacillus Polymyxa Initiates Biocontrol Against Crown Rot Disease. Journal of Appl Microbiol (UK) 104 (4): 961-969.

Haggag, Wafaa M, Malaka A. Saleh and Omima Hafez (2014a). Development of *Tilletiopsis Pallescens* as Bio-fungicides for Controlling of Grape Powdery Mildew Advances in Natural and Applied Sciences, 8(1) January 2014, Pages: 32-37.

Haggag, Wafaa M., Malaka A. E. Saleh, Inas Mostafa, Noran Adel (2013). Mass Production, Fermentation, Formulation of *Pseudomonas putida* for Controlling of Die Back and Phomopsis Diseases on Grapevine. Advances in Bioscience and Biotechnology, 2013, 4, 741-750.

Haggag, Wafaa, M. (2002b). Hyperproducing Chitinase *Trichoderma* Mutants Induced by Gamma-ray for Efficient Biocontrol of Botrytis Cinerea on Tomato and Cucumber Plants Growing in Plastic Houses. Arab Journal of Biotechnology. 5 (2): 151-164.

Haggag, Wafaa, M. and Saber, M.S.M. (2000). Evaluation of Three Composts as Multi-strain Carries for Biofertilizer and Biocontrol Agents Against Fusarium Wilt Disease of Some Legume Plants. *Arab Journal of Biotechnology*, 3: 133-144.

Haggag, Wafaa, M., Mohamed, H.A.A. (2007). Biotechnological Aspects of Microorganisms Used in Plant Biological Control (Article). *American-Eurasian Journal of Sustainable Agriculture,* 1(1):7-12.

Haggag, Wafaa, M., Mohamed, H.A.A. and Saker, M. (2005). Biocontrol Activity and Molecular Characterization of Colchicine-induced Ploidy Yeast Strains of Tilletiopsis Pallescens on Powdery Mildew and Rhodotorula Glutinis on Grey Mould Diseases of Green House Sweet Pepper. Egyptian Journal of Biotechnology, 19: 183-208.

Harger JRE, Meyer, FM., 1996, Definition of Indicators for Environmentally Sustainable Development, Chemosphere, 1749-1775.

Harrington, J.M., D.L. Parker, J.R. Bargar, A.A. Jarzecki, B.M. Tebo, G. Sposito and O.W. Duckworth. (2012). Structural Dependence of Mn Complexation by Siderophores: Donor Group Dependence on Complex Stability and Reactivity . *Geochimica et Cosmochimica Acta.* 88: 106-119.

Hedin L.O., Brookshire E.N.J., Menge D.N.L., Barron A.R. (2009). The Nitrogen Paradox in Tropical Forest Ecosystems. Annual Review of Ecology, Evolution and Systematics, 40, 613-635.

Higa, T. (1991). Effective Microorganisms: A Biotechnology for Mankind. p. 8-14. In J.F. Parr, S.B. Hornick, and C.E. Whitman (ed.) Proceedings of the First International Conference on Kyusei Nature Farming. U.S. Department of Agriculture, Washington, D.C., USA.

Higa, T. 1994. Effective Microorganisms: A New Dimension for Nature Farming. pp. 20-22. In J.F. Parr, S.B. Hornick, and M.E. Simpson (ed.) Proceedings of the Second International Conference on Kyusei Nature Farming. U.S. Department of Agriculture, Washington, D.C, USA.

Higa, T. and G.N. Wididana (199l). Changes In the Soil Microflora Induced by Effective Microorganisms. pp.153-162. In J.F. Parr, S.B. Hornick, and C.E. Whitman (ed.) Proceedings of the First International Conference on Kyusei Nature Farming. U.S. Department of Agriculture, Washington, D.C., USA.

Hiltner, L. (1904). Über neuere Erfahrungen und Probleme auf dem Gebiete der Bodenbakteriologie unter besonderer Berücksichtigung der Gründüngung und Brache. *Arb DLG.* 98: 59-78.

Ishiwata, S. (1901). On a Kind of Severe Flacherie (Sotto Disease) (I.). *Dainihon Sanshi Kaiho.* 9: I-5. [Japanese]

Jahan, M., M.N. Mahallati, M.B. Amiri and H.R. Ehyayi. (2013). Radiation Absorption and Use Efficiency of Sesame as Affected by Biofertilizers Inoculation in a Low Input Cropping System. *Industrial Crops and Products.* 43: 606-611.

Koulman, A., T.V. Lee, K. Fraser, L. Johnson, V. Arcus, J.S. Lott, S. Rasmussen and G. Lane. (2012). Identification of Extracellular Siderophores and a Related Peptide from the Endophytic Fungus *Epichloe festucae* in Culture and Endophyte-infected *Lolium perenne. Phytochemistry.* 75: 128-139.

Kupriyanov A.A., Semenov A.M., Van Bruggen A.H.C. (2010). Transition of Entheropathogenic and Saprotrophic Bacteria in the Niche Cycle: Animals–excrement–soil–plants–animals. Biology Bulletin, 3, 263-267.

Leung, M.(2004). "Bioremediation: Techniques for Cleaning up a Mess," Journal of Biotechnology, Vol. 2, pp. 18-22.

Malisorn, C. and Suntornsuk, W. (2008) . Optimization of β-carotene production by *Rhodotorula glutinis* DM28 in fermented radish brine. Bioresource Technology, 99 (7): 2281-2287.

Marques, M.P.C, P. Fernandes and de C.C.C.R. Carvalho. (2010). Lab-scale Bioproduction of Siderophores. *Journal of Biotechnology.* 150: 424.

Mohammed S.H., Seady M.A., Enan M.R., Ibrahim N.E., Ghareeb A., Moustafa S.A. (2008). Biocontrol Efficiency of Bacillus Thuringiensis Toxins Against Root-knot Nematode, Meloidogyne Incognita. Journal of Cell and Molecular Biology, 7: 57-66.

National Academy of Sciences. (1989). Alternative Agriculture. Committee on the Role of Alternative Agriculture Farming Methods in Modern Production Agriculture. National Research Council, Board on Agriculture. National Academy Press, Washington, D.C., USA. 448 p.

National Academy of Sciences. (1993). Pesticides in Diets of Infants and Children National Research Council, Board on Agriculture. National Academy Press, Washington, D.C., USA. 373 p.

Noble A.D., Ruaysoongnern S. (2010). The Nature of Sustainable Agriculture. In Soil Microbiology and Sustainable Crop Production, pp. 1-25. Eds R.Dixon and E.Tilston. Berlin, Heidelberg, Germany: Springer Science and Business Media B.V.

Olguin, E.J. (2000). Cleaner Bioprocesses and Sustainable Development. In '*Environmental Biotechnology and Cleaner Bioprocesses*' (E.J.Olguin, G.Sanchez & E.Hernandez, eds.), pp. 3-18. Taylor & Francis Inc, Philadelphia.

Peay K.G., Bidartondo M.I., Arnold A.E. (2010) Not Every Fungus is Everywhere: Scaling to the Biogeography of Fungal–plant Interactions Across Roots, Shoots and Ecosystems. New Phytologist, 185, 878-882.

Podile R. and K Kishore, (2007). Plant Growth-promoting Rhizobacteria. *In: Plantassociated bacteria.* Springer Netherlands, pp. 195-230.

Prestes, O.D., J.A. Padilla-Sanchez, R. Romero-Gonzalez, S.L. Grio, A.G. Frenich, and J.H. Martinez-Vidal. (2012). Comparison of Several Extraction Procedures for the Determination of Biopesticides in Soil Samples by Ultrahigh Pressure LC-MS/MS. *Journal of Separation Science.* 35: 861-868.

Provorov N.A., Tikhonovich I.A. (2003). Genetic Resources for Improving Nitrogen Fixation in Legume–rhizobia Symbiosis. Genetic Resources and Crop Evolution, 50, 89-99.

Provorov N.A., Vorobyov N.I. (2009). Host Plant as an Organizer of Microbial Evolution in the Beneficial Symbioses. Phytochemistry Reviews, 8, 519-534.

Provorov N.A., Vorobyov N.I. (2010). Simulation of Evolution Implemented in the Mutualistic Symbioses Towards Enhancing Their Ecological Efficiency, Functional Integrity and Genotypic Specificity. Theoretical Population Biology, 78, 259-269.

Renshaw, J.C., G.D. Robson, A.P.J. Trinci, M.G. Wiebe and F.R. Livens, D. Collison and R.J. Taylor. (2002). Fungal Siderophores: Structures, Functions and Applications. *Mycological Research.* 106: 1123-1142.

Ryan R.P., Germaine K., Franks A., Ryan D.J., Dowling D.N. (2008) Bacterial Endophytes: Recent Developments and Applications. FEMS Microbiology Letters, 278, 1-9.

Sasson, A. (1990). *Feeding Tomorrow's World.* Unesco Paris.

Schell, J. & J.Mayer (1987) Chances and Risks of Biotechnology for Agricultural Production in the Tropics and Subtropics. *Natural Resources and Development* 26, 7-13

Shtark O.Y., Borisov A.Y., Zhukov V.A., Provorov N.A., Tikhonovich I.A. (2010) Intimate Associations of Beneficial Soil Microbes with Host Plants. Soil Microbiology and Sustainable Crop Production, pp. 119-196. Eds R.Dixon and E.Tilston. Berlin, Heidelberg, Germany: Springer Science and Business Media B.V.

Speeding CRW., (1993). What is Sustainability?, Europe Gatt, Sustainability and the Future of Farming, Proceedings of Rozal Agricultural Society of England National Agricultural Conference.

Tircso, G., Z. Garda, F.K. Kalman, Z. Baranyai, I. Pocsi, G. Balla and I. Toth. 2013. Lanthanide (III) Complexes of Some Natural Siderophores: A Thermodynamic, Kinetic and Relaxometric Study. *Journal of Inorganic Biochemistry.* 127: 53-61.

UNEP (1996). Sustainable Production and Consumption. *Industry & Environment* 19(3), 4.

Valueva, T. and Mosolov, V. (2004). Role of Inhibitors of Proteolytic Enzymes in Plant Defense Against Phytopathogenic Microorganisms. Biochemistry: 69, No. 11, pp. 1305-1309.

Vance C.P. (1998) Legume Symbiotic Nitrogen Fixation: Agronomic Aspects. In The Rhizobiaceae. Molecular Biology of Model Plant-Associated Bacteria, pp. 509-530. Eds H.P.Spaink, A.Kondorosi and P.J.J. Hooykaas. Dordrecht, the Netherlands: Kluwer Academic Publishers.

Vidali, M. (2001) "Bioremediation. An Overview," Pure and Applied Chemistry, Vol. 73, No. 7, pp. 1163-1172.

Vidya Sagar. K, (2005). *National Conference on Environmental Biotechnology*, Bangalore.

Warner, W.S., 2000 Cultural Influences that Affect the Acceptance of Compost Toilets: Psychology, Religion and Gender. at http://www.nwnet.co.uk/earthwise/10articl/wwarner.htm

WHO 2001 see http://www.who.int/disasters/commdiseases.cfm

Xiang, W. Li Zhao, Xin Xu, Yonghua Qin, Guanghui Yu (2012). Mutual Information Flow between Beneficial Microorganisms and the Roots of Host Plants Determined the Bio-Functions of Biofertilizers. American Journal of Plant Sciences, Vol. 3, No. 8.

Yang J., Kloepper J.W., Ryu C.M. (2009) Rhizosphere Bacteria help Plants Tolerate Abiotic Stress. Trends in Plant Science, 14, 1-4.

Zayed, M.S. (2012). Improvement of Growth and Nutritional Quality of *Moringa oleifera* Using Different Biofertilizers. *Annals of Agricultural Sciences*. 57: 53-62.

Zhuang, L., S. Zhou, Y. Wang, Z. Liu Z and R. Xu. (2011). Cost-effective Production of *Bacillus thuringiensis* Biopesticides by Solid-state Fermentation Using Wastewater Sludge: Effects of Heavy Metals. *Bioresource Technology*. 102: 4820-4826.

Pages: 35-51

BIOTECHNOLOGY, AGRO-ECOLOGY AND ENVIRONMENT

Edited by: Dr. Avnish Chauhan; Dr. Pawan Kumar 'Bharti'

ISBN: 978-93-5056-757-9

Edition: 2015

Published by: Discovery Publishing House Pvt. Ltd., New Delhi (India)

2

Biopesticidal Effect of Black Pepper Extract on Growth Parameters and Diseases of Tomato

Gayatri Nahak[1] and Rajani Kanta Sahu[1, 2*]

ABSTRACT

Black pepper (*Piper nigrum* L.) native of south India popularly known as" king of spices". Pepper is mostly used in the curry recipes as masalas and also as ingredient in the prescriptions of folk medicine, Ayurveda and traditional medicinal systems. Traditionally it used in folk medicine as aphrodisiac, carminative, stomachic, antiseptic diuretic and for the treatment of cough, rheumatoid arthritis, peripheral neuropathy, melanoderma and leprosy due to the presence of volatile compounds, tannins, phenols and other unknown substances. The current investigation was to assess the effects of aqueous extract of *Piper nigrum* L. plant on the growth, yield and disease control of a common vegetable plant tomato (*Solanum lycopersicum* L.). The black pepper extract increased shoot height, number of branches, number of leaves, number of buds, number of flowers and number of fruits of tomato plant over controls in different treatments. Numbers of diseases were calculated as percentage and disease/plant. The percentage of reduction of disease was calculated

1 KIIT School of Biotechnology, KIIT University, Bhubaneswar, Odisha, (India).

2 P.G. Department of Botany, Berhampur University, Berhampur - 760 007, Odisha, (India).

after the spray of black pepper extract on plants. Black pepper extract was found effectively in controlling canker (55.76%), early blight (63.71%), wilt (58.95%), leaf spot (22.55%), fruit spot (52.58%), blossom end rot (57.82%) and sun scald (59.50%) in comparison to controls under field condition. Thus biopesticides can contribute in reducing use of chemical pesticides and subsequently minimize its hazards to the environment and human health.

Key words: Biopesticide, Black pepper extract, *Tomato, Diseases, Growth parameters.*

INTRODUCTION

In their search for pest control agents with limited undesirable effects on the environment and non-target organism, researchers are continuously evaluating botanical resources (Grainge et al., 1986), and exploring new botanicals possessing high pesticidal activity to resolve the pesticide dilemma (Berenbaum, 1989). For pest control massive use of synthetic pesticides has imposed so many detrimental effects on the environment and cause intoxication of non-targeting organisms (Farage Elawar, 1989; Markowitz, 1992; Rajeskaran and Baker, 1994; Gupta et al., 2001). However, these chemicals are declared ecologically unsafe because these persist for longer period in the environment and enter in to the food chain. Such products are greatly disadvantageous for mankind and the environment, therefore research is necessary to identify new products with insecticide effect by studying plants natural defenses, particularly those rich in bioactive organic compounds of insecticide effect, fungicide, growth inhibitor and repellent, amongst others (Almeida et al., 2005). The need for new and less toxic molecules with lesser environmental impact is fundamental, thus stimulating and increasing the interest in research on insecticides plants (Pungitore et al., 2005). During last few decades various synthetic pesticides have been applied to protect stored grains and other agricultural products from insect infestation. But it has been reported that certain insect pests have acquired resistance against most of the insecticides (Brattsten et al., 1986; Zettler and Cuperus, 1990; White, 1995). Thus it is necessary to develop certain new safe alternatives of these synthetic pesticides, which might have no adverse effect on the environment and non-target animals.

Black pepper is one of the important spices rich in aromatic and medicinal components along with appreciable levels of several other functional components having health promoting properties (*Roy and Vijayalaxmi, 2013;* Meghwal and Goswami, 2012). The uses of black pepper in various fields such as food processing, pharmaceutical industry etc, is increasing steadily due to its recognition as an important source of natural antioxidant having anticarcinogenic activity (*Srinivasan*, 2007; *Nair and Gupta, 2003; Abbasi et al., 2010*). Large number of studies has been undertaken in the laboratory against the causal organism affecting the tomato plant. However the effectiveness of the peppercorn extracts on individual crops in different agro-climatic zones and cultivars in field condition have not been investigated much. Hence the objective of the study was to determine to efficacy of aqueous extract of peppercorn for controlling some important diseases like canker, early blight, leaf spot, fruit spot, blossom end rot, wilt and sun scald as well as its effect on growth and yield of tomato plant.

MATERIALS AND METHODS

Preparation of Experimental Plots and Plantation

The grasses and weeds of experimental plot were removed and the land ploughed to a depth of 15-30cm and several holes with the dimension of 30 × 30 × 30cm were made every 150 inches interval. In each hole, required amount of cow-dung and organic fertilizer at the rate of 6-12t/ha was applied. Optimum spacing 90 × 60cm with one plant/hill was maintained. About 10 days old tomato seedlings were planted.

Preparation of Aqueous Peppercorn Extract

Hundred grams from each of the dried, powdered peppercorn were weighed and were mixed in a1000ml distilled water. Then the solution was boiled, cooled and filtered through the cheese cloths followed by filtration by the Whattman No.1 filter paper. Then filtrate was kept under normal room temperature and sprayed on the plants on a weekly basis from 15th day onwards.

Growth, Yield and Disease Parameters

Morphological measurements of tomato plants (*Solanum lycopersicum* L.) were taken during 10-100 days with 10 days intervals after transplantation till harvest time. The growth parameters were taken into consideration and they are as follows: shoot height, number of leaves, number of buds, number of flowers and number of fruits. The percentage of infection (Canker, Early blight, Wilt, Leaf spot, Fruit spot, Blossom end rot and Sun scald) were investigated after 4 weeks of transplantation. Numbers of diseases were calculated as (%) and diseases/plant.

Preparation Crude Extract

The collected peppercorn seeds were shade dried under normal environmental condition, ground into uniform powder using Thomas-Wiley machine. The powdered peppercorn (50g) was extracted with distilled water by using Soxhlet extraction apparatus for 10-12 hrs. Then collected solutions were filtered through Whattman No-1 filer paper. The extracts were evaporated to dryness under reduced pressure at 90°C by Rotary vacuum evaporator to obtain the respective extracts and stored in a freeze condition at -18°C until used for further analysis.

Quantitative Phytochemical Estimation of the Crude Extract

Phytochemical analysis of crude extract of *Piper nigrum* L. was carried out using standard quantitative methods as described by Hagerman *et al.* (2000); Kumaran and Karunakaran (2006); Obdoni and Ochuko (2001). The components analyzed for phytochemicals were phenol, flavonoids, tannins, alkaloids and saponins.

RESULTS AND DISCUSSION

Growth and Yield

Tomato (*Solanum lycopersicum* L.) is the second most important vegetable crop in the world because of its special nutritive value. It is one of the most versatile vegetable with wide usage in Indian culinary tradition which is consumed as a fresh vegetable, in ketchup, as a puree, and in many other forms. One of the main constraints to tomato cultivation is damage caused by pathogens, including viruses, bacteria, nematodes and fungi, which cause severe losses in production worldwide. Major fungal diseases affecting tomato production are late blight, early blight, septoria leaf spot, fusarium wilt, and verticillium wilt, corky root rot, damping-off, leaf mold and powdery mildew (Panthee and Chen, 2010). Controlling of plant diseases mainly depend on fungicides treatments (El-Mougy *et al.*, 2004). However, fungicidal applications cause hazards to human health and increase environmental pollution. Therefore, alternatives, eco-friendly approach treatments for control of plant diseases are needed (Abd-El-Kareem, 2007; Mandal *et al.*, 2009). Biological control methods are being increasingly used in agriculture as an alternative to chemical fungicides to control diseases caused by fungal plant pathogens. Recently, there have been many reports stated that some plant extracts and safe chemicals become a necessary to control many diseases of vegetable plants (Aba AlKhail, 2005; Abogharsa1 *et al.*, 2006; Deepak *et al.*, 2005; Deepak *et al.*, 2007; Mandal et al., 2009).

The experiment was conducted on growth and yield of tomato cultivation of neem extract and the results on effectiveness of various treatments were described. There was significant increase in the plant height, number of branches and leaf number at all growth stages from 10-100 days in pepper extract treatment in comparison to control (Figs. 2.1, 2.2 & 2.3). Number of buds from 40-80 days, number of flowers from 50-90 days and number of fruits 90-120 were recorded. All measured parameters gave significant differences from their respective controls (Figs. 2.4, 2.5 & 2.6). Peppercorn aqueous extract showed a promotive effect on shoot lengths (30.04%), branches (27.72%) leaf numbers (11.82%), number of buds (18.01%), number of flowers (10.30%) and number of fruits (23.07%) with increasing time compared to untreated or control ones. The promotive effect could be due to triterpene which acts by delaying the transformation of ammonium nitrogen into nitrate nitrogen as reported by Akhtar, (1999). Growth stimulating effect of ten medicinal plant extracts (*P. pinatta, A. marmelos, A. indica, B. campestris, P. nigrum, E. tirucalli, V. negundu, A. conyzoides, T. patula and Z. jujube*) on *Lycopersicum esculentum* L. have been observed (Pattnaik *et al.*, 2012). Similar experiment carried out by Okunlola and Thomas (2013) showed the effect of *A. indica* and *Piper guineense* on the growth and yield of jute under sole and mixed cropping. All growth parameters increased in comparison to control. In another experiment ethanolic extracts of *Melia azedarch, Eucalyptus robosta, Sapium sebiferum* had no significant influence on growth and development of Soybean seedlings (Wan *et al.*, 2012). Effect of tea seed extracts on growth of beet, mustard, oat and barley were studied. Different concentrations of these extracts increased the growth, yield and biomass of the crops. The growth stimulating effect is not exclusively by its adverse effect on pathogen or by an increase in nutrient uptake. However substances with hormone like properties can stimulate of effect biomass allocation in plants. In addition to hormones, medicinal plant extracts contain saponins and polyphenols which could be the active compounds causing the effect on growth (Anderson, 2010).

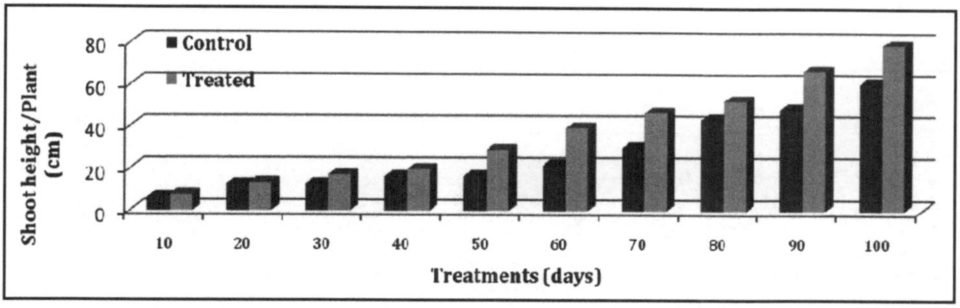

Fig. 2.1: Effect of *P.nigrum* Aqueous Extract on Plant Height of *Lycopersicon esculentum*

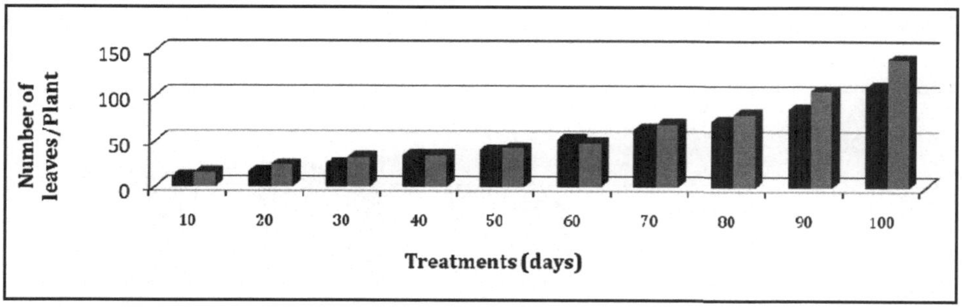

Fig. 2.2: Effect of *P.nigrum* Aqueous Extract on Number of Leaves of *Lycopersicon esculentum*

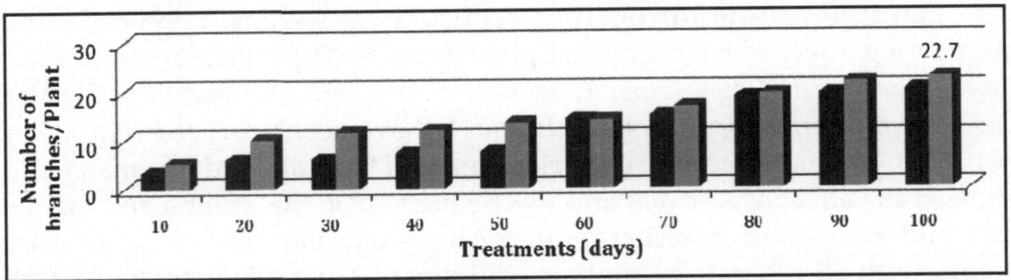

Fig. 2.3: Effect of *P.nigrum* Aqueous Extract on Number of Branches of *Lycopersicon esculentum*

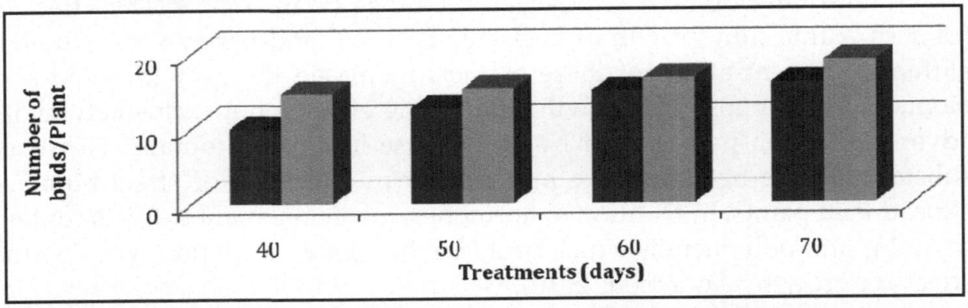

Fig. 2.4: Effect of *P.nigrum* Aqueous Extract on Number of Buds of *Lycopersicon esculentum*

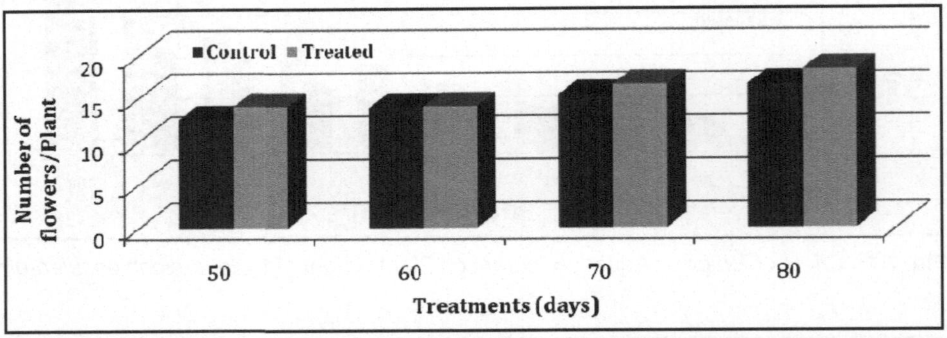

Fig. 2.5: Effect of *P.nigrum* Aqueous Extract on Number Flowers of *Lycopersicon esculentum*

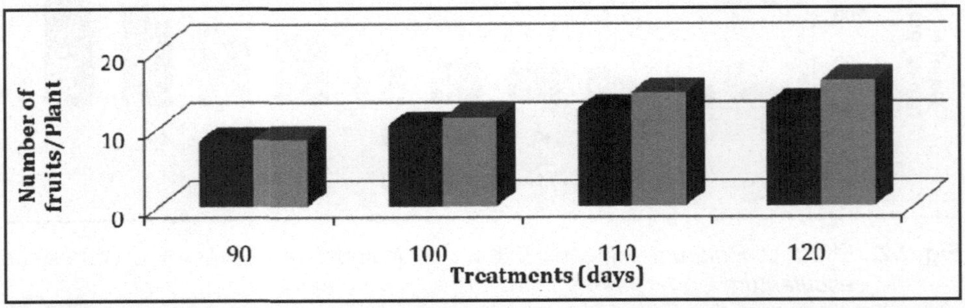

Fig. 2.6: Effect of *P.nigrum* Aqueous Extract on Number Fruits of *Lycopersicon esculentum*

Diseases

Because of its fleshy nature, tomato fruit is attacked by a number of insect pests and diseases. Pathogenic diseases develop through soil borne and above ground infections, and, in some instances, are transmitted through insect feeding. Major tomato diseases include those that attack the root system (fusarium wilt, verticiliun wilt, bacterial wilt, rhizoctonia), above-ground stems and foliage (early blight, leaf spot, bacterial canker, late blight), and fruit (bacterial spot, bacterial speck, anthracnose) (Pandey *et al.*, 2006). Thus, the disease control programme is important at each stage of growth (Tomato Diseases and Disorders).

Canker caused by *Clavibacter michiganense* subsp. michiganense (Cmm), is a serious pathogen of tomatoes which causes serious losses in some tomato plantings. It is often first seen as dark, necrotic lesions at the margins of older leaves. This disease can cause lesions or cankers on any portion of the plant, including the fruit, or it can result in a general wilt or decline of the plant (Gleason *et al.*, 1993; Jones *et al.*, 1991). In our field experiment peppercorn reduced canker disease by 55.76% in comparison to control (Figs. 2.7 & 2.15). Different combinations of natural treatments could give better effects against bacterial canker (*Clavibacter michiganensis* subsp. michiganensis) and bacterial speck (*Pseudomonas syringae* pv. tomato) of tomato such as natural compounds (Tinivella *et al.*, 2009), plant extracts (Hartman *et al.*, 1995), essential oils (Schmitt *et al.*, 2009) and natural acids (Roberts *et al.*, 2006). It was studied that the essential oils from *T. spicata* and *O. syriacum* had the highest inhibitory activity against *Clavibacter michiganensis* subsp. Michiganensis corresponding to 83.6% and 82.8% increase in the zones of inhibition over the control (Soylu *et al.*, 2005).

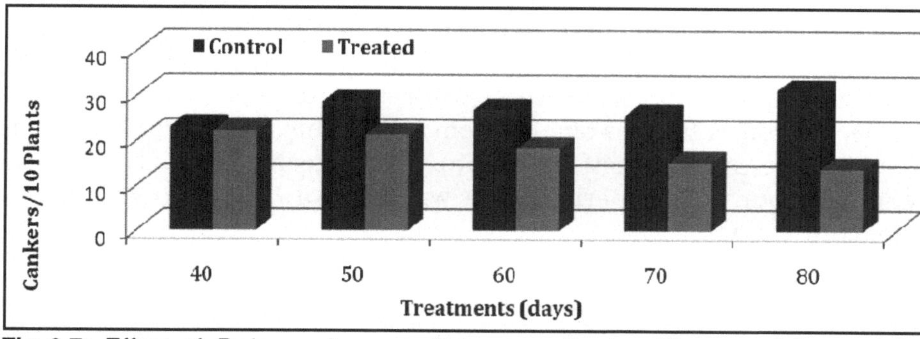

Fig. 2.7: Effect of *P.nigrum* Aqueous Extract on Canker Disease of *Lycopersicon esculentum*

Early blight caused by the fungus *Alternaria solani*, is common foliage diseases which first appears in the older leaves and are characterized by irregular shaped brown spots with concentric rings (Sunil and Srivastava, 2013). These infections often occur near the stem of the tomato fruit. Reported carrot plants sprayed with sea weed extracts showed less disease due to

Alternaria and Botrytis compared to SA and the control (Jayaraj *et al.*, 2008). Previous reports have shown that seaweed extracts can reduce disease and promote plant growth. Jayaraj *et al.*, 2008 reported sea weed evaluated in carrot plants reduced leaf blights caused by Alternaria and Botrytis as effectively as the fungicide chlorothalonil. The result obtained from our investigation showed that the aqueous peppercorn extract act as good antifungal agent by reducing early blight by 63.71% in tomato plant (Figs. 2.8 & 2.16). Similarly garlic and neem oils have also been shown to be effective in reducing the severity of early blight disease of tomato (Wszelaki and Miller, 2005).

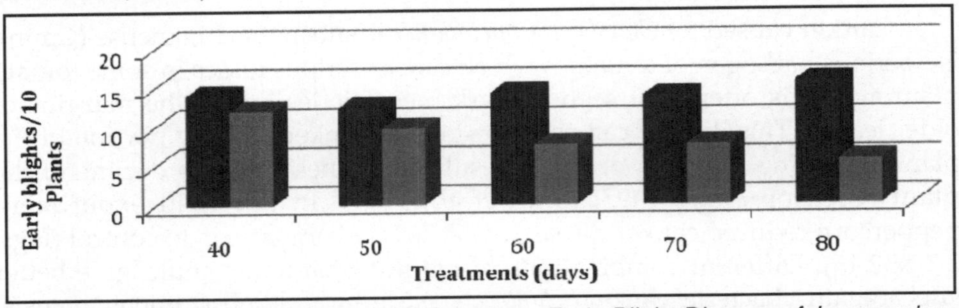

Fig. 2.8: Effect of *P.nigrum* Aqueous Extract on Early Blight Disease of *Lycopersicon esculentum*

Wilt is caused by the soil borne fungus *Fusarium oxysporum* f. sp. *Lycopersici*. The leaf extracts of *Piper nigrum* L. substantially reduced the number of infected leaves and number of lesions on foliage, and curtailed disease development, which in turn, protected flowers and capsules from infection (Enikuomehin, 2005). Similarly our result also showed a positive effect on reducing Fusarium wilt by 58.95% (Figs. 2.9 & 2.17). The results obtained from EI-Khalal, 2007; Croxton *et al.*, 2011 who reported that the growth rate of shoot and root was markedly inhibited in tomato seedlings in response to fusarium wilt diseases. Effect of crude extract of neem and neem seed at concentrations ranging from 5-30% inhibited growth of *Fusarium oxysporum* the causal agent of tomato wilt (Ogechi, 2006). This further strengthens our field experiment on wilt control of tomato by aqueous peppercorn extract.

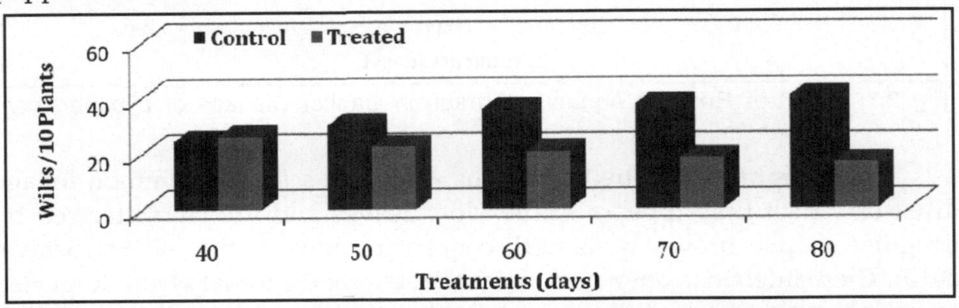

Fig. 2.9: Effect of *P.nigrum* Aqueous Extract on Wilt Disease of *Lycopersicon esculentum*

Leaf spot caused by the fungus *Septoria lycopersici* which are noticeable by small, circular spots on the upper surface of the lower leaves. Heavily infected leaves turn yellow, wither, and eventually fall off. Reduction of leaf spot disease was observed from 40th day onwards and maximum reduction was observed on 80th day in comparison to control (55.48%) (Figs. 2.10 & 2.18). A study was undertaken to evaluate the effectiveness of 33 plant extracts against leaf spot of ground nut. All treatments including *Piper nigrum* gave considerable reduction in disease incidence (Hussain *et al.*, 2013). Suppression of septorial leaf disease of tomato by aerated compost tea reduced 22.55% of diseases by foliar spray (Gangaiah *et al.*, 2004). It can be concluded that peppercorn extract was found more effective in comparison to other plants.

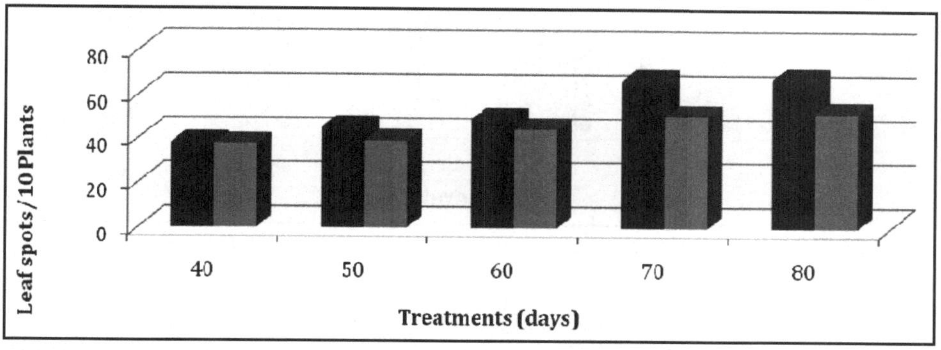

Fig. 2.10: Effect of *P.nigrum* Aqueous Extract on Leaf Spot Disease of *Lycopersicon esculentum*

Fruit spot caused by *Pseudomonas syringae pv.* is the most common disease in tomatoes. Spots on tomato fruit are not very deep. They can be cut out and the tomato can be eaten (Reddy *et al.*, 2001). Suppression of bacterial spots of tomato with foliar sprays of compost extract under green house and field condition was investigated. The population of infected leaves was reduced significantly by extracts prepared from cow manure (Jaber H. Aldahmani *et al.*, 2003). In our present study peppercorn extract treated tomato plants showed significantly better performance over control by 52.58% (Figs. 2.11 & 2.18).

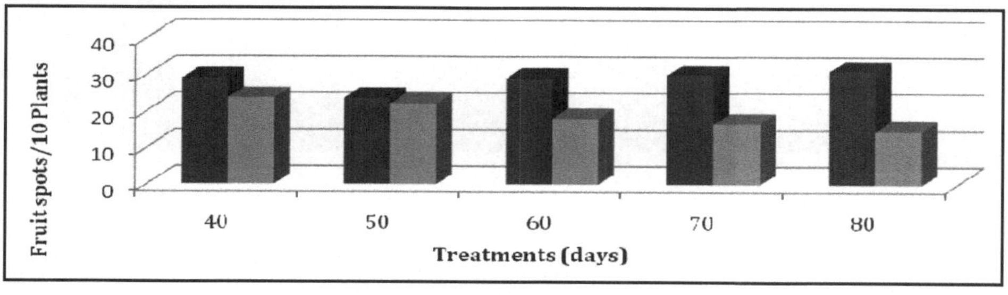

Fig. 2.11: Effect of *P.nigrum* Aqueous Extract on Fruit Spot Disease of *Lycopersicon esculentum*

Blossom end rot which caused by a calcium deficiency that is related to wide fluctuations in available moisture which can be caused by excessive use of Nitrogen. Brownish black spots on the blossom end of the fruits which may gradually increase in size invade the lesion and cause complete rotting of the fruit (Reddy *et al.*, 2001). Reduction in incidence of blossom end rot of tomato by foliar application of plant extract mixed with Ca and sugar ester reduced the incidence of blossom end rot in comparison to control (Ikeda and Osawa, 1988). However peppercorn extract only reduced BER by 57.82% without any addition of minerals and micro nutrients (Figs. 2.12 & 2.19).

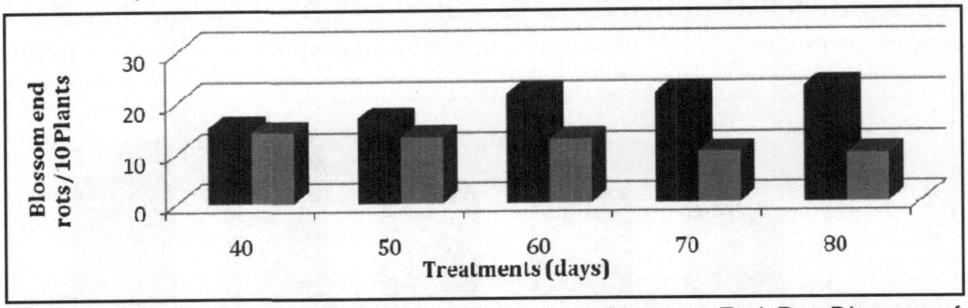

Fig. 2.12: Effect of *P.nigrum* Aqueous Extract on Blossom End Rot Disease of *Lycopersicon esculentum*

Sunscald appears as light patches on green or ripening fruit. As the patches grow, they may blister and may become grayish-white. Affected sunscald tomatoes can develop black mold (Sunburn or Sunscald-Peppers and Tomatoes). In various studies it was shown that neem based pesticides like neem cake, neem seed kernel extract (NSKE), neem leaf extract, neem oil etc., act as a repellent and antifeedent and its oil is effective against fruit borer (Elshafie and Basedow, 2003). Similar observation was noticed in our experiment where the foliar application of peppercorn extract reduced 59.50% of sun scald (Figs. 2.13 & 2.19).

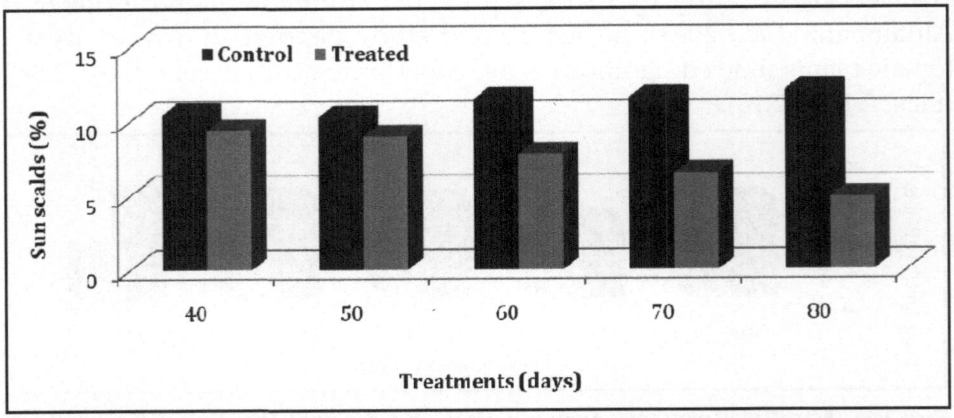

Fig. 2.13: Effect of *P.nigrum* Aqueous Extract on Sun Scald Disease of *Lycopersicon esculentum*

The phytochemical screening and quantitative estimation of the percentage crude yields of chemical constituents of the plants studied showed that the leaves, stems and seeds were rich in alkaloids, flavonoids, tannins and saponins. They were known to show medicinal activity as well as exhibiting physiological activity (Sofowara, 1993; Nahak and Sahu, 2011). The result obtained from Fig. 2.14 showed the presence of some important phytochemical compounds in the leaf extract of *Piper nigrum* L. such as alkaloids (16.27mg/g), flavonoids (10.04mg/g), saponins (4.05mg/g), steroids (5.3mg/g), terpenoids (6.12mg/g) and tannins (2.93mg/g). These class of compounds independently or in combination may be responsible for the broad range of medicinal properties of peppercorn which exhibit an extra ordinary array of pharmacological activities. Treatment with pepper aqueous extract provided an effective control of canker (55.76%), early blight (63.71%), wilt (58.95%), leaf spot (22.55%), fruit spot (52.58%), blossom end rot (57.82%) and sun scald (59.50%) diseases of *Solanum lycopersicum* L. and this can be attributed to the fact that pepper has numerous monoterpenes hydrocarbons such as *sabinene, pinene, terpenene, limonene, mercene,* etc., which altogether gives aromatic property to the pepper. These compounds help the body removes harmful free radicals and helps protect from cancers and diseases (Nisar Ahmad et al., 2010).

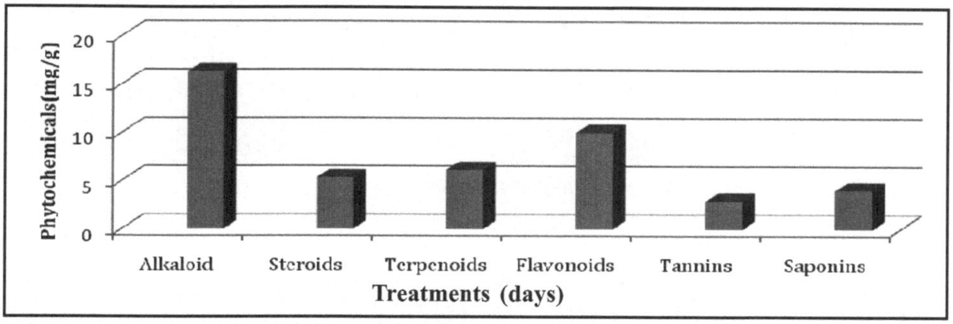

Fig. 2.14: Quantitative Phytochemical Constituents of Ethanol Extract of *Piper nigrum* Leaves

Fig. 2.15: Bacterial Canker in Leaf and Fruit of Tomato Plant

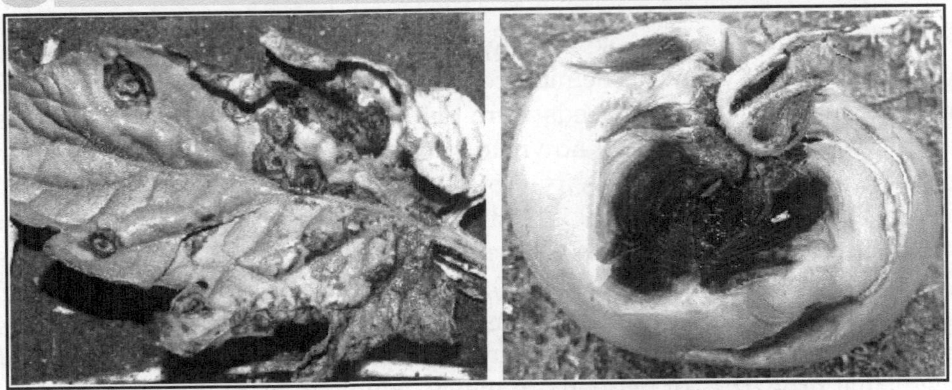

Fig. 2.16: Early Blight Infection in Leaf and Fruit of Tomato Plant

Fig. 2.17: Wilt Diseases in Tomato Leaf and Fruits

Fig. 2.18: Leaf Spot and Fruit Spot Diseases in Tomato Plant

Fig. 2.19: Blossom End Rot and Sun Scald in Fruits of Tomato Plant

CONCLUSION

Black pepper is one of the important spices which is in great demand due to its innumerable medicinal properties. It is composed of numerous organic chemicals including essential oil, alkaloids, flavonoids, phenols, lignans, acids, amides and other aromatic compounds. The results of the present studies showed that Black pepper based formulations in all the treatments were found to be superior over control not only on shoot height, number of leaves, number of buds, number of flowers and number of fruits of *Solanum lycopersicum* L. but in respect of diseases control also such as wilt and leaf spot which suggest that use of pepper extracts are good alternative to synthetic pesticides because they are easily available, safe to environment, cost effective, nonhazardous, natural enemies, have low to moderate mammalian toxicity. Through such based line data it is suggested that the further researches on black pepper should be directed towards identification and quantification of active principles responsible for standardization and formulation of the pepper extract would make it easier to use and, therefore, more acceptable to farmers.

REFERENCES

1. Aba AlKhail, A.A. (2005): Antifungal Activity of Some Extracts Against Some Plant Pathogenic fungi // Pakistan J. Biol. Sci., 8(3): 413-417.
2. Abbasi, B.H., Ahmad, N., Fazal, H. and Mahmood, T. (2010): Conventional and Modern Propagation Techniques in Piper Nigrum. J. Med. Plant Res., 4: 007-012.
3. Abbasi, P.A., Cuppels, D.A. and Lazarovits, G. (2003): Effect of Foliar Applications of Neem Oil and Fish Emulsion on Bacterial Spot and Yield of Tomatoes and Peppers. Can. J. Plant Pathol., 25: 41-48.
4. Abd-El-Kareem, F. (2007): Induced Resistance in Bean Plants Against Root Rot and Alternaria Leaf Spot Diseases Using Biotic and Abiotic Inducers Under Field Conditions. Research Journal of Agriculture and Biological Sciences, 3(6): 767-774.
5. Aboellil, A.H. (2007): Trilogy, a Product of Neem (*Azadirachta indica*) Induces Resistance in Cucumber Against *Podosphaera xanthi*. Research Journal of Microbiology, 2 (5): 402-414.

6. Abogharsa1, I.A., Saeed, M.A. and Buhidma, M.S. (2006): Control of Fusarium Wilt Fungus on Tomato Plant by Plant Extracts // Ninth Arab Congress of Plant Protection, Damascus, Syria.
7. Ahmad, N., Fazal, H., Abbasi, B.H., Rashid, M., Mahmood, T. and Fatima, N. (2010): Efficient Regeneration and Antioxidant Potential in Regenerated-tissues of Piper Nigrum L. Plant Cell, Tissue and Organ Culture, 102: 129-134.
8. Akhtar, M. and Mahmood, I. (1995): Evaluation of a Neem Based Product Against Root-knot Nematode *Meloidogyne incognita*. Tests of Agrochemicals and Cultivars, Suppl. Annal. Appl. Biol., 16: 6-7.
9. Almeida, F.A.C., Almeida, A.S., Santos, N.R., Gomes, J.P. and Araújo, M.E.R. (2005): Efeitos de extratos alcoólicos de plantas sobre o caruncho do feijão Vigna (*Callosobruchus maculatus*). Rev. Bras. Eng. Agríc. Ambient, 9(4): 585-590.
10. Anderson, M. (2010): Plant Growth is Stimulated by Tea-seed Extract: A New Natural Growth Regulator? Hort. Science, 45(12): 1848-1853.
11. Anderson, M. (2010): Plant Growth is Stimulated by Tea-seed Extract: A New Natural Growth Regulator? Hort. Science, 45(12): 1848-1853.
12. Arden, F. Sherf. (1987): Text for Septoria Leaf Spot from: Foliar Blights of Tomato. Department of Plant Pathology, Cornell University; Text for Septoria Leaf Spot from: Foliar Blights of Tomato, V38, 1987, Ohio State University.
13. Berenbaum, M.R. (1989): North American Ethnobotanicals Assources of Novel Plant Based Insecticides, pp. 11-24. In: Insecticides of Plant Origin (Arnason J.T., Philogene B.J.R., Morand P, Eds). ACS Symposium Series 387, American Chemical Society, Washigton, USA.
14. Bohra, B., Vyas B.N. and Mistry, K.B. (2006): Ecofriendly Management of Damping- off in Winter Vegetables and Tobacco Using Microbial Agents and Neem Formulations. J. Mycol. Pl. Pathol., 36: 178-181.
15. Brahmachari, G. (2004): Neem- An Omnipotent Plant: A Retrospection. Chem. Biochem., 5: 408-421.
16. Brattsten, L.B., Holyoke, C.W., Leeper, J.R. and Raffa, K.F. (1986): Insecticide Resistance: Challenge to Pest Management and Basic Research. Science, 231: 1125-1160.
17. Chaturvedi, R., Razdan, M.K. and Bhojwani, S.S. (2003): Production of Haploids of Neem (*Azadirachta indica* A. Juss.) by Anther Culture. Plant Cell Rep., 21: 531-537.
18. Croxton, S.D., Foshee, III, W.G., Blythe, E.K., Murphy, J.F. and Sibley, J.L. (2011): Evaluation of Selected Tempera Paints Applied to Tomatoes to Reduce the Occurrence of Tomato Spotted Wilt Virus. International Journal of Vegetable Science, 17: 177-189.
19. Deepak, S.A., Oros, G., Sathyanarayana, S.G., Shetty, H.S. and Sashikanth, S. (2007): Antisporulant Activity of Watery Extracts of Plants Against *Sclerospora graminicola* Causing Downy Mildew Disease of Pearl Millet // American Journal of Agricultural and Biological Sciences, 2(1): 36-42.
20. Deepak, S.A., Oros, G., Sathyanarayana, S.G., Shetty, N.P., Shetty, H.S. and Sashikanth, S. (2005): Antisporulant Activity of Leaf Extracts of Indian Plants Against *Sclerospora graminicola* Causing Downy Mildew Disease of Pearl Millet // Archives of Phytopathology and Plant Protection, 38(1): 31-39.
21. El Shafie, H.A.F. and Basedow T. (2003): The Efficacy of Different Neem Preparations for the Control of Insects Damaging Potatoes and Eggplants in the Sudan. Crop Prot., 22, 1015-1021.
22. El-Khallal, S.M. (2007): Induction and Modulation of Resistance in Tomato Plants Against *fusarium* Wilt Disease by Bioagent Fungi (*Arbuscular Mycorrhiza*) and/or Hormonal Elicitors (Jasmonic Acid & Salicylic Acid): 2-changes in the Antioxidant Enzymes, Phenolic Compounds and Pathogen Related-proteins. Australian Journal of Basic and Applied Science, 1 (4): 717-732.
23. El-Mougy, N.S., Abd-El-Karem, F., El-Gamal, N.G. and Fotouh, Y.O. (2004): Application of Fungicides Alternatives for Controlling Cowpea Root Rot Diseases Under Greenhouse and Field Conditions. Egypt. J. Phytopathol., 32: 23-35.

24. Elshafie, H.A.F. and Basedow, T.H. (2003): The Efficacy of Different Neem Preparations for the Control of Insects Damaging Potatoes and Eggplants in the Sudan. Crop protection, 22: 1015-1021.

25. Enikuomehin, O.A. (2005): Cercospora Leaf Spot Disease Management in Sesame (*Sesamum indicum* L.) with Plant Extracts. Journal of Tropical Agriculture, 43(1-2): 19-23.

26. Farage Elawar, M. (1989): Enzyme and Behavioural Changes in Young Chicks as a Result of Carbaryl Treatment. Journal of Toxicology and Environmental Health, 26: 119-132.

27. Gangaiah, C., Carey, E. and Tisserat, N.A. (2004): Suppression of Septoria Leaf Spot Disease of Tomato Using Aerated Compost Tea. Kansas State University. ASHS Annual Meeting. Available on http://www.ashs.org/annualmeeting/conference/index.lasso.

28. Gleason, M.L., Gitaitis, R.D. and Ricker, M.D. (1993): Recent Progress in Understanding and Controlling Bacterial Canker of Tomato in Eastern North America. Plant Disease, 77: 1069-1076.

29. Grainge, M., Ahmed, S., Mitchell, W. C. and Hylin, J.W. (1986): Plant Species Reportedly Possessing Pest Control Properties. An East-West Central University of Hawaii Database. East-West Center, Honolulu, HI, USA.

30. Gupta, A., Upadhyay, R.K. and Saxena, P.N. (2001): Toxicity Evaluation of Certain Blood Biochemical Parameters in *Passer domesticus* (Linn.). Journal of Scientific and Industrial Research, 60: 668-674.

31. Hagerman, A., Muller I. and Makkar, H. (2000): Quantification of Tannins in Tree Foliage. A Laboratory Manual, Vienna: FAO/IAEA, pp: 4-7.

32. Hartman, M, Szoboszlai, S. and Kriszt, B. (1995): Biogazdák által alkalmazott növényi kivonatok értékelése laboratóriumi körülmé- nyek között, Növényvédelem, 31(2): 59-65.

33. Hussain, B., War, A.R. and Sharma, H.C. (2013): *Jasmonic and Salicylic Acid-induced Resistance in Sorghum Against the Stem Borer Chilo Partellus.* Phytoparasitica. pp: 1-22.

34. Ikeda, H. and Osawa, T. (1988): The Effects of NO_3/NH_4 Ratios and Temperature of the Nutrient Solution on Growth, Yield and Blossom End Rot Incidence in Tomato. J. Jpn. Soc. Hort. Sci., 57: 62-69.

35. Jaber, H. Al-Dahmani, Pervaiz A. Abbasi, Sally A. Miller and Harry Hoitink A. J. (2003): Suppression of Bacterial Spot of Tomato with Foliar Sprays of Compost Extracts Under Greenhouse and Field Conditions. Plant Disease, 87(8): 913-919.

36. Jayaraj, J.A., Wan, M. and Rahman Punja, Z.K. (2008): Seaweed Extract Reduces Foliar Fungal Diseases on Carrot. Crop Protection, 27: 1360-1366.

37. Jones, J.B., Jones, J.P., Stall, R.E. and Zitter, T.A. (1991): Compendium of Tomato Diseases. American Phytopathological Society Press. St. Paul, MN.

38. Kokate, C.K., Purohit, A.P., Gokhale, S.B. (2008): Pharmacognosy, 42nd Edition, Nirali Prakashan, pp: 11.56-11.58.

39. Kumaran, A. and Karunakaran, R. (2006): Anti Oxidant and Free Radical Scavenging Activity of an Aqueous Extracts of *Coleus aromaticus.* Food Chemistry, 97: 109-114.

40. Mandal, S., Mallicka, N. and Mitraa A. (2009): Salicylic Acid Induced Resistance to *Fusarium oxysporum* f. sp. *lycopersici* in tomato // Plant Physiology and Biochemistry, 47(7): 642-649.

41. Markowitz, S.B. (1992): Poisoning of an Urban Family due to Misapplication of Household Organophosphate and Carbamate Pesticides. Clinical Toxicology, 32: 295-300.

42. Meghwal, M. and Goswami, T.K. (2012): Chemical Composition, Nutritional, Medicinal and Functional Properties of Black Pepper: A Review. Open Access Scientific Reports, 1: 172.

43. Nahak, G. and R.K. Sahu (2010: Antioxidant Activity in Bark and Roots of Neem (*Azadirachta indica*) and Mahaneem (*Melia azedarach*).J of American Sci., 4: 28-34.

44. Nair, R.R. and Gupta, S.D. (2003): Somatic Embryogenesis and Plant Regeneration in Black Pepper (Piper nigrum L.). Direct Somatic Embryogenesis from Tissue of Germinating Seeds and Ontogeny of Somatic Embryos. J. Hortic. Sci. Biotchnol., 78: 416-421.

45. Nisar Ahmad, Hina Fazal, Bilal Haider Abbasi, Shahid Farooq. (2010): Efficient Free Radical Scavenging Activity of *Ginkgo biloba, Stevia rebaudiana* and *Parthenium hysterophorous* Leaves Through DPPH (2, 2-diphenyl-1-picrylhydrazyl). International Journal of Phytomedicine, 2: 231-239.
46. Obdoni, B. and Ochuko, P. (2001): Phytochemical Studies and Comparative Efficacy of the Crude Extracts of Some Homostatic Plants in Edo and Delta States of Nigeria. Global J. Pure Appl. Sci., 8: 203-208.
47. Ogechi, N., Agbenin and Marley, P.S. (2006): In-vitro Assay of Some Plant Extracts Against *Fusarium oxysporum* f. Sp. Lycopersici Causal Agent of Tomato Wilt. Journal of Plant Protection Research, 46(3): 215-220.
48. Okunlola, I.A. and Thomas, I.O. (2013): Effect of Mixed Cropping and Plant Extracts on the Growth, Yield and Pest Control of Jute (*Corchorus olitorius* L.). Folia Hort., 25 (1): 49-60.
49. Pandey, A.K., Namgyal, D., Mehdi, M., Mir, M.S. and Shikh, B.A. (2006): A Case Study: Major Insect Pest Associated with Different Vegetable Crops in Cold Arid Region, Ladakh of Jammu and Kashmir. J. Entomol. Res., 30: 169-174.
50. Panthee, D.R. and Chen. F. (2010): Genomics of Fungal Disease Resistance in Tomato. Curr. Genomics, 11: 30-39.
51. Pattnaik, M., Kar M. and Sahu, R. K. (2012): Bioefficacy of Some Plant Extracts on Growth Parameters and Control of Diseases in *Lycopersicum esculentum*. Asian Journal of Plant Science and Research, 2(2): 129-142.
52. Pungitore, C.R., García, M., Gianello, J.C., Sosa, M.E. and Tonn, C.E. (2005): Insecticidal and Antifeedant Effects of *Junellia aspera* (Verbenaceae) Triterpenes and Derivatives on *Sitophilus oryzae* (Coleoptera: Curculionidae). J. Stored Prod. Res., 41: 434-443.
53. Rajeskaran, M. and Baker, P.P. (1994): Biochemical Changes in the Liver of House Sparrows (Passer domesticus) Treated with Combinations of Pesticides. Indian Journal of Environmental Toxicology, 4: 37-40.
54. Reddy, M.S. Ryu, C.M., Rodríguez-Kábana, R., Dawkins, T. and Kloepper, J.W. (2001): Can Beneficial Bacteria from Auburn Boost Tomato Growth and Yield? www.bashanfoundation.org/reddy/reddyyield.pdf.
55. Roberts, S.J. et al. (2006): Physical and Biological Seed Treatments for Control of Bacterial Diseases of Carrots and Brassicas Caused by Xanthomonas app., 11th International Conference on Plant Pathogenic Bacteria, Edinburgh, Scotland.
56. Roy, U.B. and Vijayalaxmi, K.K. (2013): Review of Phytochemistry and Medicinal Properties of Piper Nigrum, the Black Gold. IJESR, 3(7): 326-331. Schmitt, A., Koch, E., Stephan, D., Kromphardt, C., Jahn, M., Krauthausen, H.J., Forsberg, G., Werner, S., Amein, T., Wright, F. Tinivella, Van der Wolf J. and Groot, S.P.C. (2009): Evaluation of Non-chemical Seed Treatment Methods for the Control of *Phoma valerianellae* on Lamb's Lettuce Seeds. Journal of Plant Diseases and Protection, 116 (5), 200-207.
57. Sofowara A. (1993): Medicinal Plants and Traditional Medicine in Africa. Spectrum Books Ltd, Ibadan, Nigeria. pp: 289.
58. Soylu, S., Soylu, E.M., Bozkurt, I.A. and Kaya, A.D. (2003): Antibacterial Activities of Essential Oils from Oregano, Thyme, Rosemary and Lavender Plants Against *Pseudomonas savastanoi* pv. phaseolicola, the Causal Agent of Halo Blight of Bean. Ovidius Univ. Ann. Med. Sci. Pharm., 1: 40-44.
59. Srinivasan, K. (2007): Black Pepper and its Pungent Principle-piperine. A Review of Diverse Physiological Effects. Crit. Rev. Food Sci. Nutr., 47: 735-748.
60. Sunil, K. and Srivastava, K. (2013): Screening of Tomato Genotypes Against Early Blight (*Alternaria solani*) Under Field Condition. The Bioscan., 8(1): 189-193.
61. Tinivella, F., Hirata, L.M. Celan, A., Wright, S.A.I., Amein, T., Schmitt, A. Koch, E. Van Der Wolf, J., Groot, S.P.C., Stephan, D. Garibaldi, A. and Gullino, M.L. (2009): Control of Seed-borne Pathogens on Legumes by Microbial and Other Alternative Seed Treatments. Eur. J. Plant Pathol. 123: 139-151.

62. Wan, J., Xu, J., Yang, M., Yang, Z., Huang, Q. and Zhao, S. (2012): Effects of Three Plant Extracts on Growth and Development of Dodder and Soybean and on Protective Enzymes of Host. Legume Genomics and Genetics, 3(2): 8-13.

63. White N.D.G. (1995): Insects, Mites and Insecticides in Stored Grain Ecosystem, pp. 123-168. In: Stored Grain Ecosystem (Jayas D.S., White N.D.G., Muir W.E., Eds). Marcel Dekker, New York, USA.

64. Wszelaki, A.L. and Miller, S.A. (2005): Determining the efficacy of Disease Management Product in Organically-produced Tomatoes. Plant Health Progress. Plant Health Progress, (July): 1-7.

65. Zettler, J.L. and Cuperus, G.W. (1990): Pesticide Resistance in *Tribolium castaneum* (Coleoptera: Tenebrionidae) and *Rhyzopertha dominica* (Coleoptera: Bostrichidae) in Wheat. Journal of Economic Entomology, 83: 1677-1681.

Pages: 52-72

BIOTECHNOLOGY, AGRO-ECOLOGY AND ENVIRONMENT

Edited by: Dr. Avnish Chauhan; Dr. Pawan Kumar 'Bharti'

ISBN: 978-93-5056-757-9

Edition: 2015

Published by: Discovery Publishing House Pvt. Ltd., New Delhi (India)

3

Diseases Management in Betelvine *An Overview*

Shivnath Das[1]; Sanjeev Kumar[2]
Rakesh Deo Ranjan[3] and Archana Rani[4]

ABSTRACT

Betelvine (*Piper betle* L.) is an important cash crop of India. The deep green heart shaped leaves of betelvine are popularly known as *Pan* in India. It is an evergreen dioecious and perennial creeper, grown in conservatories (Baroj) under shady and humid conditions that are necessary for the growth of plant. The shady and moist atmosphere also favour the development of many diseases incited by fungi, bacteria, viruses and nematodes that greatly affect the growth of plants and produces heavy losses to farmers. The major diseases like leaf and foot rot caused by *P. palmivora or P. parasitica*, anthracnose caused by *Colletotrichum capsici* (Syd.) Butler and Bisby and bacterial leaf spot caused by *Xanthomonas campestris* pv. *betlicola* (Patel, Kulkarni and

1 Junior Scientist cum Assistant Professor, Agronomy, Bihar Agriculture University, Sabour, Bhagalpur, Bihar.

2 Assistant Professor/Scientist, Plant Pathology, Jawahar lal Nehru Krishi Vishwavidyalaya-Jabalpur, M.P.

3 Junior Scientist cum Assistant Professor, Plant physiology, Bihar Agriculture University, Sabour, Bhagalpur, Bihar.

4 Ph.D, Department of Agricultural Biotechnology and Molecular Biology, (FBS & H), Rajendra Agricultural University, Pusa - 848 125, Bihar (India).

Dhande) Dye, basal rot or collar rot caused by *Sclerotium rolfsii* and root knot caused by *Meloidoyne incognita* and others plant parasitic nematodes are the main yield limiting factors of the betelvine cultivation all over the India. Here, an attempt is made to reviewed the major diseases incited the betelvines and their symptomatology, etiology, epidemiology and management.

INTRODUCTION

Betelvine (*Piper betle* L.) is an important traditional and ancient cash plantation crop of India. It belongs to family Piperaceae. The deep green heart shaped leaves of betelvine are popularly known as *Pan* in India. It is also known as Nagaballi, Nagurvel, Saptaseera, Sompatra, Tamalapaku, Tambul, Tambuli, Vaksha Patra, Vettilai, Voojangalata etc in different parts of the country (Gunther, 1952; CSIR, 1969; Krishnamurthi, 1969; Guha and Jain, 1997). Betelvine is cultivated in many parts of world including India, Bangladesh, Malaysia, Srilanka, Pakistan, Mauritius and Myanmar for its leaves, which are used for mastication along with areca nut due to its stimulatory aromatic taste (Satyabrata *et al.* 1995; Mithila *et al.* 2000). Betel leaves is also known for its medicinal attributes contain some vitamins, enzymes, thiamine, riboflavin, tannin, iodine, iron, calcium, minerals, protein, essential oil and medicine for liver, brain and heart diseases (Chopra *et al.*, 1956; Khanra, 1997). Its leaves also contain anti-oxidant properties due to the presence of phenols; particularly hydroxylchavicol (4-allyl pyrocatechol) and its aromatic volatile oil contain a phenol called chavicol which has powerful antiseptic properties. The presence of aromatic volatile oil also gives rise to a sensation of warmth and well-being in the mouth and stomach. It is also known to produce a primary stimulation of the central nervous system and the betel leaf is also believed to be a common household remedy for various ailments (Guha, 2006; Ramamurthi and Usha Rani, 2012).

Betelvine is a native crop of tropical south East Asia. Geographically betelvine cultivation is restricted in the region between 68°E and 118°E longitude and 30^{0}N and 12°S latitude. The most probable place of origin of betel is Malayasia (Chattopadhyay and Maity, 1967). India is the largest producer of betel leaves in the world (Arulmozhiyan *et al.*, 2005) and betelvine is cultivated by following the traditional methods under artificially erected structure known as 'baroj' which is a kind of hut with its sides and roof are made of jute stick or straw on a light frame of bamboo. It is cultivated in India on about 75,000 ha area with an annual production worth about Rs. 1000 million (Dasgupta, 2012; Vijaykumar and Arumugam, 2012). On an average about 66% of such production is contributed by the state of West Bengal, where it is cultivated on about 20,000 ha area (Guha, 2006). There are about a hundred varieties of betelvine grown across the world, of which about 40 are found in India, and of these, 30 grown in West Bengal alone. It is also cultivated in other states like Assam, Bihar, Madhya Pradesh, Maharashtra, Orissa, Tripura and Uttar Pradesh (Maity, 1989; Samanta, 1994; Guha 1997; Ramamurthi and Usha Rani, 2012).

The betelvine is an evergreen dioecious and perennial creeper, grown in conservatories (Baroj) under shady and humid conditions that are necessary for the growth of plant. The shady and moist atmosphere also favour the development of many diseases incited by fungi, bacteria, viruses and nematodes that greatly affect the growth of plants and produces heavy losses to farmers (Mathew *et al.* 1978; Maiti and Sen, 1979; Singh and Rao, 1988; Chattopadhayay and Maiti, 1990; Goswami *et al.*, 2002; Akhter *et al.*, 2011). The major diseases like Phytophthora leaf and foot rot caused by *P. palmivora or P. parasitica*, anthracnose caused by *Colletotrichum capsici* (Syd.) Butler and Bisby and bacterial leaf spot caused by *Xanthomonas campestris* pv. *betlicola* (Patel, Kulkarni and Dhande) Dye, basal rot caused by *Sclerotium rolfsii* and root knot nematodes are the main yield limiting factors of the betelvine cultivation all over India.

FUNGAL DISEASES

Betelvine is subjected to attack of many fungal diseases including foot rot and leaf rot, anthracnose leaf spot, powdery mildew and collar rot or wilt.

Foot Rot and Leaf Rot

Dastur (1927) first reported foot rot and leaf rot diseases of betelvine (*P. betle* L.) from Durg, caused by *P. parasitica* var. *piperina*. The disease has been also reported from almost all betelvine growing countries in the world including Indonesia, Myanmar (Su, 1937), Sri Lanka (Paul, 1939) and Bangladesh (Roy, 1948; Turner, 1969) etc. Waterhouse (1963) reported is caused by *Phytophthora nicotianae* var. *parasitica*. Maiti and Sen (1979) considered it is as *P. palmivora* while Marimuthu (1991) called the pathogen *P. palmivora* MF_4. In recent literature *P. palmivora* MF_4 has been called *P. capcici* (Melhotra and Aggarwal, 2003). The highest intensity of foot and leaf rot has been also recorded in Midnapore and Nadia district of West Bengal (Dasgupta and Sen, 1997, 1999) and other states of India. The extent of losses may vary from 30-100% in case of foot rot and leaf rot leading to almost total crop failure (Maiti and Sen, 1982; Maiti and Sen, 1979; Dasgupta *et al.*, 2000).

Symptomatology: Dastur (1935) gave an accurate description of the symptoms of the disease includes foot rot or wet rot associated with wilting of vines is common. The leaves and shoots turn yellow, wither and finally dry out to a pale brown colour. In the diseased plants fine young roots are infected first. Gradually the rotting spreads through older roots and ultimately reaches the foot or collar region of the plant. In a diseased plant, the whole underground portion gets more or less completely rotten. The soft tissues of old roots and the inter-nodal portion of the cuttings are completely decomposed by the pathogen, leaving only the fibrous portion.

Table 3.1: Losses Caused due to Diseases in Betelvine

Sl.No	Major Diseases	Causal Organism	Approx. Losses	References
Fungal Diseases				
1.	Foot rot and Leaf rot	*P. parasitica* var. *piperina*	30-100%	Dasgupta *et al.*, 2000
2.	Leaf spot/Anthracnose	*Colletotrichum capsici*	10-60% yield loss	Maiti and Sen, 1982
3.	Powdery mildew	*Odium piperis*	10-20%	Mitra (1930)
4.	Sclerotial wilt/Stem rot/ Collar rot/Basal rot	*S. rolfsii*	42-62%.	Singh and Chand (1982)
5.	Leaf spot	*Fusarium semitectum. Drechslera rostrat, Alternaria alternata*	10-50%	Saleem and Zareen, 1999
Bacterial Diseases				
6.	Bacterial leaf spot/ stem canker/bacterial blight	*Xanthomonas axonopodis* pv. *betlicola*	75%	Amarasinghe (2009)
Viral Diseases				
7.	Betel vine mosaic	*Cucumber mosaic virus*	5-10	Singh and Rao, 1988).
Nematode Diseases				
8.	Root knot nematode	*Meloidogyne incognita*	3.9 to 40.28	Jonathan *et al.*, 1990
9.	Reniform nematode	*Rotylenchulus* renifoms	3.9 to 50.28	Akhter *et al.*, 2011

Fig. 3.1: Leaf Rot

Letter the symptoms are also characterized by Vijaykumar and Arumugam (2012) as the diseased plant at this stage exhibits a general pallor and drooping of the tender shoots. The aerial parts, leaves or stem do not show any other sign of infection such as lesions or rotting. Such plants when pulled out easily break at the collar region and underground parts are found to be in the state of decay. The roots and rootlets are found to be black or brown, and in decaying condition. Wilting is dependent on the extent of infection, rapidity of infection in the internodes and the position of the internodes. If the internodes just below the ground surface are infected, the plants wilt very suddenly as if they are cut off from all possible sources of water and food. When the infection is first evident in internodes away from the soil surface, the aerial parts of the plants appear to remain normal and healthy for a long time as the internodes above the diseased portion still continue to function. The disease in internodes can be easily detected by the blackening of the tissues inside. The infection to aerial parts does not usually extend beyond one or two internodes because the plant is killed before the disease progresses further.

The disease leaf rot is characterized by the presence of circular black or brownish water soaked spots. These spots rapidly increase in size and coalesce with each other, involving a major area in the leaf blade, which undergoes rotting when the weather is continuously wet. The central rotten portion of the spot drops out, leaving a hole with irregular edges. The symptoms develop on any part of the leaves, including tips and margins. If the conditions still continue to be favorable, the rot proceeds to the petiole and eventually to the stem. If drier conditions are present, the infected leaf shows wrinkles and becomes reduced in size. The infection also remains localized and the infected black area is surrounded by a brown zone and presents a dry parched appearance. Infection is mainly confined mainly to the leaves which are located within a couple of feet from the ground surface.

Etiology and epidemiology: Foot rot and leaf rot is caused by the fungus *Phytophthora parasitica* var. *piperina* or *Phytophthora palmivora* that survive in the soil as a saprophyte during adverse climatic by means of oospores and chlamydospores and attacks roots, stem and leaves. It produces large number of spores at low temperatures under moist conditions. Secondary spread is carried from vine to vine by disseminated sporangia and zoospores through irrigation water and rains accompanied by wind (Rangaswami and

Mahadevan, 2006). It occurs in a very virulent form and if not controlled, causes widespread damage and even total destruction of the betelvine plantations. A foot rot syndrome is also produced by a number of pathogens including *Phytophthora parasitica* var. *piperina*, *Phytophthora nicotianae* var. *parasitica*, species of *Rhizoctonia*, *Pythium* and *Sclerotium rolfsii* Sac. (Dasgupta *et al.* 2008). Melhotra and Tiwari (1967) demonstrated that the pathogen *Phytophthora* was survived as mycelium in the host tissue tissues and after five weeks, chlamyospores or resting sporangia were formed as well as pathogen could be isolated up to 17 weeks from the host tissues. Chaurasia (1976) reported the oospore of the pathogen in nature first time from India. The disease is primarily carried through plantation of infected cutting (Chawdhury, 1944 a,b,c; Asthana and Mahmud, 1945; Asthana, 1947). The appearance and spread of the disease is dependent on external factors. Low temperature (15.6-27.40C), high humidity (91.0-99.3) and diffused light that prevail inside the baroj favours vine growth and are also congenial for the growth of the pathogen (Datta *et al.* 2010). The disease appears at the onset of monsoon and remains in high intensity throughout the rainy season. It wanes during the winter and may also occur in summer months when sudden hail storms occur. Whereas, under dry conditions the progress of the disease is slow. During rainy season when very wet conditions prevail for a number of days, leaves of betel vine is infected by the disease known as leaf rot. The incidence of leaf rot was observed in the month of June, July and August. The peak infection was noted in the second week of August when the average temperature, relative humidly and rainfall were 29.60°C, 94.6% and 13.4 mm respectively (Kumar and Kumar, 2004; Huq, 2011).

***Management*:** the phyto-sanitary approach including Collection, removal and destruction of dead and dying plants burned or buried in the soil is recommended to reduce the incidence of foot rot or leaf rot disease in betel orchard (Melhotra and Aggarwal, 2003). Thyagarajan *et al.* (1972) recommended the combined application of phosphorus and nitrogen. The mortility of vines was more when high doses of nitrogen were applied but was considerably lowered with phosphorus alon or in combination with a low dosage of nitrogen. Saksena and Melhotra (1970) recommended the removal of collateral hosts such as *Colocasia* species growing around the orchard. Singh and Chand (1973) suggested judicious use of water to prevent dissemination of the pathogen. The pathogen overwinters or oversummers in the soil so; judicious rotation of the crop in betelvine orchards may check the spread of disease. Paddy and banana rotation in Salem and Tanjore districts in Tamil Nadu state has been found to considerable safeguard the crop against the incidence of disease (Melhotra and Aggarwal, 2003). A combined effect of flooding followed by hot weather and deep plouging has been found to reduce the incidence of the disease (Tiwari and Mehrotra,

1974). Screenings of betel cultivar led to the identification of a few that are tolerant to this disease such as Halisahar Sanchi, Pachaikodi and Karapaku (Maiti, 1994). Volatile oils, like those from *Luvanga scandans* and *Mentha arvensis* were sown to inhibit growth of *Phytophthora* sp. (Chaurasia and Vyas, 1977). Many workers suggested that biocontrol agents like *Trichoderma harzianum* and *Pseudomonas fluorescens* were applied with oil cakes at quarterly intervals for management of this disease (Tiwari and Mehrotra 1968; Mohanty *et al.* 2000; D'Souza *et al.* 2001; Dasgupta *et al.* 2003; Sengupta *et al.* 2011). Phytophthora rot of betel vine is also reduced by dipping of cuttings in a *T. viride* spore suspension before planting (Mehrotra and Tiwari, 1976). The effect of different antagonists on corn straw and til oil cake amendments showed that *T. viride* gave best control (Mehrotra and Tiwari, 1976). Plant growth-promoting rhizobacteria (PGPR) *Serratia marcescens* strain NBRI1213 was evaluated for plant growth promotion and biologic control of foot and root rot of betelvine. Bacterization of betelvine (*Piper betle* L.) cuttings with *S. marcescens* NBRI1213 induced phenylalanine ammonia-lyase, peroxidase, and polyphenoloxidase activities in leaf and root (Lavania, 2006). Chaurasia (1976) demonstrated the effectiveness of *Aspergillus flavus*, *A. oryzae* and *Penicillium* sp. in the control of disease. The foot rot caused by *Phytophthora* species were claimed to be ameliorated by soil drenching by 1% Brodeux Mixture (Dastur, 1935; Dasgupta, 1993; Dasgupta and Sen, 1999; Dasgupta and Maiti, 2008). Chaurasia (1976) and Saksena (1977) obtained best results by dipping the cutting in Streptomycin sulphate solution (500 ppm) followed by 1% Brodeux mixture application twice a month. The chemical spray near the root zone with fosetyl-Al (%) was also effective in controlling this disease (Dasgupta *et al.*, 1988; Mohanty and Dasgupta, 2008). Narasimhan *et al.* (1976) recommended the spray of 0.5% Dexon (Sodium-p-dimethyl-amino-benzine) to be effective. Ayyavoo and Samiyappan (1981) reported the efficacy of Deconil-2787 90.1%) during winter at 15 days of interval was effective. Johri and Chaurasia (1984) have recommended Akomine which is an inorganic source of plant nutrients with phosphorus as the active ingredient. Being inorganic in nature there are not residual or side effects. The product has been tested for its efficiency in management of betelvine *Phytophthora* along with Aliette and Captaf by which about 80% mortality of vine checked. The disease is also controlled by spraying of 0.5% Brodeux mixture, Peronox (0.35%), Fytolan (0.2%), Dithan Z-78 (0.2%) or Blitox-50 (0.25%) 3to 4 time at 8-10 days interval (Balasubrahmanyam *et al.*, 1988; Rangaswami and Mahadevan, 2006). Tiwari and Mehrotra (1973) obtained promosing result by using CS_2 (carbon disulphide) and formalin as soil fumigants in pots. Formaline however is phytotoxic in the dosages used for controlling the disease. Magdum *et al.* (2009) emphasized on integrated disease management; sanitation followed by one soil application of 1.0% bordeaux mixture at pre-monsoon then one soil application of *T. horzianum* at one month after the application of bordeaux mixture and one soil application of 1.0% bordeaux mixture at 2 months after its first application that significantly reduced the incidence both leaf rot and foot rot.

Leaf spot/Anthracnose

Leaf spot caused by *Colletotrichum capsici* is a major disease of the betelvine (Bhale *et al.*, 1987). Leaf spot of betelvine was first identified by Roy (1948) in Bangladesh. It is also known as anthracnose of 'Pan'. The epidemic form of the disease in country has been also reported (Hossain *et al.*, 1986). It may cause 10-60% yield loss and reduced market value of the crop (Singh and Joshi, 1971; Maiti and Sen, 1982).

Fig. 3.2: Anthracnose

Symptomatology: The diseased leaves are characterized by the presence of circular to irregular, light to dark brown lesions on the leaves that is surrounded by a yellow hallo. The centre of such spots latter turned straw yellow in colour. The spots often coalesced to form bigger patches. On stems, branches and petiole small black, irregular specks are seen which occasionally ruptured the cortex underneath. Often the spot grow along the length of stem in which case the part of vine above, the diseased internodes is also wilted (Naik and Hiremath, 1986).

Etiology and epidemiology: leaf spot or anthracnose is caused by *Colletotrichum capsici* (Syd.) Butler and Bisby. The pathogen *C. gloeosporioides* was also reported on this crop from Karnataka (Naik and Hiremath, 1986) with incidence of disease 19%. The fungus colony was grayish black and smooth. Conidia were oblong hyaline, non-septate with rounded ends, having oil globules in the centre, formed in culture and measured (8.6-19.9 × 3.5-6.5µ) (Naik and Hiremath, 1986). The disease usually appears after rains and only the leaves are affected. It is reported that environmental factors like temperature, relative humidity and rainfall have crucial role in development of leaf spot of betelvine (Maiti and Sen, 1982). Roy (1948) recorded severe leaf spot of betelvine due to anthracnose when rain fall was high. Dasgupta and Sen (1985) found that 92% relative humidity was critical moisture level for severe leaf spotting and heavy loss of betel vine. Under dry weather the progress of disease severity is slow where as during moist weather leave spot enlarges rapidly causing rotten of whole leaves (Basak *et al.* 1992). Goswami *et al.* (2002) reported maximum disease severity observed in the months of June and July when all the three weather factors were higher as compare to other months of year where as the incidence of leaf spot was also observed during months of March, April and May. But gradually infection reached maximum when average temperature, relative humidly and rainfall parameters were 26.7°C, 88.3% and 19.4mm respectively (Huq, 2011).

***Management*:** The fungicides- Benomyl and Thiophanate-methyl was found to be quite effective in the control of anthracnose of betel vine (Miati *et al*., 1978; Saleem, 2000). Acharya and Das (1995) revealed significant anthracnose disease control of betelvine by foliar sprays of 0.05% bitertanol, followed by 0.2% mancozeb, 0.1% ziram (as Cuman-L) and 0.5% Bordeaux mixture (0.5%). Balasubrahmanyam *et al*. (1988) reported Copper oxychloride 50 WP (0.25%) was found effective against this disease.

Leaf spot by other pathogen: Chattopadhayay and Sengupta, (1955) reported leaf spot of betelvine is also caused by *Fusarium semitectum*. *Drechslera rostrata* (*Exserohilum rostratum*) was found to cause leaf spot in Madhya Predesh, India (Singh and Joshi, 1974a), whereas, *Alternaria alternata* and *Culvularia lunata* have also been reported to produce leaf spot on betelvine (Ojha *et al*. 1988). Leaf spot caused by *Cephalosporium acremonium* was first reported from Jabalpur, India by Singh and Joshi (1974b). Saleem and Zareen (1999) reported many fungi like *Fusarium solani*, *F. sporotrichoides*, *Bipolaris australiensis*, *B. hawaiiensis*, *B. papendorfii*, *Curvularia pallescens*, *C. tuberculata*, and *Botryodiploidia theobromae* cause leaf necrosis on betel vine. Many fungi associated with leaf spot of betel vine and significantly controlled by application of Benomyl and Topsin-M (Saleem and Zareen, 1999).

Powdery Mildew

The disease is caused by a species of *Odium*, which was first reported from Ceylon by Stevenson (1926) and letter by Mitra (1930) from Burma and by Narasimhan (1933) from Mysore as well as from Bombay by Uppal and Kamat (1938).

Symptomatology: The disease is easily recognized by the appearance of yellow spots, which are slightly raise and irregular in outline, and correspond in extent to white powdery patches of mildews on upper surface of leaves. The patches of mildew are also sometimes found on the upper surface of leaves. These patches are first small but increase in extent as they grow together. The disease appears on the undersurface of the leaves as white to brown powdery patches. These patches gradually increase in size and often coalesce with each other. They vary in size from a few to 40mm in diameter and are covered by dusty growth which is fairly thick in cases of sever attack. Areas on the upper surface corresponding to patches on the under surface appear yellowish, raised and irregular in outline. Young leaves when attacked fail to grow and become deformed, the surface being cracked and the margin turned inwards. Such leaves present a pale appearance and drop with slight disturbance. The disease is more prevalent in old plantations (Uppal and Kamat, 1938).

Etiology and epidemiology: The causative fungus *Odium piperis* of betelvine is an ectophytes, which feeds by sending globular haustoria into epidermal cells of the leaves. The disease has been reported to be in the leaves only and it has been found to disappear during the hot season.

Management: The disease was managed by dusting of sulphur (200 mesh) on leaves and plucking of infected leaves as soon as they are ready for harvest. Maiti (1994) reported betelvine cultivars- male clones of Kapoori, Tellaku, Vellairettala, Ambadi Badam and Kulgedu were found resistant to powdery mildew.

Sclerotial Wilt/Stem Rot/Collar Rot/Basal Rot

Singh and Chand (1982) reported in a survey of betel gardens in different localities *S. rolfsii* was found to be responsible for plant losses of 42-62%.

Symptomatology: Betelvine of all ages are vulnerable to infection particularly at the collar region. The first visible symptom of collar rot disease was observed as yellowing or wilting of lower leaves. Later on, the yellowing progressed to upper leaves. The fungal mycelium first appeared at the base of the vines near the soil line. The pathogen then grew upwards covering the stem with a cottony-white mass of mycelia. Later on, water-soaked and grey lesion appeared on the vines, which turned brown, resulting in the rotting of whole plant system. A large number of small, light brown, mustard-seed like sclerotia developed in the collar zone. After the pathogen established itself, its subsequent advancement and production of mycelia and sclerotia were quite rapid. The infected vines, which were 3-4 weeks old ultimately toppled down and died (Singh, 2002).

Etiology and epidemiology: Basal rot is caused by *Sclerotium rolfsii Dastur.* Mridha and Alamgir (1987) studied the growth and sclerotia production of *S. rolfsii* isolated from betelvine on different media, various pH and different light regimes. They observed that fungus produced a luxuriant mycelia growth and large number of sclerotia on PDM medium at pH 6 and in alternate light and dark conditions.

Management: Mridha and Alamgir (1987) reported that ammonia solution of 0.5% gave effective control when applied in soil. Brahmankar *et al.* (2011) reported that wilt or root rot management was done by integrated approach of disease management including soil solarization during summer followed by application of *Trichoderma* 10 kh/ha (set and soil application), neem cack 200 kg/ha, NPK @ 100:50:50 kg/ha and deep irrigation found significantly superior not only in controlling the wilt causing fungus and nematode but also had a favorable effect on growth parameters. Mopsin proved to be the superior in controlling the collar rot disease in field as it gave 100% disease control at 0.10% concentration (Singh, 2002). Rhizolex 50 WP (0.4%) used for soil drenching were effective against basal rot disease (Gangwar and Dasgupta, 1989). HaralPatil and Raut (2008) reported the fungicides, Metalaxyl + Mancozeb (0.1%), Difenoconazole (0.05%), Propiconazole (0.05%), Hexaconazole (0.05%) and Metiram (0.1%) to be effective in controlling *S. rolfsii. In biological control, Trichoderma lignorum, Gliocladium virens* and *T. viride* were most effective against *S. rolfsii*. However, in case of botanicals, the plant extracts of *Allium sativum, Azadirachta indica* and *Catheranthus roseus* (all at 10% concentration) were promising against *S. rolfsii*.

BACTERIAL DISEASES

Bacterial Leaf Spot/Stem Canker/Bacterial Blight

A bacterial leaf spot of betelvine was first reported by Patel *et al.* (1951) from India and named the pathogen as *Xantomonas betlicola*. The pathogen *X. c.* pv. *betlicola* has been renamed as *Xanthomonas axonopodis* pv. *betlicola* by Vauterin *et al.* (1995). This was considered as minor disease, even though there were subsequent reports of its occurrence in 1971 from Jabalpur area of M.P. (Singh and Chand, 1971) and in 1978 from Kerala by Mathew *et al.* (1978). Nadugala and Amarasinghe (2009) reported up to 60% incidence of this disease from major betel cultivating areas and it can be increase to about 75% during the rainy seasons. The phenotypic and virulence variation were also found among isolates of *Xanthomonas axonopodis* pv. *betlicola* (Nadugala and Amarasinghe, 2009).

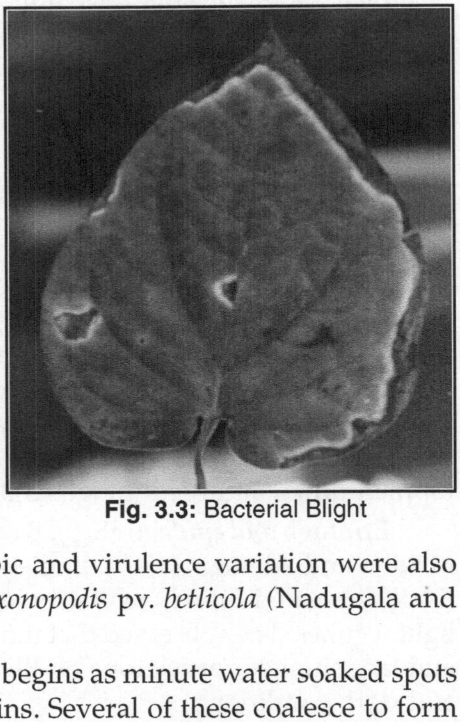

Fig. 3.3: Bacterial Blight

Symptomomatology: The infection begins as minute water soaked spots all over the leave blade delimited by veins. Several of these coalesce to form larger irregular brownish spots. The advance lesions are invariably accompanied by yellowish halos and result in ultimate defoliation. The symptoms are found to vary with varieties. In certain cases the infection is confined to the leave margin, defused and quickly spreading in an irregular fashion. Often grayish black lesions are seen on stem and petioles. When the disease becomes serious the leaves and internodes fall off and finally the vine dies (Mathew *et al.* 1978).

Morphological and Cultural Characteristics of Organism

The colour of colony is yellow and slimy, colony shape-circular and shiny, shape of organism-short rods; motility-motile; temperature range-26-30 °C; temperature optimum- 28°C, gram reaction-negative; growth on nutrient broth-turbid yellow growth.

Physiological and Biochemical Properties

Starch hydrolysis-strong and positive; catalase production-positive; Kovac's oxidase test-negative; H_2S production-positive; fermentation of sugars, Lactose-fermented with acid production and no gas formation; sucrose fermented with acid production and no gas formation (Patel *et al.*, 1951; Singh and Chand, 1971; Mathew *et al.* 1978).

Biochemical analysis of betel leaves infected by leaf spot and blight caused by *Xanthomonas campestris* pv. *betlicola* showed a decrease in moisture, chlorophyll, protein, phenol and total carbohydrate contents as compared with healthy leaves. The decrease in these five parameters was 31-42%, 29-70%, 20-79%, 30-53% and 53-87%, respectively (Wasnikar *et al.* 1993).

Management: The leaf spot of betelvine has also been reported to be caused by a fungus-bacterium complex (Bhale *et al.*, 1985; Deka *et al.*, 2005.). In such leaf spot, *C. capsici* is always associated with the bacterium *X. a.* pv. *betlicola*. The diseases complex can be effectively controlled by the chemicals like 0.5% Bordeaux mixture or 0.1% copper oxychloride (Yadav *et al.*, 1993). *In vitro* screening of four bioagents *viz.*, *Trichoderma harzianum*, *Aspergillus terreus*, *Bacillus subtilis* and *Pseudomonas fluorescens* and extracts of four plant species *viz.*, *Chromolaena odorata*, *Ageratum houstonianum*, *Polygoum hydropiper* and *Tagetes erecta* was done against *Colletotrichum capsici*, *Xanthomonas axonopodis* pv. *betlicola* and complex of *C. capsici* + *X. axonopodis* pv. *betlicola*. *B. subtilis* significantly inhibited the growth of *C. capsici* (79.5%) and *X. axonopodis* pv. *betlicola* (68.1%) and their complex (76.4%). Among the phytoextracts, *P. hydropiper* was the best in restricting the growths of both pathogens (72.3 and 72.2%) and their complex (70.4%) respectively over control. Under field condition, sanitation + *B. subtilis* provided best control strategy of leaf spot complex showing 9.7 percent disease index (PDI), followed by 11.1% PDI in sanitation alone and sanitation + *P. hydropiper*. Highest fresh leaf yield and cost: benefit ratio were obtained in sanitation + *B. subtilis* with 33.5 lakh/ha/year and 1:1.29, respectively (Deka *et al.*, 2008). Tripathi *et al.* (1984) reported that during field evaluation, streptomycin was found to be most effective (80-90% disease control) followed by menadione (78-80%) and resorcinol (68-72%). Incidence of bacterial leaf spot decreased significantly as phosphorus level (25-125 kg/ha) increased (Wasnikar *et al.* 1993). It is reported that most of the betel varieties that are cultivated at commercial level are susceptible to *X. campestris* pv. *betlicola* (Nema, 1988). Balasubrahmanyam *et al.* (1988) reported Copper oxychloride 50 WP (0.25%) with 500 ppm streptocycline was best against bacterial leaf spots. Maiti (1994) reported betelvine cultivar Simurali Bangla was resistant to bacterial leaf spot

VIRAL DISEASES

Betel Vine Mosaic

Singh and Rao (1988) first time observed mosaic, a viral disease in betelvine from Andhra pradesh and Karnataka.

Symptoms: Initially the leaves show vein clearing symptom followed by mosaic mottling which the characteristic symptom of disease. Bright yellow to light green and dark green patches develop on entire leaf lamina. Conspicuous bold blisters are also observed on infected leaves. The leaves become puckered and distorted and very much reduced in size. The infected plants appear week with shortened internodes and show stunted growth. The yield is reduced considerably as only a few leaves (5-10) are produced per plant and these leaves are unmarketable (Singh and Rao, 1988).

Association of two kinds of viruses with isometric (25 nm in diameter) and rigid rod (350 × 15 nm^2) shaped particle have been also reported on betelvine from India (Singh and Rao, 1988; Srinivas and Reddy, 1991). Based coat protein gene sequence identities, Cucumber mosaic virus- CMV infecting both Indian long pepper and betel vine belonging to sub group-1 (Hareesh *et al.*, 2006).

NEMATODE DISEASES

The crop of betelvine is highly susceptible to the attack of several endoparasitic and other nematodes causing 3.9 to 40.28 per cent loss in yield. Estimated losses can be decrease to betel vine industry were more than 20% with banana plantation by root-knot and other parasitic nematodes (Dhande and Sulaiman, 1961; Jagdale *et al.* 1986). The root knot nematode *(Meloidogyne incognita)* is the most serious pest of betelvine orchard alone has been reported to result in 26-38% yield losses. High population of root knot and reniform nematode *(Rotylenchulus* renifoms) was noted from March to June in betel orchard (Jonathan *et al.*, 1990, Nakat and Madne, 1993; Maiti and Shivshankara, 1998; Bhatt and Vadhera, 2004; Shahina and Erum, 2005). *Sesbania grandiflora* and *S. sesban* act as reservoir for the nematodes (Rao *et al.* 1991). Several other plant parasitic nematodes have been also reported to be associated with betelvine like *Pratylenchus coffeae*, *Helicotylenchus multicinctus*, *Aphelenchus avenae* and *Longidorus siddiqii* (Balasubrahmanian, 1984; Akhter *et al.*, 2011). Nema (1997) reported eight species of plant parasitic nematodes from Madhya Pradesh of which *R. reniformis* was the dominant parasite. The root knot nematode· *(M. incognita)* and reniform nematode *(R. reniformis)* were most destructive in all the betelvine growing areas except Andhra Pradesh, while *Helicotylenchus microcephalus* was found to be dominant in Maharashtra (Maiti and Shivshankara, 1998). Amer-Zareen (1999) reported species of

Aphelenchoides, Aphelenchus, Helicotylenchus, Hoplolaimus, Rotylenchulus, Tylenchorhynchus and *Xiphinema* from Pakistan. These infestations are due to the use of untreated green manure, infested tools and some time infested cultivars of *Piper betle.*

The main symptoms of namatodes attack are reduction in size of betel leaves, chlorosis and black spot near the mid leaves. In root knot disease there is formation of tumor in the root tips of host plants known as root galls (Doosani *et al.*, 1992). The nematodes have been found vital role in the development of wilt and root rot diseases caused by fungi and bacteria (Ray *et al.* 1993). It was evident that the nematode predisposes the vine to *Phytophthora paimivora* which infects through wounds caused by *Meloidogyne incognita* (Marimuthu, 1991; Jonathan *et. al.*, 1996). Sitaramaiah and Devi (1994) observed positive correlation between the populations of *M. incognita* with wilt disease incidence. Studies have also been made on *M. incognita* and *Sclerotium rolfsii* inter relationship. Maximum reduction in fresh and dry weight of root and shoot length occurred with simultaneous inoculations of the fungus and 4,000 nematodes per pot (Sitaramaiah and Devi, 1990). More damage was observed when *Xanthomonas campestris* pv. *betlicoia* was combined with *M. incognita* and *S. roifsii* (Acharya *et al.*, 1987). The absorption of minerals is disturbed due to choking of xylem vessels and the attack of other stylet bearing nematodes, which produces the holes in root-lets, causes the absorption of the spores of soil born fungi with minerals due to the pressure and finally plants become week (Maiti and Sen, 1979).

Management of nematode diseases: Solarization by mulching the land with 100 gauge black and white polythene before planting for 15 days was found to reduce plant parasitic nematode population in India (Shivakumar and Marimuthu, 1987; Rao *et al.*, 1996). Application of neem oil cake at 1 tonne/ha and saw dust at 2 tonnes/ha can reduced the nematodes population and root galls and increased the number of leaves harvested significantly (Jagdale *et al.* 1985a,b; Acharya and Padhi, 1988a). Bed amendment with chopped and shade-dried leaves of *Calotropis gigantea* (Madar) at 2.5 tonnes also reduced the 60% nematode population (Shivakumar and Marimuthu, 1986; Murthy and Rao, 1992). When different levels of Potash were tried, 75 kg/ha was observed to be most effective in reducing the larval population and number of root galls. A combination of neem cake (0.5 t/ha) + NPK (150:100:50) + Carbofuran @ 0.75 kg a.i./ha also reduced nematode population and root gall index (Nakat and Madne, 1993). Mixed cropping of *Tagetes* sp. Sadaphuli and baken neem (*Melia azadarichta*) in betelvine gardens suppressed the nematode population in soil (Nakat and Madne, 1993). Neem cake was the most effective in reducing the root galls and producing maximum number of marketable leaves (Acharya and Padhi, 1988a; Murthy and Rao, 1992). Rao *et al.* (1996) observed that *Calotropis* leaves @ 80 kg/ha significantly reduced the population of plant parasitic nematodes in soil including root knot nematode and was superior to neem and castor leaves. Recently *Paecilomyces* lilacinus has been found effective biocontrol agent in pots as well as under field conditions (Jonathan *et al*., 1995; Nakat *et al*., 1998, Pathak and Saikia, 1999; Bhatt and Vadhera, 2004). Application of *Trichoderma viride* multiplied on linseed oil cake was applied in the soil at an interval of 60, 90 and 120 days after planting found to be highly effective in reducing root-knot nematodes in betelvine (Bhatt *et al*., 2002). Unfortunately none of the cultivars was found resistant to root knot nematode. Out of the cultivars tested Sanchi and Birkoli were moderately resistant and rest of the cultivars showed susceptible reaction against *M. incognita* (Acharya and Padhi, 1988b). Nakat and Madne (1993) recorded less number of galls in Kuljedu, Maghai, Bhadana and Karapaku cultivars of betelvine. Aldicarb was observed to be most effective nematicide in the nematode management (Jagdale *et al*., 1984; Murthy and Rao, 1994; Bhatt and Vadhera, 2004). Nakat and Madne (1993) and Rao *et al*. (1993) observed that carbofuran @ 1.5 kg a.i./ha was effective in reducing larval population of root knot nematode.

FUTURE PERSPECTIVE

Betelvine's leaves are generally used for mastication along with areca nut as raw form. The chemical pesticides when applied in higher doses or frequently in orchards for management of diseases give residual effects. Therefore, in perspective to environmental and human health, management of betelvine's disease in future will be required judicious application of chemical and eco-friendly management strategies or integrated approaches as well as proper identification pathogen by new emerging tools will be also help in proper management of disease.

REFERENCES

Acharya, A. and Das, J.N. 1995. Control of Anthracnose of Betelvine by Fungicidal Chemicals. *Current Agricultural Research* 8(2): 58-60.

Acharya, A. and Padhi, N.N. 1988a. Effect of Neemcake and Saw Dust Against Nematode, *Meloidogyne incognita* on Betelvine (*Piper betle* L.). *Indian J. Nematol.* 18: 105-106.

Acharya, A. and Padhi, N.N. 1988b. Screening of Betelvine Varieties for Resistance Against Root-knot Nematode, *Meloidogyne incognita. Indian Journal of Nematology* 18: 109.

Acharya, A., Dash, S.C. and Padhi, N.N. 1987. Pathogenic Association of *Meloidogyne incognita* with *Sclerotium rolfsii* and *Xanthomonas betlicola* on betelvine. *Indian Journal of Nematology* 17(2): 196-198.

Akhter, M., Nawab, B. Perveen, S. and Khan, H.A. 2011. Plant Parasitic Nematodes Associated with Diseased Betel vine Conservatories in Karachi, Thatta, Hub Area and Ketty Bunder. *Pak. J. Nematol.* 29(1): 53-61.

Amer-Zareen., Shahina, F. and Shahzad, S. 1999. New Records of Nematodes Associated with Betelvine in Pakistan with Observation s on *Aphelenchoides helicosoma. Pak. J. Nematol.* 17: 47-50.

Arulmozhiyan, R., Chitra, R., Prabhakar, K., Jalaluddin, S.M. and Packiaraj, D. 2005. SGM. BV.2 – A New Promising Betel Vine Variety. *Madras Agric. J.* 92(2): 498-503.

Ashthana, R.P. 1947. The Role of Cutting in the Dissemination of Foot Rot of *Piper Betle. Indian Journal of Agriculture science* 18: 223-225.

Asthana, R.P. and Mahmud, K.P. 1945. Vegetative Propagation of *Piper Betle* in Central Provinces. *Proc. Indian Acad. Sci.* 22: 70-75.

Ayavoo, R., Samiyappan, R. and Seshadri, K. 1981. Chemical Controls of Betelvine Wilt Disease. *Pesticides* 16: 14-15.

Balasubrahmanian, P. 1984. Namatodes Problems of Betel Vine in Tamil Nadu. In: *Improve. Betel Culti.,* Lucknow, India. pp. 87-90.

Balasubrahmanyam, V.R., Chaurasia, R.S., Tripathi, R.D. and Johri, J.K. 1988. Evaluation of Some Fungicides and Antibiotics Against Fungal and Bacterial Pathogens of Betelvine (*Piper betle* L.). *Tropical Pest Management* 34(3): 315-317.

Basak, A.B., Mridha, M.A.U. and Jlali, M.A. 1992. Studies on the Leaf Spot Disease of *Piper betel* L. Caused by *Colletotricum piperi* Petch. *Chittagony University Studies Part II: Science Volume* 16(2): 87-91.

Bhale, M.S., Chaurasia, R.K. and Nayak, M.L. 1985. Association of *Colletotrichum capsici* with *Xanthomonas campestris* pv. *betlicola* Incitant of Leaf Spot of Betelvine (*Piper betle* L.). *Indian Phytopath.* 38: 565-566.

Bhale, M.S., Khare, M.N., Nayak, M.L. and Chaurasia, R.K. 1987. Diseases of Betelvine (*Piper betle* L.) and Their Management. *Rev. Trop. Plant Pathol.* 4: 199-220.

Bhatt, J. and Vadhera, I. 2004. Nematodes of Betelvine and Their Management –A Review. *Agric. Rev.,* 25(3): 231-234.

Bhatt, J., Sengupta, S.K. and Chaurasia, R.K. 2002. Management of *Meloidogyne incognita* by *Trichoderma viridae* in betelvine. *Indian Phytopathology* 55: 348-350.

Brahmankar, S.B., Dange, N.R., Tathod, D.G. 2011. Remove from Marked Records Integrated Management of Betel Vine Wilt in Vidarbha. *International Journal of Plant Protection* 4(1): 146-147.

Chattapdayay, S.P. and Maiti, S. 1967. Diseases of Betelvine and species. ICAR New Delhi.

Chattopadhayay, S.B. and Maiti, S. 1990. Diseases of Betel Vine and Spices. ICAR, New Delhi. pp. 60.

Chattopadhayay, S.B. and Sengupta, S.K. 1955. A New Disease of *Piper betle* in West Bengal. *Indian Phytopathology* 8: 105-111.

Chaurasia, S.C. 1976. Studies on Foot Rot and Leaf Rot Diseases of Pan (*Piper betle*) with Special Reference to Pathogenesis and Control Measure. Ph.D. Thesis, Univ. of Sagar.

Chaurasia, S.C., and Vyas, K.M. 1977. *In vitro* Effect of Some Volatile Oil Against *Phytophthora parasitica* var. *piperina. Madhya Bharati* 22: 63-65.

Chawdhury, S. 1944a. Disease of Pan (*Piper betle*) in Sylhet, Assam. I. The Problem an its Economic Importance. *Proc. Indian Acad. Sci.* 19: 147-151.

Chawdhury, S. 1944b. Disease of Pan (*Piper betle*) in Sylhet, Assam. II. *Phytophthora* Foot Rot and Leaf Rot. *Proc. Indian Acad. Sci.* 19: 152-164.

Chawdhury, S. 1944c. Disease of Pan (*Piper betle*) in Sylhet, Assam. III. Effect of Manuring on Incidence of *Phytophthora* Foot Rot and Leaf Rot. *Proc. Indian Acad. Sci.* 19: 165-170.

Chopra, R.N., Nayar, S.L. and Chopra, I.C. 1956. Glossary of Indian Medicinal Plant. CSIR, New Delhi. p. 194.

CSIR, 1969. *The Wealth of India, Vol. VIII.* CSIR (Council of Scientific and Industrial Research, New Delhi), New Delhi. pp. 84-94.

Das Gupta, B. and Sen. C. 1985. Relationship of Inoculums Density of *Colletotricum capsici* and Moisture on Leaf Spot Development in Betel Vine. *Indian Phytopathology* 38(2): 364.

Dasgupta, B. 1993. Chemical Control of Root Rot and Leaf Rot of Betelvine Caused by *Phytophthora palmivora* Using Bordeaux Mixture, in: Singh, H.B., Upadhyay, D.N. and Saha, L.R. (eds.), *Current Trends in Life Sciences,* Vol. 19. *Recent Trends in Plant Disease Control.* Today and Tomorrow Printers and Publishers, New Delhi. pp. 75-88.

Dasgupta, B. and Maiti, S. 2008. Research on Betel Vine Diseases Under AINP on Betel Vine. Proc. National Seminar on "*Piperaceae-Harnessing Agro-technologies for Accelerated Production of Economically Important Piper Species*", 21-22 November, 2008, Indian Institute of Spices Research, Calicut - 673012, Kerala, India, pp. 270-79.

Dasgupta, B. and Sen, C. 1997. Betelvine Diseases and Their Management: A Retrospect in Perspective, in: M.K. Dasgupta (ed.), *Pest Management in Changing Agricultural Situation*. pp. 43-50.

Dasgupta, B. and Sen, C. 1999. Assessment of *Phytophthora* Root Rot of Betelvine and its Management Using Chemicals. *Journal of Mycology and Plant Pathology* 29: 91-95.

Dasgupta, B., Dutta, P. and Das, S. 2011. Biological Control of Foot Rot of Betelvine (*Piper betle* L.) Caused by *Phytophthora parasitica* Dastur. *The Journal of Plant Protection Sciences* 3(1): 15-19.

Dasgupta, B., Dutta, P.K., Muthuswamy, S. and Maiti, S. 2003. Biological Control of Foot Rot of Betelvine (*Piper betle* Linn.). *Journal of Biological Control* 17: 63-67.

Dasgupta, B., Mohanty, B., Dutta, P.K. and Maiti, S. 2008. *Phytophthora* Diseases of Betelvine (*Piper betle* L.): A Menace to Betelvine Crop. *SAARC Journal of Agriculture* 6: 71-89.

Dasgupta, B., Roy, J.K. and Sen, C. 2000. Two Major Fungal Diseases of Betelvine, in: M.K. Dasgupta (ed.), *Diseases of Plantation Crops, Spices, Betelvine and Mulberry*. pp. 133-137.

Dastur, J.F. 1927. A Short Note on the Foot Rot Diseases of Pan in Central Provinces. *Agric. J. India* 22: 105-108.

Dastur, J.R. 1935. Disease of Pan (*Piper betle*) in the Central Provinces. *Proceedings of Indian Academy of Sciences* 1: 26-31.

Datta, P., Dasgupta, B., Majumder, D., Das, S. 2010. Disease Prediction Model of Foot Rot and Leaf Rot of Betelvine (*Piper betle* L.) caused by *Phytophthora parasitica* in West Bengal. *SAARC Journal of Agriculture* 8(2): 87-96.

Deka, S.N, Dutta, P.K., Bora, L.C. and Saikia, L. 2005. Studies on Leaf Spot of Betelvine caused by *Xanthomonas-Colletotrichum* in Assam. *Karnataka J. Hort.* 2: 14-15.

Deka, U.K., Dutta, P.K., Gogoi, R. and Borah, P.K. 2008. Management of Leaf Spot Disease Complex of Betelvine by Bioagents and Plant Extracts. *Indian Phytopath.* 61(3): 337-342.

Dhandhe, G.W. and Sulaiman, M, 1961. Occurrence of Root-knot Nematodes on Betel Vine in Maharastra. *Curr. Sci.* 30: 351-352.

Doosani, Z.A., Shahzad, S., Vahidy, A.A. and Ghaffar, A. 1992. Diseases of Betel Vine in and Around Karachi Area and Their Control, in: Ghaffar, A. and Saleem, S. (eds.), *Status of Plant Pathology in Pakistan*. Proc. National Symposium, 3-5th Dec., 1991. Dept. of Botany, University of Karachi, Karachi, pp. 87-92.

D'Souza, A., Roy, J.K., Mohanty, B. and Dasgupta, B. 2001. Screening of Isolates of *Trichoderma harzianum* Rifai Against Major Fungal Pathogens of Betelvine. *Indian Phytopathology* 54: 340-45.

Gangwar, S.K. and Dasgupta, B. 1989. Rhizolex 50 WP-a New Fungicide to Control the Foot Rot of Betelvine (*Piper betle* L.) caused by *Sclerotium rolfsii* Sacc. *Proceedings: Plant Sciences* 99(3): 265-269.

Goswami, B.K., Kader, K.A., Rahman M.L., Islam, M.R. and Malaker, P.K. 2002. Development of Leaf Spot of Betelvine Caused by *Colletotrichum capsici*. *Bangladesh J. Plant Pathol.* 18(1&2): 39-42.

Guha, P. 2006. Betel Leaf: The Neglected Green Gold of India. *J. Hum. Ecol.* 19(2): 87-93.

Guha, P. and Jain, R.K. 1997. *Status Report On Production, Processing and Marketing of Betel Leaf (Piper betle L.)*. Agricultural and Food Engineering Department, IIT, Kharagpur, India (1997).

Gunther, E. 1952. *The Essential Oils, Vol. V.* D. Van Nostrand & Co, Inc. New York, pp. 160-161.

HaralPatil, S. K. and Raut, S.P. 2008. Efficacy of Fungicides, Bio-agents and Botanicals Against Collar Rot of Betelvine. *Journal of Plant Disease Sciences* 3(1): 93-96.

Hareesh, P.S., Madhubala, R. and Bhat, A.I. 2006. Characterization of *Cucumber mosaic virus* Infecting Indian Long Pepper (*Piper longum* L.) and Betel Vine (*Piper betle* L.) in India. *Indian Journal of Biotechnology* 5: 89-93.

Pages: 73-107

BIOTECHNOLOGY, AGRO-ECOLOGY AND ENVIRONMENT

Edited by: Dr. Avnish Chauhan; Dr. Pawan Kumar 'Bharti'

ISBN: 978-93-5056-757-9

Edition: 2015

Published by: Discovery Publishing House Pvt. Ltd., New Delhi (India)

4

Nutrient Use Efficiency of Canola Crop

El Habbasha S.F.[1]; Wafaa Haggag[2] and Faten Ibrahim[3]

ABSTRACT

Canola is one of the main oil crops where characterized by high seed oil and protein content and its oil is a nutritionally valuable complement of human nutrition because its low content of saturated and high content of unsaturated fatty acids. Although, it has considered a highly demanding fertilizers crop it categorized as a low NUE crop, (from 12 to 40%) and PUE (from 8% to 16%) while KUE is generally considered a higher use efficiency because it is immobile in most soils and is not subjected to the gaseous losses or the fixation reactions.

Nutrient use efficiency is low in arid and semiarid regions due to loss of fertilizer by volatilization, leaching, run off and reacts with other elements to create relatively insoluble compounds. At low levels of nutrient supply, rates of increase in yield and nutrient uptake are large because the nutrient of interest is the primary factor limiting growth. The balance between different nutrients

1 Field Crops Research Department, National Research Centre, Dokki, Egypt.

2 Pathology Department, National Research Centre, Dokki, Egypt.

3 Medicinal and Aromatic Plants Research Department, National Research Centre, Dokki, Egypt.

have a strong influences on quality characters as well as yields, one of these important equilibriums, the balance between nitrogen and sulphur elements however, the application of sulphur needs to be balanced with nitrogen for optimum yields consequently enhances nitrogen use efficiency in canola.

Many strategies to increase nutrient use efficiency of the most suitable fertilizer and minimize nutrient losses are manipulation of the application techniques integrated nutrient management between chemical, biofertilizers and organic fertilizers in attendance with different micronutrients also, split application and placement, manipulation of particle size, use of coating materials and other chemicals, efficient agronomic practices and use of varieties with higher nitrogen use efficiency.

Key words: Canola, Nutrient Use Efficiency, Micronutrients.

INTRODUCTION

Canola (*Brassica napus* L.; genome AACC, 2n=38) is one of the main oil crops (the world's third-leading source of both harvested oilseeds and vegetable oils in 2011) where it records 13.1 and 15.4% for harvested oilseed and global production of vegetable oils, respectively (FAOSTAT, 2011). Canola a promising oil crop characterized by high seed oil (40-45%) and protein content (19-21%). Canola oil is a nutritionally valuable complement of human nutrition because of its low content of saturated Palmitic (C16:0) and Stearic (C18:0) and high content of unsaturated Oleic (C18:1), Linoleic (C18:2) and Linolenic (C18:3) fatty acids. It is almost lacking in nutritionally undesirable very long-chain fatty acids which meets all the requirements of a prime edible oil (Ackman, 1990; Downey and Bell, 1990; Trautwein, 1997). Despite the beneficial nutritional properties of á-Linolenic acid (18:3n–3), the oxidative stability of the oil can be improved by decreasing the linolenate content from an average of 10% to less than 3%, which results in enhanced shelf life (Rakow et al., 1987; Pleines and Friedt, 1988). It is a particularly important nutritional quality characteristic of high-temperature frying oils in the fast-food and food processing industries (Mensink and Katan, 1993). Moreover, its protein is a biologically valuable plant protein with an optimal perspective for human nutrition (Barth, 2007).

Mineral fertilizers have sustained world agriculture, global population and growth of wealth for more than 100 years (Smil, 2001; Stewart et al., 2005). The fertilizer industry supports application of nutrients as the best management practice for achieving optimum nutrient efficiency at:

1. The right rate. Most crops are location and season specific depending on cultivar, management practices, climate, etc., and so it is critical that realistic yield goals are established and that nutrients are applied to meet the target yield.

2. The right time. Split applications of fertilizer during the growing season, rather than a single, large application prior to planting, are known to be effective in increasing nutrient use efficiency (Cassman et al., 2002).
3. The right place. Numerous placements are available, but most generally involve surface or sub-surface applications before or after planting. Prior to planting, nutrients can be broadcast, applied as a band on the surface, or applied as a subsurface band, usually 5 to 20 cm deep).

Nitrogen use efficiency (NUE) is defined as the ratio between seed N yield (kg N ha^{-1}) and N fertilizer input (kg N ha^{-1}) in canola (Gan et al., 2008). In short-lived plants this value is simply the inverse of tissue concentration, but in perennial plants it is most appropriately defined as total net primary production (above- and belowground) per unit nutrient absorbed annually (Hirose 1975; Birk and Vitousek 1986). Nutrient-use efficiency may exert important ecosystem controls; for example, high nutrient-use efficiency drives infertile systems towards even greater nutrient deficiency because low litter nutrient content and reduced nutrient mineralization rates depress nutrient circulation (Pastor et al., 1984; Shaver and Melillo, 1984; Chapin, 1986). The differentiation between 'available' and 'not-immediately available' nutrients is useful in nutrient balance studies, but has only been attempted occasionally (Janssen, 1999; Hoa et al., 2006). Increased nutrient use efficiency with decreasing nutrient availability has been demonstrated (Chapin et al., 1982; Gray and Schlesinger, 1983; Birk and Vitousek, 1986).

Efficiency of nutrient uptake and nutrient use efficiencies in plants are widespread throughout much of the agricultural regions in the world, especially in developing countries where fertilizers may not be affordable (Welch et al., 1991; Snapp et al., 2002). Nutrient deficiencies may be the result of an inherently low nutrient status of the soil, low mobility of nutrients within the soil or poor solubility of the given chemical form of the nutrient. The solubility and mobility of nutrients within the soil is governed by a number of factors, including mass flow of water, adsorption capacity of the soil, soil pH (Jungk, 2001; Shuman, 1991), the chemical form of nutrients (Crowley and Rengel, 1999) and plant-induced changes in the soil immediately surrounding roots (Rengel and Marschner, 2005). In field studies, nutrient use efficiencies are either calculated based on differences in crop yield and/ or nutrient uptake between fertilized plots and an unfertilized control, or by using isotope-labeled fertilizers to estimate crop and soil recovery of applied nutrients. For the same soil and cropping conditions, nutrient use efficiency generally decreases with increasing nutrient amount. At low levels of nutrient supply, rates of increase in yield and nutrient uptake are large because the nutrient of interest is the primary factor limiting growth (de Wit, 1992). Nutrient use efficiency can be improved by checking the pathways of nutrient losses from soil-plant system, nutrients available through making integrated systems from all possible sources, optimal allocation of nutrients to crops and maximizing the utilization of applied and native nutrients by the crops. Nutrient use efficiencies is significantly enhanced by the application of tablet forms of NPK sources than other slow release forms as well as standard fertilizer materials. Nutrient availability in the soil-plant system is dictated by complex interactions between plant roots, soil microorganisms, chemical reactions and pathways of losses. The concentration dependents of most of the processes that nutrients undergo in soil include transformations induced by microbes (N fixation, nitrification, denitrification, immobilization etc.), chemical processes (exchange, fixation, precipitation, hydrolysis, etc.) and physical processes (leaching, runoff, volatilization etc.).

Role of Nitrogen on Growth and Nutrient Use Efficiency of Canola

Nitrogen is the most important element that plants require in greatest amounts for crop growth and high yield with good quality. It serves as a constituent of many plant cell components, including amino acids, nucleic acids and increases photosynthetic rate, metabolites synthesized, merstematic activity and translocated assimilates to the seed. Nitrogen comprises 7% of total dry matter of plants and is a constituent of many fundamental cell components and photosynthetic pigments (Bungard et al., 1999). High nitrogen supply favors the conversion of carbohydrates into proteins, which in turn promotes the formation of protoplasm (Arnon, 1972) and ultimately improves crop plant growth and yield parameters (Bakhsh et al., 1999; Khan et al., 2000). Therefore, nitrogen deficiency rapidly inhibits plant growth.

Nitrogen level in canola plants is highest in the early seedling stage when young leaves are the majority of the plant dry matter. As the plant grows into flowering stages, the overall nitrogen level declines due to stem material and leaf loss. Canola has a relatively high requirement of chemical fertilizers where the content of these nutrients in seeds and plant tissues is greater than in most grain crops because of which it is considered to be a high demanding nutrients crop. In canola, the requirement for nitrogen per unit yield is higher than in cereal crops (Hocking and Strapper, 2001).

Nitrogen fertilizer mainly increases canola leaf area index, leaf duration, plant weight, growth rates, number of flowering branches, plant height, number of flowers, number and weight of pods and seed yield. Therefore, good nitrogen fertility is necessary to produce a large, photosynthetically efficient leaf area that will support high numbers of flowers, pods and seed yield. Nitrogen is mobile within the plant and can be moved from older to younger leaves and pods. If such a deficiency persists, most species show yellowing of the leaves, especially in the older leaves near the base of the plant. Under severe nitrogen deficiency, these leaves become completely yellow and fall off the plant. Younger leaves may not show these symptoms initially because nitrogen mobilized from older leaves. Therefore, nitrogen deficiency symptoms first show up in older leaves as pale green to yellow colouring, and sometimes purpling. Overall plant growth becomes slow, with short thin stems, small leaves, and few branches and the amount and time of flowering gets restricted with lower number of pots.

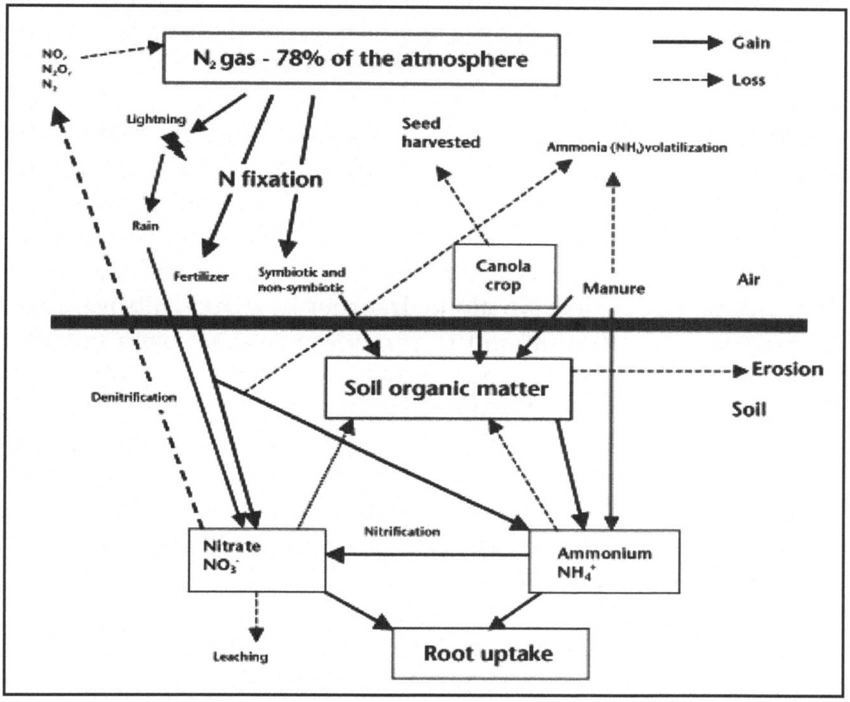

Fig. 4.1: Nitrogen Cycle and Transformations (CCC, 2003)

Heavy nitrogen fertilization can reduce canola yields when excellent spring moisture conditions are followed by drought. Under this condition, the nitrogen produces larger leaves, increases transpiration and moisture use. As a result, soil moisture is depleted, leaving little for flowering, podding and seed fill. Excessive nitrogen fertilization can also reduce yields by promoting lodging, delaying maturity that may increase foliar disease due to the dense canopy and lodging. Nitrogen fertilization generally increases the protein content of canola seed and meal while it may slightly decrease the canola seed oil content, especially at higher rates. Depending upon the fertilization technique and environmental conditions, nitrogen losses through ammonia volatilization varies from negligible to more than 50% of the applied nitrogen (Black et al., 1989; Freney et al., 1992). Soil texture, moisture content of the soil, pH buffering capacity, cation exchange capacity, nitrification rate and presence of plant and plant residues are some of the factors which also affect ammonia volatilization (Freney and Black, 1988). It is a major risk because mineral nitrogen, especially nitrate (NO_3^-) and urea ($CO(NH_2)_2$) are very soluble and can run off through surface water. Water contaminated by nitrate is not potable and at high concentrations can be a serious risk for human health (Al-Redhaiman, 2000 and Umar and Iqbal, 2007). During the growing season, most of the available nitrogen is in the nitrate form. Nitrate produced during nitrification process leaches down to ground water or denitrifies to produce N_2O type greenhouse gases. Nitrate can move downward at a rate greater than that which is used by the crop and the depth it moves is dependent upon the amount of water entering the soil and texture. Nitrogen use efficiency is low in arid and semiarid regions due to loss of fertilizer nitrogen by ammonia volatilization, nitrate leaching, run off and gaseous emission via denitrification. Due to rapid nitrification process nitrogen is available in soil as nitrate for most of the time whereas mixed nitrogen nutrition is considered better for plant growth and development than either nitrate or ammonium alone. In order to reduce nitrogen loss via leaching and/or denitrification and to provide mixed nitrogen nutrition to crop plants nitrification inhibition is desirable. Among the plant nutrients applied to the soil, nitrogen is the only essential element that volatilizes into the atmosphere as ammonia (NH_3). Consequently, NH_3 is the third most abundant nitrogen gas [after dinitrogen (N_2) and nitrous oxide (N_2O)] in the atmosphere (Liu et al., 2007). Ammonia volatilization from fertilizers applied to crops and from livestock waste, contributes about 90% of global NH_3 emission (Schlesinger and Hartley, 1992; Ferm, 1998). Thus, NH_3 volatilization not only causes nitrogen loss, reduction in nitrogen influx and use efficiencies but also exacerbates air quality and human well-being. Soil pH, water regimes, and temperature are important factors influencing NH_3 volatilization from agricultural soils (He et al., 1999; Liu et al., 2007a). Thus soil, water and fertilizer management becomes important for enhancing nitrogen uptake and utilization efficiency by reducing NH_3 volatilization.

Continuous heavy application of only one nutrient disturbs the nutrient balance and leads to depletion of other nutrients as well as to under-utilization of fertilizer nitrogen. The response of a crop to nitrogen not only depends on the status of nitrogen but also on the deficiency or sufficiency of other associated plant nutrients (Yadav et al., 1998). The amount of mineral nitrogen fertilizers applied to agricultural crops, in the last four decades has increased by 7.4 fold, whereas the overall yield increase has been only 2.4 fold (Tilman et al., 2002), which means that nitrogen use efficiency has declined sharply. This obviously implies that NUE is higher at reduced levels of crop production when use of nitrogen fertilizer is much lower. NUE is the product of absorption efficiency (amount of absorbed nitrogen/quantity of available nitrogen) and the utilization efficiency (yield/absorbed nitrogen) (Gallais and Coque, 2005). Canola nitrogen requirement is higher than cereals and it is considered as a high nitrogen demanding crop (Hocking et al., 1997; Rathke et al., 2005). Nutrient use efficiency (NUE) in canola is specifically biased towards nitrogen as the main nutrient; hence NUE in the discussion relates more to nitrogen use efficiency. Understanding nitrogen use characteristics of canola will help to improve nitrogen use efficiency and minimize production costs (Masson and Brennan, 1998; Fismes et al., 2000) especially when production regions are characterized by different soil and climatic properties. Nitrogen use efficiency in crop production is generally low (Peng et al., 1996; Raun, and Johnson, 1999) which might cause severe yield limitations where there is a lack of nitrogen supply.

Moreover, this might increase environmental pollution where high nitrogen fertilizer doses are applied to attain maximum yields (Hirel et al., 2007; Horst et al., 2003). Canola NUE ranges from 12 to 40% (depending on the cultivar and management regime). Canola is categorized as a low NUE crop (Gan et al., 2007). On a global scale, at least 50% of the nitrogen fertilizer applied is lost from agricultural systems and most of these losses occur during of fertilizer application. However, it has also been demonstrated through under research of new nitrogen management technologies that 30 to 50% increase in nitrogen use efficiency can be achieved (Dobermann and Cassman, 2004; Giller et al., 2004). There is great interest in improving the efficiency with which productivity, profitability, sustainability, and environmental protection can be accomplished. There have also been genuine concerns over nutrient use efficiency, in general, and nitrogen use efficiency (NUE) in particular for economic as well as environmental reasons. Improving NUE of canola can be achieved by increasing the seed yield for current nitrogen inputs or maintaining current seed yields using lower quantities of nitrogen. An improved NUE will also provide economic benefits to the grower as fertilizer and fuel costs continue to be an issue. Nitrogen use efficiency technology that makes plants hungrier for nitrogen and absorb more of it out of the soil has been established in canola and is poised for commercialization within the next decade.

Some approaches to minimize nitrogen losses and increase use efficiency (Roy and Pederson, 1992) of the most suitable fertilizer material are manipulation of the application techniques including split application and placement, manipulation of particle size, use of coating materials and other chemicals, judicious and economic application of fertilizers for synergistic interactions, application of organic sources along with mineral fertilizers and efficient agronomic practices like tillage, irrigation, mulching, weed control, plant population and use of varieties with higher nitrogen use efficiency.

Some plant species and genotypes have special capacity to grow and yield well on soils with low fertility. These species and genotypes are considered tolerant to nutrient deficiency, hence they are nutrient efficient. Efficient genotypes grow and yield well on nutrient deficient soils by employing specific physiological mechanisms that allows them to gain access to sufficient quantities of nutrients leading to more uptake efficiency and utilization efficiency (Sylvester-Bradley and Kindred, 2009). Yau and Thurling (1987) evaluated the variations in fertilizer nitrogen response among spring rape cultivars and its relationship to nitrogen uptake and utilization and they noted a cultivar difference. Their work showed the ability of genotype to yield adequately even under low nitrogen input become of inherited capacity to utilize nitrogen more efficiently for dry matter production. Houman et al. (2013) conducted and experiment with four genotypes of *B. napus* (cultivars Topas, Sentry, Polo and the experimental line 04C204) having varying level of seed oil content to study nitrogen use efficiency.

Topas, with lowest seed oil content potential, had higher biomass accumulation in shoots and roots and higher NUE than line 04C204. The higher NUE in cv. Topas would suggest a greater efficiency in the production of the crop in field. Other strategies to improve NUE are to use genetical modifications or to breed new varieties that take up more nitrogen from the soil and utilize the more efficiently (Hirel et al., 2007 and Good et al., 2004). In canola, the overexpression of a gene encoding the enzyme alanine aminotransferase (AlaAT) from barley, directed by a rape root-specific promoter, led to a dramatic increase in biomass production and seed yield (Good et al., 2007). Improvement in plant productivity was only observed under low nitrogen fertilization which was attributed to a higher flux of nitrate, associated or induced by a decrease in the content of glutamine and glutamate in the stem. In the field when the applied nitrogen rate was reduced by 40%, the agronomic performance of the transgenic rapeseed plants overexpressing AlaAT was similar to that of untransformed control plants grown under higher nitrogen rates.

Role of Phosphorus on Growth and Nutrient Use Efficiency of Canola

Phosphorus functions in the plant as a structural element and in energy transfer. The structural components that rely on phosphorus include nucleic acids (the building blocks of DNA) and phospholipids (fats and oils) which are important membrane constituents. The phosphorus energy transfer compounds are phosphate esters about 50 different esters have been identified out of which ATP (adenosine triphosphate) is the principal phosphate energy compound used for starch synthesis and nutrient uptake. However energy produced during respiration and photosynthesis is captured by these phosphate compounds, which then are transported to areas that are building plant tissues. The energy stored in the phosphate compound is released and the molecule is recycled back to be charged. The recycling of phosphate energy compounds is accomplished at extremely fast rates and a small amount can satisfy the plant energy needs. The main phosphorus forms taken up by roots from the soil solution are the primary and secondary phosphate ions ($H_2PO_4^-$ and HPO_4^{-2}). These phosphate anions exist transiently in the soil solution due to rapid removal by roots and microbes or reaction with other soil minerals. The phosphorus level is highest in young vegetative material and in the canola seed and this level remains fairly high in the leaves (0.3 to 0.4%) until late flowering when significant translocation to developing pods and seeds occurs. By maturity, 75 to 80% of the phosphorus in aboveground dry matter is in the seed. Canola seed contains 0.7 to 0.8% P, while stems and pods at harvest contains only 0.1 to 0.2%, respectively.

Canola is an efficient scavenger of soil phosphorus even though *Brassica* species are non-mycorrhizal (mycorrhizae are symbiotic associations between certain soil fungi and plant roots where the fungi contribute to the phosphorus nutrition of the plant). Canola endowed with several mechanisms to achieve this efficient phosphorus uptake, has abundant fine roots with the ability to branch and proliferate in zones of higher nutrient content such as around fertilizer bands or granules. In addition to root proliferation in fertilizer zones due to branching, canola roots can increase the root hair number and length in response to low phosphorus conditions. The second mechanism that enhances phosphorus uptake is solubilization of relatively insoluble mineral phosphorus forms. It has the ability to acidify the rhizosphere just behind the root tip near the zone of root hair formation.

The acid generated by roots is predominantly caused by exudation of organic acids such as malic and citric acid and also released enzymes (phosphatases) that mineralize phosphate from organic phosphorus pools. Exudates for mobilization and scavenging inorganic phosphorus (Pi) from soil is one of the ways in which plants respond to low supplies in soil phosphorus by increasing the availability of inorganic and organic forms of phosphorus into the rhizosphere (Rengel and Marschner, 2005; George and Richardson, 2008). Several plant species, including some legumes and rapeseed/canola, can increase the exudation of organic acid anions (citrate, malate, malonate, and oxalate) in response to low available phosphorus (Pearse et al., 2006; Kirkby and Johnston, 2008). Immature plants adequately supplied with phosphorus have 85 to 95% of the total inorganic phosphate stored in the vacuoles. In contrast, in phosphorus deficient plants, almost all the phosphate in leaves is found in active pools (cytoplasm and chloroplasts) and at maturity, most of the plant phosphorus is stored in organic form as phytate in the grain.

Canola plants suffering from strong phosphorus deficiency can experience slow leaf expansion along with smaller and fewer leaves. Deficiency symptoms appear by the second week of growth since canola seedlings are able to obtain sufficient phosphorus from seed reserves during the first week of growth. Root growth is less affected by phosphorus deficiency than shoot growth, leading to a typical decrease in shoot-root ratio. With a more severe deficiency, root development becomes restricted, but not as dramatically as stem and leaf growth. Although overall root branching is restricted in phosphorus deficient soils, root hair length and density usually increase. Phosphorus deficiency affects the maturity and development of reproductive tissue. Even a mild phosphorus deficiency can delay the maturity by several days compared to plants with adequate phosphorus. In addition to a delay in flowering, a phosphorus deficiency can reduce the number of flowers and seeds per pod. Also, a phosphorus deficiency can cause leaves to die and drop early, which contributes to the overall yield loss.

The majority of phosphorus fertilizer is not absorbed by canola in the application year itself. Instead, most of the fertilizer phosphorus reacts with soil constituents to form relatively insoluble salts or stabilized phosphorus compounds. Timing and placement are two management strategies used to maximize phosphorus fertilizer uptake and yield response. Since phosphate reacts with soil constituents to form insoluble compounds over time, phosphorus fertilizer efficiency can be increased by limiting the time from application to crop uptake. Phosphorus supply during the first two to six weeks of canola growth is critical to achieve optimal yield and it has an ability to absorb native soil phosphorus through acidification of the rhizosphere.

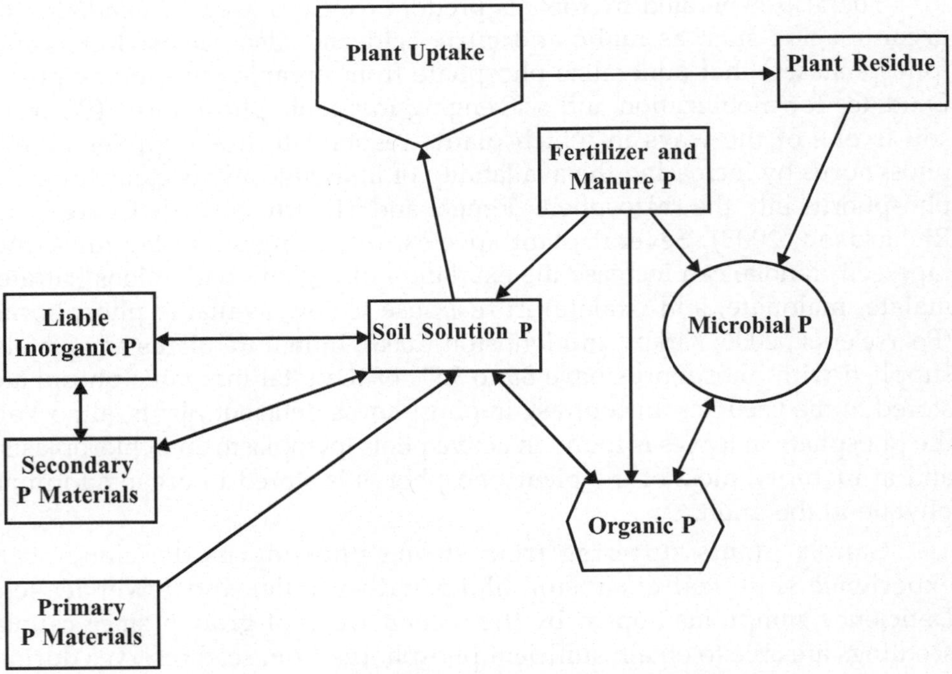

Fig. 4.2: The Soil Phosphorous Cycle (CCC, 2003)

Both organic and inorganic phosphorus forms occur in soil and both are important sources of plant available phosphate in soil solution. Primary and secondary phosphate ions ($H_2PO_4^-$ and $H_2PO_4^{-2}$) can be present in soil solution, with $H_2PO_4^-$ the major form at pH< 7.2. This solution has several possible fates: it may be absorbed by roots, adsorbed to mineral surfaces, precipitated with various cations such as Ca^{+2}, or immobilized into microbial biomass and soil organic matter. Soil phosphate supply is usually highest in the pH range of 6.5 to 7.0. At high pH levels (>7.5), calcium and magnesium cations can precipitate phosphate to form salts with low solubility. In contrast, in acidic soils (pH<6), iron and aluminium cations react with the phosphate to form insoluble compounds. The diffusion coefficient of phosphorus in soil is very low, hence the root zone phosphorus is depleted and plants cannot get phosphorus when it is needed (Clarkson, 1981). When soluble granular phosphorus fertilizers are applied to soil, a large proportion of the phosphorus dissolves quickly but there are many fates for that dissolved phosphorus once it gets into the soil solution pool.

The concentration of phosphorus around the fertilizer granule is high, and phosphorus may be lost from the soil solution pool by precipitation reactions, where soluble phosphorus combines with other elements in the soil (calcium, aluminium and iron) to produce new solid compounds. As phosphorus moves away from the granule through soil pores it binds to soil surfaces by a process called adsorption. This is where phosphorus is attracted to the clay mineral surfaces of soils somewhere of the phosphorus on the surface remains in a plant available form (ie. it can move back into the soil solution pool) but some may remain very strongly bound and permanently removed from the plant available pool into the non-exchangeable pool. Part of the dissolved phosphorus is also incorporated into the soil organic matter by the soil microbial biomass but can be later mineralized to soluble phosphorus by other microbial processes or exudates from plant roots. Soil microbes however compete with crop roots for soil solution phosphorus (McLaughlin and Alston, 1986; McLaughlin et al., 1988b). A number of crop species excrete phosphorus solubilising compounds under phosphorus deficient conditions, especially canola (Hoffland et al., 1992; Lipton et al., 1987; Zhang et al., 1997) and might therefore be suited to systems where plant-available phosphorus is low.

Phosphorus availability may decrease through crop removal, soil erosion, high soil p^H, surface runoff, binding to soil particle surfaces, high clay content and formation of minerals. Mineral formation is the major factor contributing to decreased phosphorus use efficiency in soils. Specifically, phosphorus fertilizer quickly reacts with calcium (Ca^{2+}) and magnesium (Mg^{2+}) to create relatively insoluble phosphates. The concentration of inorganic phosphorus in the solution is often low (2 to 10 μM) which lead to the slow rate of diffusion into the root (Marschner, 1995). Hence phosphorus is one of the least available mineral elements in the soil and frequently limits plant growth (Vance et al., 2003; Tiessen, 2008). Low phosphorus availability limits plant growth on many soils across the world and is a common constraint to agricultural productivity, particularly in developing countries where access to phosphorus fertilizers is restricted (Lynch, 2007).

However, high phosphorus balance efficiency is often achieved in low input, low production farming systems (McIvor et al., 2011; Burkitt et al., 2007), or in productive agriculture on soils that have intrinsically low phosphorus buffering capacity (e.g. sands), or where phosphorus buffering capacity is low because sorption sites for phosphorus are close to saturation and soil phosphorus fertility is relatively high (Syers et al., 2008). Plants that are more productive in soils with low available phosphorus concentrations, either as a result of improved foraging for phosphorus in soil or by extracting phosphorus from sparingly-available sources, also have an important role to play as their use can reduce the phosphorus that occur in moderate to high phosphorus absorbing soils. In fertilized agricultural systems, phosphorus in sparingly available inorganic and organic phosphorus pools is a major contributor to the inefficient use of phosphorus for soils that have moderate to high phosphorus sorption capacity, whereas in soils with low phosphorus retention, losses due to phosphorus leaching can contribute to inefficient phosphorus use (Simpson et al., 2011).

Canola (*Brassica napus* L.) generally shows that the response to phosphorus in canola is greater than that of wheat (*Triticum aestivum* L.) and it requires up to 50% less phosphorus than wheat to reach 90% of maximum yield (Bolland et al., 1999; Brennan and Bolland, 2001; Bolland and Brennan, 2008). Canola also take up more phosphorus than wheat at a given amount a phosphorus fertilizer, suggesting that canola roots have a greater ability to utilize soil phosphorus with high responsiveness Vu et al. (2010).

Phosphorus use efficiency in simple agronomic terms can be defined as the amount of shoot biomass per unit of phosphorus present in the plant. It represents the integration of plant phosphorus uptake from soil and its translocation within the plant, processes that are both extremely complex (Holford, 1997). Furthermore, a smaller radius of fine roots and root hairs causes a slower decline in phosphorus concentration at the root/hair surface, enabling a higher rate of phosphorus influx to be maintained, which may also contribute to greater phosphorus uptake.

Therefore enhancing opportunities for phosphorus transport via soil-root contact through species or genotypes with greater lateral root formation (Gahoonia et al., 1999; Manske et al., 2000), longer root hairs (Gahoonia and Nielsen, 1997; Gahoonia and Nielsen, 2004), or reduced root diameter will give greater potential for increased phosphorus acquisition by plants.

Also, phosphorus use efficiency refers to the increase in yield of a variety following the addition of phosphorus fertilizer, assessed as the difference in yield between fertilized and unfertilized units divided by the difference in nutrient supplied in each of the treatments (Hammond et al., 2009) while, agronomic phosphorus use efficiency is a measurement of the level of responsiveness to phosphorus. Thus, a variety with high agronomic efficiency will be one that has a high yield increase in response to increased phosphorus application. A variety with a high agronomic efficiency may result in higher yields at the levels of phosphorus currently recommended and may also show a large yield response with further additions of phosphorus.

Graham (1984) defines the nutrient efficiency of a genotype as the ability to produce high yield in soil that is limiting in that element for a standard genotype. This is essentially the same as the definition proposed by Moll et al. (1982), but importantly, it differs in that the relative yield of a genotype in limiting versos with non-limiting nutrient conditions is used to determine nutrient-use efficiency. Hence, there is a need to improve phosphorus use efficiency (PUE) in farming systems. Progress in improving phosphorus use efficiency has been limited for several reasons, viz. inconsistent definitions of phosphorus use efficiency, inappropriate phenotyping, incomplete understanding of the phosphorus uptake, lack of field validation, and little consideration of genotype x environment interactions that affect the expression of phosphorus use efficiency. Only 10-20% of phosphorus is used in the year in which it is applied (McLaughlin et al. 1988). Improvements in the efficiency of phosphorus nutrition of crops come from a variety of potential sources, including changes in fertilizer technology, improvements in exploiting soil biology, and better fertilizer management practices as well as genetic improvement.

Enhanced phosphorus efficiency can be achieved by improved uptake of phosphate from soil and by improved productivity per unit phosphorus taken up (phosphorus use efficiency). Improved phosphorus use efficiency can be achieved by plants that have overall lower phosphorus concentrations, and by optimal distribution and redistribution of phosphorus in the plant allowing maximum growth and biomass allocation to harvestable plant parts. Improving the efficiency of phosphorus fertilizer use for crop growth requires enhanced phosphorus acquisition by plants from the soil (phosphorus acquisition efficiency) and enhanced use of phosphorus in processes that lead to faster growth and greater allocation of biomass to the harvestable parts {(internal phosphorus use efficiency (PUE)}, as only 15-30% of applied fertilizer phosphorus is taken up by crops in the year of its application (Syers et al., 2008). The inorganic phosphorus concentration in tissues generally reflects the phosphorus inorganic supply (White and Hammond, 2008). A greater effort to enhance the efficiency of phosphorus use for crop production will reduce environmental impacts associated with phosphorus fertilizers and phosphorus waste, increase the nutritional value of grains, and improve farm economies.

More efficient use of phosphorus within the plant adds to the gains that can be made by improving phosphorus acquisition efficiency, thereby reducing phosphorus fluxes on crop land and in the environment. The largest yield benefits of improved PUE are expected for crops growing in soils that have very low phosphorus content and where little or no phosphorus fertilizer is applied. PUE averages 8% when P is broadcast and incorporated and 16% when phosphorus was either knifed with anhydrous ammonia or applied with the seed bed preparation (Sander, Penas, and Eghball, 1990; Sander, Penas, and Walters, 1991). We can summarize some strategies which plants and microorganisms may improve phosphorus use efficiency (i) root-foraging strategies that improve phosphorus acquisition by lowering the critical phosphorus requirement of plant growth and allowing agriculture to operate at lower levels of soil phosphorus (ii) phosphorus mining strategies to enhance desorption, solubilisation or mineralization of phosphorus from sparingly-available sources in soil using root exudates (organic anions, phosphatases) (iii) improving internal phosphorus utilization efficiency through plants that yield more per unit of phosphorus uptake.

Role of Potassium on Growth and Nutrient Use Efficiency of Canola

Potassium (K) like that of nitrogen is also required in large amounts by canola. In spite of the large requirement, canola yield responses to potassium fertilizer (potash) are inconsistent infrequent, due to ample soil potassium reserves on the prairies, and strong ability of the crop to absorb it. Potassium is different from most other essential nutrients since it does not become part of structural components in the plant. Instead, most of the potassium in plants remains dissolved in the cell sap and performs several major functions. It is the most abundant inorganic cation in plants, comprising up to 10% of plant's dry weight (Watanabe et al., 2007). One major function of potassium is that of enzyme activation and more than 60 enzymes are activated by K. Potassium helps maintain a favorable water status in plants in several different ways.

Potassium cations dissolved in cell sap perform major osmotic functions where, dissolved ions of attract water and act as an osmotically active substance. It also maintains the water relations in plants by regulating water loss (called transpiration) from pores (stomata) in the leaves. Potassium cations, in combination with chlorine, calcium and certain hormones governs, the opening and closing of stomata. Potassium (K^+) is the main ion that counterbalances the H^+ flux during photosynthesis in the chloroplasts, maintains a favorable pH gradient in the chloroplasts for making phosphate energy compounds and in the process affects photosynthsis of several levels and is needed for nitrogen uptake and protein synthesis the major counter ion that balances nitrate during transport and storage in vacuoles. The potassium level is highest in canola seedling but declines steadily towards maturity. Potassium uptake by canola is rapid during the early growth stages and tapers off by the end of flowering. Under high potassium fertility and good growth, canola can absorb more K than apparently needed, a situation termed luxury consumption. As canola matures, the potassium level in leaves declines while in the stem it increases.

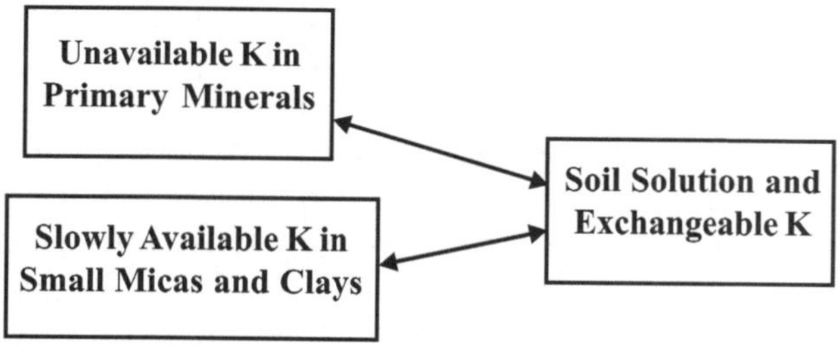

Fig. 4.3: Potassium Soil Cycle (CCC, 2003)

Figure 4.3 shows that the various pools are in dynamic equilibrium. As K^+ is removed by plant uptake and through leaching on sandy soils, additional potassium is released from the mineral soils to become available and moves to plant roots by diffusion through the soil.

Canola has a high potassium demand which is more than cereals, although only modest amounts are retained in grain. The nutrient content of canola hay is four times the grain potassium content, and nutrient removal can be ten times higher if a canola crop is cut for hay compared to being harvested for grain. Potassium deficiency reduces overall canola growth but to a lesser degree than nitrogen or phosphorus deficiency. The first observable symptom of potassium deficiency is mottled or marginal chlorosis, which then develops into necrosis at the leaf tips, at the margins, and between veins. The yellowing occurs first in middle leaves followed by older ones if observed at bolting to flowering stages. Because potassium can be mobilized to the younger leaves, these symptoms appear initially on the more mature leaves toward the base of the plant. The leaves may also curl and crinkle. The stems of potassium-deficient plants may be slender and weak, with abnormally short internodal regions.

Potassium is relatively immobile in the soil since the K^+ cations are readily adsorbed at the negative surface charges on clay particles and organic matter. It can also be fixed into the clay lattice structure of certain clay types, but it is more mobile in sandy soil and thus can be leached in these soil textures. Low soil K levels occur where there has been large off-takes of K and particularly on light soils under high rainfall where K can be leached. Most soils are well supplied with K, but deficiency of this nutrient in canola can occur is only likely it is grown in deep sandy acid soils of high rainfall regions. In most soils, K^+ is much less mobile than nitrate but somewhat more mobile than phosphate. This relative immobility means that fertilizer placement will greatly affect uptake efficiency if the application methods minimize contact with soil but increase contact with root. Similarly banding and seed-placed methods can also achieve good uptake efficiency.

The potassium efficiency is described as the proportion of yield potential that can be achieved under potassium deficiency stress. Considerable genotypic variation in efficiency of potassium uptake and utilization (as the amount of biomass or economic yield per unit of potassium taken up) has been identified in a variety of crop species, including canola (Damon et al., 2007). Potassium efficient genotypes can have higher acquisition of potassium from soil (uptake efficiency) with higher dry matter per unit of potassium taken up (utilization efficiency). Crop genotypes with the capacity to take up relatively more potassium where availability is low (Trehan and Sharma, 2002) have been identified together with those that produce a relatively large biomass per unit of potassium taken up (Woodend et al., 1987). There is little information available about potassium use efficiency. However, it is generally considered to have a higher use efficiency than nitrogen and phosphorus because it is immobile in most soils and is not subjected to the gaseous losses that nitrogen takes or the fixation reactions that affect phosphorus. First year recovery of applied potassium can range from 20% to 60%. In most developed countries, particularly in Europe, potassium use has been historically large and sufficient to sustain soil fertility and crop production at high levels. However, potassium use has declined in recent years. As a result, average potassium removal by crops rate approach or exceed potassium inputs in these areas and many farmers appear to take advantage of mining soil potassium that had been accumulated over time.

Uptake efficiency of soil-grown plants may consist of increased capacity to mobilize/solubilize non-available nutrient forms into plant-available ones, and/or increased capacity to transport nutrients across the plasma membrane of root cells and into other plant parts. For potassium, it appears that the increased capacity to convert unavailable into available forms is of greater importance for efficient uptake because potassium is transported to roots by diffusion, which is a relatively slow process that frequently limits nutrient uptake. However, larger amounts are transported towards roots if a larger concentration gradient between the root surface and the bulk soil can be maintained by vigorous potassium uptake at the root surface (Jungk and Claassen 1997). When a capacity of root cells to take up potassium exceeds the rate of potassium replenishment at the root surface, the uptake rate will be governed by the potassium supply rather than by the capacity of plants to take potassium up (Rengel, 1993). Therefore, an increased capacity of root cells to take up potassium because of, an increased expression of high-affinity potassium uptake systems in the plasma membranes under nutrient deficiency stress is expected to be of secondary importance as an efficiency mechanism for potassium and other diffusion supplied nutrients (e.g. P, Zn, Mn and Cu). In pot experiments with oilseed rape the radial distance of the potassium (Rb) depletion zone adjacent to the root surface increased with the length of the root hairs (Jungk, 2001). The capacity to take up potassium from a potassium deficient soil is positively correlated with root hair length of oilseed rape (Hogh-Jensen and Pedersen, 2003).

Genotypic differences in capacity to utilize potassium can be attributed to differences in the (1) partitioning and redistribution of potassium at a cellular or whole-plant level, (2) substitution of potassium with other ions, and/or (3) the partitioning of resources into the economic product (Sattelmacher et al., 1994).

For optimal metabolic activity, plants maintain a potassium concentration in the range of 60-150 mM in the cytosol (Amtmann et al., 2005, Cuin et al., 2003, Karley et al., 2000, Leigh 2001). Differences in the potassium requirements of tissues are generally attributable to differences in the potassium requirements in the vacuoles and apoplast as well as the capacity to maintain cytosolic potassium at a certain level. Efficient utilization of potassium during the vegetative stage may not translate into potassium efficiency for economic yield. The genotypic differences in harvest index influenced the efficiency with which potassium could be utilized to yield grain more than the capacity to utilize potassium to produce biomass.

Role of Sulpher on Growth and Nutrient Use Efficiency of Canola

Sulphur is the fourth major nutrient in crop production where most crops require as much sulphur as phosphorus. The nitrogen and sulphur requirements of crops are closely related, because both nutrients are required for protein synthesis. Sulphur is involved in the synthesis of chlorophyll and is also required for the synthesis of oil (Marschner, 1986). Sulphur is a key component of two essential amino acids (cysteine and methionine) and is needed for protein synthesis. In canola, sulphur is a constituent of certain amino acids needed for protein synthesis. It also affects the quality of canola seed due to its effect on the oil content. Both of these amino acids are also precursors for coenzymes and secondary plant substances. Glutathione, an important antioxidant in plants and animals, is synthesized from cysteine. It is found primarily in the chloroplasts where its antioxidant ability is needed to detoxify free radicals generated during photosynthesis. Glutathione also functions as transient sulphur storage. Thioredoxins, another important group of sulphur compounds related to glutathione, help activate several enzymes in carbon metabolism. Sulphur also is part of several enzymes and coenzymes such as ferrodoxin, biotin (vitamin H), coenzyme A, urease, and thiamine (vitamin B_1).

An important group of secondary plant sulphur compounds in canola is glucosinolate. Plants contain over 100 different glucosinolate compounds. Glucosinolates are a group of secondary metabolites containing β-thioglucose, a sulphonated oxime moiety and a side chain, their concentration is closely related to the S supply, what is not surprising, since each glucosinolate molecule contains two or three S atoms (Zhao et al., 1997). Glucosinolates are stored in cell vacuoles, and can be broken down by an enzyme (myrosinase) to yield glucose, sulphate and volatile compounds such as isothiocyanate. Glucosinolates contribute to defense or attractant systems for certain insects and diseases and it levels are highest in growing points, roots, and youngest leaves, all of which are most vulnerable to insects and diseases.

Canola is more sensitive than cereals to sulphur deficiency and frequently responds to sulphur. Therefore, pay equal attention to nitrogen, phosphorus and sulphur. The main sulphur form absorbed by canola roots is sulphate. Low plant sulphur contents also increase the root uptake rate. Negative feedback signals for sulphur uptake may be sulphate or glucosinolate levels in vacuoles, or the levels of organic sulphur compounds such as cysteine, methionine or glutathione. The sulphur level in canola plants is highest in the early seedling stage when young leaves comprise most of the dry matter. As plants develop the overall sulphur level declines but not as dramatically as with nitrogen. By maturity, canola straw contains approximately 0.3 to 0.4% sulphur while pod chaff contains slightly more sulphur (0.5 to 0.6%). Canola seed contains about 0.4 to 0.6% sulphur. At harvest, canola straw and pod chaff contain roughly twice as much sulphur per acre as that in the seed (McGrath & Zhao, 1996; Zhao et al., 1993). However, as the effects of sulphur are related to nitrogen levels, such recommendations would be based on nitrogen recommendations of an appropriate variety, also considering inherent soil sulphur levels, climatic regions and yield potential.

Sulphur has several effects on canola growth. Since chlorophyll synthesis requires sulphur, deficiency will affect visible leaf colour and photosynthesis. Sulphur is involved in photosynthesis and, deficiencies decrease chlorophyll content and leaves turn yellow showing inter-veinal chlorosis. Protein synthesis requires sulphur containing amino acids, and, therefore, sulphur deficiency affects rapidly growing parts, especially reproductive structures. By the bolting stage, sulphur deficiency begins to affect yield parameters such as branches per plant, fertile flowers per plant, seeds per pod and individual seed weight. Under mild to moderate sulphur deficiency, thousand kernel weight is normally not significantly affected since plants compensate by reducing the seed number per pod. Sulphur availability has been identified as a key factor critical for canola production; with deficiencies frequently lowering canola yield (Fismes et al., 2000).

Sulphur deficiency symptoms vary depending upon the severity and timing of the deficiency relative to crop growth stage. In the vegetative stage, foliar symptoms show up under severe sulphur deficiency. Since sulphur has a low mobility within the plant, symptoms are observed more readily on the youngest leaves, which become greenish-yellow compared to the normal bluish-green in *B. napus*. The yellowing (chlorosis) starts from the leaf edges and the tissue around leaf veins remains green. Subsequently, the leaf edges and bottoms may turn purple. The purple colour is caused by enhanced pigment (anthocyanin) synthesis due to sugar accumulation resulting from sulphur limited amino acid and protein synthesis. Under S deficient conditions, the amount of amino acids and nitrates in leaves increases dramatically and protein degradation within chloroplasts occurred. Besides, sulphur affects photosynthetic characteristics. Sulphur deficiency limits protein synthesis by limiting the amount of methionine and cysteine available for the assembly of new proteins (Fismes et al., 2000).

Sulphur fertilization can affect canola quality (oil, protein and glucosinolate contents). The balance between nitrogen and sulphur has a strong influence on quality as well as yield. Deficiency of sulphur will reduce nitrogen uptake and for this reason, the application of sulphur needs to be balanced with nitrogen for optimum yields (Fismes et al., 2000). Significant effects on quality are usually found when sulphur fertilizer is applied to extremely deficient soil, or when excessive sulphur fertilizer is applied. Sulphur fertilization can increase protein content of the meal, which is desirable, but can also increase undesirable glucosinolate contents. Sulphur application can increase seed glucosinolates (Jan et al., 2002), and the high glucosinolate lines become more responsive to sulphur than that of low glucosinolate lines. Sulphur supply may increase glucosinolate (GLS) content of canola (Fismes et al., 2000) however the high level of glucosinolate hydrolysis products can adversely reduce the feeding value of rapeseed meal rendering the meal unpalatable. Increasing sulphur application has been shown to increase oil, protein and glucosinolates of canola seeds (Haneklaus et al., 1999).

Canola has high requirements for sulphur (Grant & Bailey, 1993), become of a combination of high protein content with high proportions of cysteine and methionine (Clandinin, 1981). Sulphur increases the percentage of oil content of the seed (Chaudhry et al., 1992) and glucosinolate content (Marschner, 1986). A strong interaction between sulphur and nitrogen for seed and oil production in oilseed crops has been reported by various workers Ahmad et al. (1998), Abdin et al. (2003), Farahbakhsh et al. (2006), Malhi et al. (2005, 2007). Oil, protein and glucosinolate concentrations in seed increase with sulphur fertilization (Malhi et al., 2007; Haneklaus et al., 1999). Thus, insufficient sulphur nutrition leads to a decline in seed yield whilst an excessive sulphur supply can affect meal quality by increasing seed GLS content which means that there should be a balance in sulphur and nitrogen levels in order to maintain desirable yields and good quality. Sulphur is a constituent of certain amino acids needed for protein synthesis in canola. It improves the quality of canola seed, including oil content. Deficiencies will greatly reduce nitrogen uptake hence the application of sulphur needs to be balanced with nitrogen for optimum yields (Ceccoti, 1996; Fismes et al., 2000). The N:S ratio is diverse (Fismes et al., 2000), but the typical ratio ranges from 7:1 to 5:1.

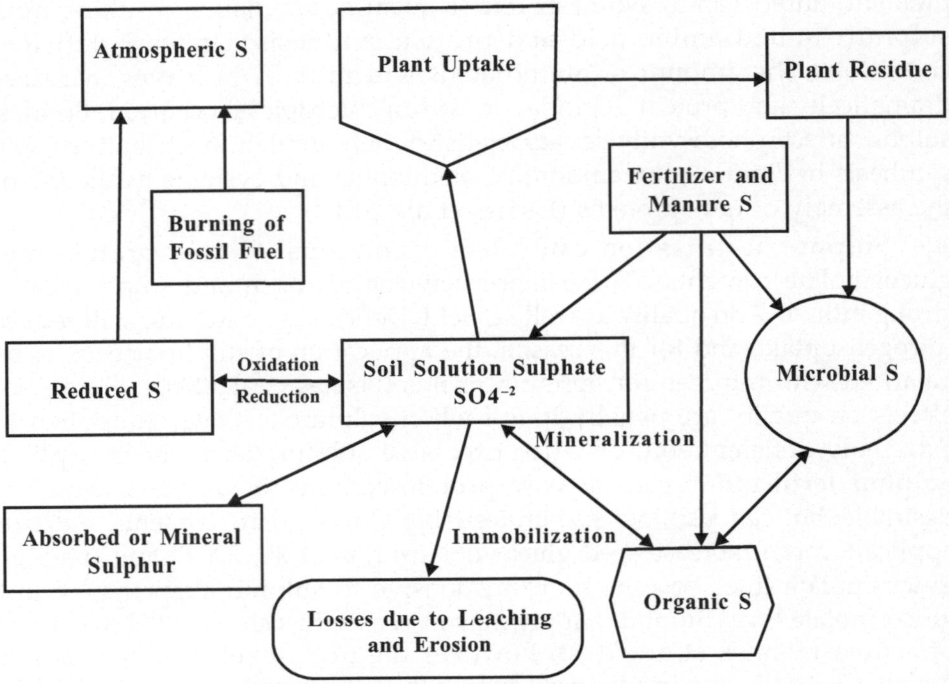

Fig. 4.4: Soil Sulphur Cycle (CCC, 2003)

A key component of the soil sulphur cycle for plant growth is the mineralization path. Soil organic matter and plant residues are decomposed by soil microbes, releasing sulphate. The sulphur mineralization rate is quite slow, and cannot match the uptake rate of growing plants. Sulphate released from residues will depend on the sulphur content. When plant residues contain more than about 0.15% sulphur (C:S ratio about 300:1), there will be a net release of sulphate through mineralization. Below 0.15% sulphur, decomposition is slower and there will be immobilization of soil sulphate by soil microbes.

The oxidation path is an important aspect of the soil sulphur cycle. In soils, sulphides, elemental sulphur and thiosulphate can be oxidized to sulphate by various soil microbes, but the main actors are bacteria from the genus Thiobacillus. The oxidation of these inorganic sulphur compounds produces considerable sulphuric acid. Sulphur oxidizing bacteria are most active under warm, moist, well aerated conditions and it is the oxidizing ability of these bacteria that permits the agricultural use of elemental sulphur for crop growth. In flooded soils, sulphate can be reduced by soil microbes to sulphides at an extremely low redox potential. However, soil microbes will utilize nitrate, iron and manganese compounds before reducing sulphate.

Highest fertilizer use efficiency generally results when sulphate fertilizer is placed near roots for easy just before the period of plant uptake for agree occurs. Under dry spring conditions, broadcast sulphate fertilizer can be stranded and result in poor uptake. However, under such dry conditions, canola germination and establishment will also be severely affected. Under average to good moisture conditions, sulphate fertilizer can be broadcast and incorporated in the spring with good results. On sandy soils, sulphate leaching can occur during wet periods. Therefore, apply fertilizer just prior to crop needs. Although sulphate fertilization just prior to or at seeding is best, post-seeding applications can be effective. Sulphate fertilizer can be soil applied up to the rosette stage with good response provided there exists sufficient water to leach the fertilizer down to the root zone before bolting. Foliar sulphate fertilizer solutions can be applied up to the bolting stage with moderate effectiveness, and can serve as a rescue treatment for deficient fields that were not adequately fertilized at or before seeding.

The conversion rate from elemental sulphur to sulphate depends on the particle size, the degree of dispersion in the soil, and the growing conditions for the bacteria (moisture, temperature). The surface area of these individual particles is the place where the soil bacteria feed and convert the elemental sulphur to sulphate. Small particles have the largest surface area and the fastest oxidation rate. The strong influence of elemental sulphur placement and timing on sulphate release subsequently affects canola yield. Sulphur fertilization enhances nitrogen efficiency in canola (Ceccoti, 1996), leading to increased nitrogen assimilation into leaf protein. Generally, for immediate crop uptake, sulphate formulations are recommended. As nitrogen and sulphur are both involved in plant protein synthesis, the shortage in sulphur supply for crops decreases the nitrogen use efficiency of fertilizers (Ceccoti, 1996). Consequently, the poor efficiency of nitrogen caused by insufficient sulphur needed to convert nitrogen into biomass production may increase nitrogen losses from cultivated soils (Schnug et al., 1993).

Plants assimilate nitrogen and sulphur in amounts proportional to that incorporated into amino acids and proteins, which suggest that nitrogen and sulphur requirements are closely interrelated (Fismes et al., 2000). Increasing nitrogen fertilizer rates aggravate sulphur deficiency of oilseed rape and reduce seed yield when available sulphur is limiting (Janzen and Bettany, 1984). Nitrogen addition increases seed yield in sulphur sufficient conditions, and optimum oil quality and maximum yield responses to both nitrogen and sulphur applications are obtained when the amount of available nitrogen and sulphur are balanced. Sulphur applications enhances nitrogen use efficiency in canola (Fisme et al., 2000). Brassica species in general require sulphur during their growth (Zhao et al., 1993), for the synthesis of both protein and naturally occurring glucosinolates. Both sulphur uptake and translocation in oilseed rape varieties vary as a function of growth stage and plant part and it improves nitrogen use efficiency and thereby maintains a sufficient oil level and fatty acid quality (Fismes et al., 2000).

Role of some Micronutrients on Growth and Nutrient Use Efficiency of Canola

Micronutrients are nutrients required by plants in small quantities or traces throughout life to orchestrate a range of physiological functions, they are not needed in large quantities, but they are as important to plant nutrition and development as the primary and secondary nutrients. A deficiency of any one of the micronutrients in the soil can limit plant growth, even when all other essential nutrients are present in adequate amounts. However, micronutrients can exist in several different forms in soil:

- within structures of primary and secondary minerals;
- adsorbed to mineral and organic matter surfaces;
- incorporated in organic matter and microorganisms; and
- in the soil solution.

Soils vary in micronutrients content, and they usually contain lower amounts of micronutrients than primary and secondary nutrients. Total soil content of a micronutrient does not indicate the amount available for plant growth during a single growing season although it does indicate relative abundance and potential supplying power.

Deficiencies of micronutrients are usually addressed by the application of supplemented fertilizer or a form of the element at sowing. Although the response of canola to foliar applied micronutrients is quite good. Micronutrient deficiency is widespread in plants, animals and humans, especially in many arid countries, due to the calcareous nature of soils, high pH, low organic matter, salt stress, continual drought, high bicarbonate content in irrigation water and imbalanced application of fertilizers (Malakouti, 2008). However, the six practically relevant micronutrients deficiencies of Fe, Mn and Zn tend to occur more on neutral to alkaline soils and under arid and semi-arid conditions. A deficiency of boron and copper is more likely to occur on acid soils in humid climates although large-scale boron deficiencies have been reported from many neutral to alkaline soils. Canola in general is very sensitive to micronutrients deficiency, specially zinc, iron and boron, where these deficiencies can compensate by use the foliar application of these micronutrients where this practice has been popular with farmers since the 1950s, when it was learned that foliar fertilization was effective and economic however many researchers have shown that a small amount of nutrients, particularly zinc, iron and boron applied by foliar spraying increases significantly the yield of crops (Sarkar et al., 2007; Wissuwa et al., 2008). Among the micronutrients zinc and iron nutrition can affect the susceptibility of plants to drought stress (Sultana et al., 2001; Khan et al., 2003; Cakmak, 2008).

Zinc is known to have an important role either as a metal component of enzymes or as a functional, structural or regulatory cofactor of a large number of enzymes (Grotz and Guerinot, 2006) and it plays an important role in the production of biomass (Ckamk, 2008). Furthermore, zinc may be required for chlorophyll production, pollen function and fertilization (Sultana et al., 2001; Pandey et al., 2006). Canola has a high requirement for zinc, particularly on alkaline soils high in carbonates, and zinc is applied adjacent to the seed at sowing. Zinc deficiency is the most important micronutrient problem, particularly in the alkaline-calcareous soils (Cakmak, 1998; Anonymous, 1998). Factors which induce zinc deficiency include alkaline soil pH, soil calcareousness, low soil organic matter, sandy texture, zinc-free fertilizers, accentuated zinc mining by high-yielding varieties, and/or flooding-induced electro-chemical changes (Mortvedt, et al., 1991; Tandon, 1995; Cakmak, 1998). The various forms of soil zinc include soil minerals, organic matter, adsorbed zinc on the surfaces of organic matter and clay, and dissolved zinc in the soil solution. Organically complexed, or chelated, zinc is important for the movement of zinc to plant roots. Also, zinc availability is affected by the presence of certain soil fungi, called mycorrhizae, which form symbiotic relationships with plant roots so, removal of surface soil in land leveling may remove the beneficial fungi and limit plants' ability to zinc absorption. Grewal et al. (1997) found that application of 3.5 kg Zn ha^{-1} increased seed yield of a zinc-inefficient oilseed rape plants by 65%. Grewal and Graham (1997) reported that canola plants grown from the high zinc seed had better seedling vigour, increased root and shoot growth, greater leaf area, more chlorophyll concentration, and higher zinc uptake in shoot compared with those grown from the low zinc seed in zinc deficient soils. The concentration of zinc at flowering, pod formation stage, concentration and uptake of zinc in straw and grain at maturity and uptake of zinc in grain and straw at maturity of Indian mustard increased significantly with increase in zinc levels (Gupta and Kaushik, 2006). Application of zinc has been reported significant positive effects in most cases, on growth, yield and chemical composition of canola (Chatterjee and Khurana, 2007; El Habbasha and Abdel Salam, 2010).

Iron is the fourth most abundant element, with total iron ranging from 0.7 to 55%, it plays essential roles in the metabolism of chlorophylls. External application of iron increased photosynthesis, net assimilation and relative growth (Sultana et al., 2001). This is especially true for soils of high pH where equilibrium conditions favour the oxidation of plant-available Fe^{+2} to unavailable Fe^{+3}.

Iron is highly immobile in plants; in event of deficiency, youngest growth turns chlorotic. With change in temperature and/or moisture, chlorosis may disappear over time, but invariably produces a yield loss effect. The low solubility product of iron minerals makes the inorganic form of iron unavailable to plants and forms the most common widespread nutritional disorder world over (Welch et al., 1991). Plants subjected to iron deficiency excess respond in different ways (Abadia, 1992). It is believed that under conditions of iron stress, some plants can increase their absorption capacity for iron. The mechanism affecting the acquisition of this essential microelement is often present in aerobic soils in the form of iron (Marschner, 1995). Solubility of iron is very low and is highly pH-dependent and it solubility decreases with increasing soil pH.

Iron deficiency may be caused by an imbalance with other metals such as Mo, Cu, or Mn. Other factors like, excessive phosphorus in the soil, a combination of high pH, high lime, wet, cold soils, and high bicarbonate levels or the plant species can differ significantly in their ability to take up iron where, roots of iron-efficient plants can improve its availability and uptake by secretion of H, organic acids and organic chelating compounds may affect on the iron deficiency.

Boron one of the important micronutrient exists in minerals, adsorbed on the surfaces of clay and oxides, combined in soil organic matter, and in the soil solution. Organic matter is the most important potentially plant-available soil source of boron. Canola has a high demand for boron, and the boron deficiency has been reported for canola grown in a field trial on acidic soil, where, it tends to be more sensitive to boron deficiency than do in cereal crops (Grant and Bailey, 1993; Shorrocks, 1997) and it needs more than the cereal crops needs (Malhi, 2001; Gupta, 2007). The crop failed to set seed without the application of supplementary boron at the start of stem elongation. Boron deficiency may become a problem as canola expands onto the acidic soils of the high rainfall tablelands however, many of these soils have low boron levels, and liming to increase the pH to a level suitable for canola could induce or exacerbate boron deficiency. Most of our understanding about boron derives from deficiency symptoms, and may involve in the following mechanisms viz. cell wall synthesis and structure, RNA metabolism, respiration hormone metabolism, stomatal regulation, membrane function, sugar transport and carbohydrate metabolism (CCC, 2003). As an essential nutrient for new cell growth, boron is required for cell expansion, regulation of H^+ transport, cellular Ca^{+2} retention and control of lignin production. Boron supply is needed for cell wall stability during pollen tube growth, and therefore is also essential for seed development, transportation of sugar photosynthesis and requires to develop meristematic tissues (Havlin et al., 2005).

Boron deficiency is often associated with dry or cold weather, which slows organic matter decomposition. Symptoms may disappear as soon as the surface soil receives rainfall or soil temperatures increase and root growth continues, but yield potential is often reduced. Boron availability decreases with increasing soil pH, particularly at a pH greater than 6.3 to 6.5. Organic matter is the largest potential B source available to plants, and is positively correlated with available B in soil where, low soil moisture reduces B release from organic matter and may even result in B deficiency under arid conditions (Miller and Donahue, 1990).

Boron is one of least mobile micronutrients in plants, and therefore deficiency symptoms appear first on young growing points and meristematic tissues, such as stem tips, root tips, new leaves and flower buds (Power and Prasad, 2010). Under boron deficiency, the symptoms are often not visual until the blooming stage (Grant and Bailey 1993), leaves on the upper plant develop red margins and/or interveinal yellow mottling on the leaves, at the bottom of the plant, leaves senesce earlier (Grant and Bailey 1993), it can affects root elongation, restrict pollen tube growth and reduce pollen production, which consequently affects fertilization and seed set (Shorrocks, 1997), decrease of bleeding sap, soluble sugar and amino acids in boron-inefficient cultivars (Cao et al., 1997), also include thickened, cracked, and wilted leaves, petioles, and stems, cracking, or rotting of fruits, tubers or roots (Power and Prasad, 2010).

Application of boron is a common practice for production of many crops, such as oilseed rape, it has a high demand for boron and is thus one of the crops most sensitive to boron deficiency however, there are significant differences in the response to boron deficiency among canola cultivars (Xue and Yang, 1994; Xue et al., 1995). Many researches has been conducted in revealing the physiological mechanisms of boron efficiency in oilseed rape, it was found that boron deficiency affected root exudates and the composition of bleeding sap on oilseed rape cultivars with contrasting boron efficiency. Boron fertilization can increase plant height, branches plant^{-1}, siliques plant^{-1}, seeds silique^{-1}, oil content and final seed yield under conditions of boron deficiency (Stevenson and Cole, 1999). Boron fertilization is often reported to contribute to a small increase in seed yield, e.g. 7% (Porter, 1993) and 7 to 11% increases (Troeh and Thompson, 2005).

In addition, uptake of Ca by canola shoots and roots can be reduced after boron application (Nadian et al., 2010). Boron also has important effects on seed production and can decrease protein and increase oil percentage in seeds (Asare and Scarisbrick, 1995). Xu et al. (2002) studied boron distribution and re-use of various boron efficient cultivars at the seedling and bolting stages in pot culture, and found that under boron deficient conditions, the boron concentration in the oldest leaf of boron inefficient cultivars was higher than that of boron efficient cultivars at the two stages, but that the reverse was the case in the youngest leaf. By contrast, the boron concentration was lowest in the youngest leaf, and boron concentration in the flower and bud of the boron efficient cultivars was 2-4 times higher than that of boron inefficient cultivars. Yu et al. (1999) reported that boron accumulation and accumulation ratio in different organs of canola were different at various developmental stages. During vegetative growth, boron was mainly accumulated in the vegetative organs. In reproductive growth, boron accumulation gradually increased in reproductive organs and reached the highest level at the budding stage. The seed yield increased significantly

(16-47%) with the application of boron, where the average response to boron application ranged from 21 to 31%. The yield increase was due to 27% and 10% increase in seeds/siliqua and 1000 seed weight, respectively (AICRP-RM, 2005).

Many strategies in direction of sustainable agriculture one of the most important of them is improving the use of nitrogen fertilizer and reduce the environmental pollution in canola production is integrated fertilization systems between chemical, biofertilizers and organic fertilizers in attendance with different micronutrients where, a number of integrated fertilizer management strategies have been developed (Wiesler et al., 2001). These take into consideration improved nitrogen supply due to varied crop rotations, cultivation of nitrogen efficient cultivars and optimized crop management practices to improve nitrogen efficiency of canola plants (Rathke et al., 2006). Integrated nutrient management is important to exploit the potential of organic manures, composts, crop residues, agricultural wastes, biofertilizers and their synergistic effect with chemical fertilizers for increasing balanced nutrient supply and their use efficiency for increasing productivity, sustainability of agriculture and improving soil health and environmental safety. Using integrated fertilizer management a considerable reduction in nitrogen fertilizer demand is possible to maximize the nitrogen use efficiency of canola. Shengri et al. (2012) in an experiment on canola, nitrogen levels and sowing date found that nitrogen has no effect on nitrogen use efficiency, while, terminal heat stress and nitrogen levels interacted significantly influenced on the nitrogen use efficiency.

Micronutrient concentration could be changed through organic and inorganic fertilizers application by the influence on soil pH (Feil et al., 2005) or increasing the soil organic matter content (Li et al., 2007). Generally, in organic products iron, phosphorus, magnesium and zinc concentrations are higher, but manganese, potassium, nitrate and heavy metal concentrations less than conventional products (Zhang et al., 2001; Ryan et al., 2004). With intensive cropping and high yields, the situation has changed considerably where its great importance to supply different crops by the suitable micronutrients. Micronutrients have become yield-limiting factors and are partly responsible for a decreasing efficiency of NPK fertilizers, therefore, standard NPK-based fertilization must often be supplemented by the suitable deficient micronutrients to increase nutrient use efficiency.

Balanced fertilization at right time by proper method increases nutrient use efficiency in canola, however, experiments have been conducted with the integrated use of organic manure, green manure, crop residues and biofertilizers along with inorganic fertilizers where integrated nutrient management not only reduces the demand of organic fertilizers but also increase the efficiency of applied nutrients due to their favorable effect on physical, chemical and biological properties of soil. Integrated nutrient management improve the nutrient uptake by canola and hence enhances the use efficiency of various nutrients from the soil where Bhat et al. (2005) reported that the incorporation of 25% FYM+ 75% chemical fertilizer + 100% sulpher significantly enhanced the uptake use efficiency and nitrogen and sulpher contents in both seed and stover, also, Hasanalideh and Hojati (2012) in an experiment observed that nitrogen use efficiency was highest in the plants treated with combination of 50 kg N ha^{-1} and zinc sulphtae whereas the highest value for physiological efficiency was observed in plants treated with 50 kg N ha^{-1} + zinc sulphtae and biofertilizer.

REFERENCES

Abadia J (1992) Leaf Responses to Fe Deficiency: A Review. J Plant Nutr 15: 1699-1713.

Abdin MZ, Ahmad A, Khan N, Khan I, Jamal A, Iqbal M (2003) Sulfur Interaction with Other Nutrients. *In*: Sulfur in Plants, eds. Y.P. Abrol and A. Ahmad, pp. 359-374. Kluwer Academic Publishers, Dordrecht, Netherlands.

Ackman RG (1990) Canola Fatty Acids – An Ideal Mixture for Health, Nutrition, and Food Use. In: F. Shahidi (ed.) Canola and Rapeseed – Production, Chemistry, Nutrition and Processing Technology. Van Nostrand Reinhold, New York, pp. 81-98.

AICRP-RM (2005) Annual Progress Report of All India Coordinated Research Project on Rapeseed-mustard, pp. A1–28.

Alan ER, Jonathan PL, Peter RR, Emmanuel D, Andrew S, Sally ES, Paul RH, Megan HR, Erik JV, Hans L, Astrid O, Richard AC, Richard JS (2011) Plant and Microbial Strategies to Improve the Phosphorus Efficiency of Agriculture. Plant Soil 349: 121-156.

Al-Redhaiman KN (2000) Nitrate Accumulation in Plants and Hazards to Man and Livestock: A Review J King Saud Univ 12: 143-156.

Amtmann A, Hammond JP, Armengaud P, White PJ (2005) Nutrient Sensing and Signaling in Plants: Potassium and Phosphorus. Adv Bot Res 43: 209-257.

Anonymous, (1998) Micronutrients in Agriculture: Pakistan Perspective; National Fertilizer Development Center: Islamabad, Pakistan 51 pp.

Arnon I (1972) Plant Population and Distribution Patterns in Crop Production in Dry Regions. Vol. 1 National Book Foundation, Islamabad, Pakistan.

Asare E, Scarisbrick DH (1995) Rate of Nitrogen and Sulphur Fertilizers on Yield, Yield Components and Seed Quality of Oilseed Rape (*Brassica napus* L.). Field Crops Res 44: 41-46.

Bakhsh A, Gurmani AH, Bhatti AU, Rehman H (1999) Effect of Balanced Application of N, P and K on the Grain Yield of Wheat. Sarhad J of Agric 15: 453-457.

Barth CA (2007) Rapeseed for Human Nutrition–Present Knowledge and Future Options. Proceedings of the 12th International Rapeseed Congress 26-30 March, Sustainable Development in Cruciferous Oilseed Crops Production, Wuhan, China 5: 3-5.

Bhat MA, Singh R, Dash D (2005) Effect of INM on Uptake and Use Efficiency of N and S in Indian Mustard on an Inceptisol. Crop Res 30: 23-25.

Birk EM, Vitousek PM (1986) Nitrogen Availability and Nitrogen Use Efficiency in Loblolly Pine Stands. Ecology 67: 69-79.

Black AS, Sherlock RR, Smith NP, Cameron KC (1989) Ammonia Volatilization from Urea Broadcast in Spring on to Autumn-sown Wheat. New Zealand J of Crop and Horticultural Sci 14: 175-182.

Bolland MDA, Brennan RF (2008) Comparing the Phosphorus Requirements of Wheat, Lupin, and Canola. Aus J of Agric Res 59: 983-998.

Bolland MDA, Siddique KHM, Loss SP, Baker MJ (1999) Comparing Responses of Grain Legumes, Wheat and Canola to Applications of Superphosphate. Nutrient Cycling in Agroecosystems 53: 157-175.

Brennan R, Bolland M (2001) Comparing Fertilizer Phosphorus Requirements of Canola, Lupin, and Wheat. J of Plant Nut 24, 1885-1900.

Bungard RA, Wingler A, Morton JD, Andrews M (1999) Ammonium can Stimulate Nitrate and Nitrite Reductase in the Absence of Nitrate in *Clematis vitalba*. Plant Cell and Environment 22: 859-866.

Burkitt LL, Small DR, McDonald JW, Wales WJ, Jenkin ML (2007) Comparing Irrigated, Biodynamic and Conventionally Managed Dairy Farms. 1. Soil and Pasture Properties. Aus J Exp Agric 47: 479-488.

Cakmak I (1998) Selection and Characterization of Cereal Genotypes with High Zinc Efficiency and Evaluation of Bioavailability of Zinc in Wheat for the Central Anatolian Region; Science for Stability Programme, Cukurova University: Adana, Turkey 171 pp.

Cakmak I (2008) Enrichment of Cereal Grains with Zinc: Agronomic or Genetic Biofortification. Plant and Soil 302: 1-17.

Cao XY, Liu WD, Pi MM (1997) Composition of Root Exudates and Root Bleeding Sap of a Boron-efficient and Inefficient Oil Seed Rape Genotype. In: Bell RW, Rerkasem B, Eds. Boron in Soils and Plants. Dordrecht: Kluwer 171-174.

Cassman KG, Dobermann A, Walters DT (2002) Agroecosystems, Nitrogen Use Efficiency and Nitrogen Management. Ambio 31: 132-140.

CCC, Short for Canola Council of Canada. (2003).Canola Growers' Manual. [Online] Access: http://www.canolacouncil.org/crop-production/canola-grower's-manual-contents [October 10, 2012]

Ceccotti SP (1996) Plant Nutrient Sulphur- A Review of Nutrient Balance, Environmental Impact and Fertilizers. Fert Res 43: 117-125.

Chapin FS, Follett JM, O'Connor KF (1982) Growth, Phosphate Absorption, and Phosphorus Chemical Fractions in Two Chionochloa Species. J of Ecology 70: 305-321.

Chapin FS, Vitousek PM, Van Cleve K (1986) The Nature of Nutrient Limitation in Plant Communities. American Naturalist 127: 48-58.

Chatterjee C, Khurana N (2007) Zinc Stress–Induced Changes in Biochemical Parameters and Oil Content of Mustard. Commun Soil Sci Plant Anal 38: 751-761.

Chaudhary SK, Gogulwar NM, Singh AK (1992) Effect of Sulphur and Nitrogen on Seed Yield and Oil Content of Mustard (*Brassica juncea*). Indian J Agron 37: 839-840.

Clandinin D (1981) Canola Meal for Livestock and Poultry. P: 25. Publication No. 59, Canola Council of Canada, Winnipeg, MB, Canada.

Clarkson DT (1981) Nutrient Interception and Transport by Root Systems. In Physiological Processes Limiting Plant Productivity, ed. C. B. Johnson, 307-330. London: Butterworth's.

Crowley DE, Rengel Z (1999) Biology and Chemistry of Nutrient Availability in the Rhizosphere. In: Rengel Z (ed) Mineral Nutrition of Crops: Fundamental Mechanisms and Implications. Food Products Press, New York, pp. 1-40.

Cuin TA, Miller AJ, Laurie SA, Leigh RA (2003) Potassium Activities in Cell Compartments of Salt-grown Barley Leaves. J Exp Bot 54: 657-661.

Damon PM, Osborne LD, Rengel Z (2007) Canola Genotypes Differ in Potassium Efficiency during Vegetative Growth. Euphytica 156: 387-397.

de Wit CT (1992) Resource use Efficiency in Agriculture. Agric Syst 40: 125-151.

Dobermann A, Cassman KG (2004) Environmental Dimensions of Fertilizer N: What can be done to Increase Nitrogen Use Efficiency and Ensure Global Food Security? pp. 261-278. In Mosier AR *et al.* (ed.) Agriculture and the Nitrogen Cycle: Assessing the Impacts of Fertilizer Use on Food Production and the Environment. Island Press, Washington, D.C., USA.

Downey RK, Bell JM (1990) New Developments in Canola Research. In: F. Shahidi (ed.) Canola and Rapeseed Production, Chemistry, Nutrition and Processing Technology. Van Nostrand Reinhold, New York, pp. 37-46.

El-Habbasha SF, Abd El-Salam MS (2010) Response of Two Canola Varieties (*Brassica napus* L.) to Nitrogen Fertilizer Levels and Zinc Foliar Application. The Proceedings of the International Plant Nutrition Colloquium XVI, August, 26-30, Sacramento, California, USA.

FAOSTAT,2011 http://faostat3.fao.org/faostat-gateway/go/to/browse/R/RF/E

Farahbakhsh I, Pakgohar N, Karimi A (2006) Effects of Nitrogen and Sulfur Fertilizers on Yield, Yield Components and Oil Content of Oilseed Rape (*Brassica napus* L.). Asian J Plant Sci 5: 112-115.

Feil B, Moser SB, Jampatong S, Stamp P (2005) Mineral Composition of the Grain of Tropical Maze Varieties as Affected by Preanthesis Drought and Rate of Nitrogen Fertilization. Crop Sci 45: 516-523.

Ferm M (1998) Atmospheric Ammonia and Ammonium Transport in Europe and Critical Loads: A Review Nutrient Cycling in Agroecosystem 51: 5-17.

Fismes J, Vong PC, Guckert A, Frossard E (2000) Influence of Sulfur on Apparent N-use Efficiency, Yield and Quality of Oilseed Rape (*Brassica napus* L.) Grown on a Calcareous Soil. Eur J Agron 12: 127-141.

Freney JR, Black AS (1988) Importance of Ammonia Volatilization as a Loss Process. In: Advances in Nitrogen Cycling in Agricultural Ecosystems, Wilson J.R. (Ed.), CAB International, Wallingford, pp. 156-173.

Freney JR, Denmead OT, Wood AW, Saffigna PG, Chapman LS, Ham GJ, Hurney AP, Stewart RL (1992) Factors Controlling Ammonia Loss from Trash Covered Sugarcane Fields Fertilized with Urea. Fertilizer Res 31: 341-349.

Gahoonia TS, Nielsen NE (1997) Variation in Root Hairs of Barley Cultivars Doubled Soil Phosphorus Uptake. Euphytica 98: 177-182.

Gahoonia TS, Nielsen NE (2004) Root Traits as Tools for Creating Phosphorus Efficient Crop Varieties. Plant and Soil 260: 47-57.

Gahoonia TS, Nielsen NE, Lyshede OB (1999) Phosphorus (P) Acquisition of Cereal Cultivars in the Field at Three Levels of P fertilization. Plant and Soil 211: 269-281.

Gallais A, Coque M (2005) Genetic Variation and Selection for Nitrogen Use Efficiency in Maize: A Synthesis. Maydica 50: 531-537.

Gan Y, Malhi S, Brandt S, Katepa-Mupondwa F and Kutcher H (2007) Canola in the Northern Great Plains. Agronomy J 99(5): 1208-1218.

Gan Y, Malhi S, Brandt S, Katepa-Mupondwa F and Stevenson C (2008) Nitrogen Use Efficiency and Nitrogen Uptake of Canola under Diverse Environments. Agronomy J 100(2): 285-295.

George TS, Richardson AE (2008) Potential and Limitations to Improving Crops for Enhanced Phosphorus Utilization. In 'The Ecophysiology of Plant-phosphorus Interactions'. Vol. 7. (ed.) PJ White, JP Hammond, pp. 247-270, Springer Netherlands.

Giller KE, Chalk PM, Dobermann A, Hammond LC, Heffer P, Ladha JK, Nyamudeza P, Maene LM, Ssali H, Freney JR (2004) Emerging Technologies to Increase the Efficiency of Use of Fertilizer Nitrogen. pp. 35-52. In Mosier AR *et al.* (ed.) Agriculture and the Nitrogen Cycle: Assessing the Impacts of Fertilizer Use on Food Production and the Environment. Island Press, Washington, D.C., USA.

Good AG, Johnson SJ, De Pauw M, Carroll RT, Savodiv N, Vidmar J, Lu Z, Taylor G, Stroeher V (2007) Engineering Nitrogen Use Efficiency with Alanine Aminotransferase. Can J Bot 85: 252-262.

Good AG, Shrawat AK, Muench DG (2004) Can Less Yield more? Is Reducing Nutrient Input into the Environment Compatible with Maintaining Crop Production? Trends Plant Sci 9: 597-605.

Graham RD (1984) Breeding for Nutritional Characteristics in Cereals. In 'Advances in Plant Nutrition'. Vol. 1. (eds PB Tinker, A Lauchli) pp. 57-102. (Praeger Publishers: New York).

Grant CA, Bailey LD (1993) Fertility Management in Canola Production. Can J Plant Sci 73: 651-670.

Gray JT, Schlesinger WH (1983) Nutrient Use by Evergreen and Deciduous Shrubs in Southern California. J of Ecology 71: 43-56.

Grewal HS, Graham RD (1997) Seed Zinc Content Influences Early Vegetative Growth and Zinc Uptake in Oilseed Rape (*Brassica napus* and *Brassica juncea*) Genotypes on Zinc Deficient Soil. Plant and Soil 191: 191-197.

Grewal HS, Stangoulis JCR, Potter TD, Graham RD (1997) Zinc Efficiency of Oilseed Rape (*Brassica napus* and *Brassica juncea*) genotypes. Plant and Soil 191: 123-132.

Grotz N, Guerinot ML (2006) Molecular Aspects of Cu, Fe and Zn Homeostasis in Plants. Biochim Biophys Acta 1763: 595-608.

Gupta M, Kaushik RD (2006) Effect of Saline Irrigation Water and Zn on the Concentration and Uptake of Zn by Mustard. Presented at the 18th World Congress of Soil Sci Philadelphia PA USA.

Gupta U (2007) Boron, in A.V. Barker DJ Pilbeam (Eds.) Handbook of Plant Nutrition. CRC Press, Boca Raton, USA 241-277.

Hammond JP, Broadley MR, White PJ, King GJ, Bowen HC, Hayden R, Meacham MC, Mead A, Overs T, Spracklen WP, Greenwood DJ (2009) Shoot Yield Drives Phosphorus Use Efficiency in *Brassica oleracea* and Correlates with Root Architecture Traits. J of Exp Botany 60: 1953-1968.

Haneklaus S, Paulsen HM, Gupta AK, Bloem E, Schnug E (1999) Influence of Sulphur Fertilization on Yield and Quality of Oilseed Rape and Mustard. In: New Horizons for an Old Crop. Proceedings of 10th International Rapeseed Congress, Canberra, Australia Capital Territory.

Hasanalideh H, Hojati M (2012) Enhancing Yield and Nitrogen Use Efficiency of *Brassica Napus* L. Using an Integrated Fertilizer Management. Advances in Environmental Biology 6: 641-647.

Havlin JL, Tisdale SL, Beaton JD, Nelson WL (2005) Soil Fertility and Fertilizers. Pearson Education, Inc, Upper Saddle River, NJ.

He ZL, Alva AK, Calvert DV, Banks DJ (1999) Ammonia Volatilization from Different Fertilizer Sources and Effects of Temperature and Soil pH. Soil Sci 164: 750-758.

Hirel B, Le Gouis J, Ney B, Gallais A (2007) The Challenge of Improving Nitrogen Use Efficiency in Crop Plants: Towards a more Central Role for Genetic Variability and Quantitative Genetics within Integrated Approaches. J Exp Bot 58: 2369-2387.

Hirose T (1975) Relations Between Turnover Rate, Resource Utility and Structure of Some Plant Populations: A Study in the Matter Budgets. J of the Faculty of Science, Imperial University of Tokyo 1 I: 335-407.

Hoa NM, Janssen BH, Oenema O Dobermann A (2006) Comparison of Partial and Complete Soil K Budgets Under Intensive Rice Cropping in the Mekong Delta, Vietnam. Agric Ecosyst Environ 116: 121-131.

Hocking PJ, Kirkegaard JA, Angus JF, Gibson AH, Koetz EA (1997) Comparison of Canola, Indian Mustard and Linola in Two Contrasting Environments. I. Effects of Nitrogen Fertilizer on Dry-matter Production, Seed Yield and Seed Quality. Field Crops Res 49: 107-125.

Hocking PJ, Strapper M (2001) Effect of Sowing Time and Nitrogen Fertilizer on Canola and Wheat, and Nitrogen Fertilizer on Indian Mustard. II. Nitrogen Concentrations, N Accumulation, and N Use Efficiency. Aus J Agric Res 52: 635-644.

Hoffland E, Boogaard RVD, Nelemans JA, Findenegg GR (1992) Biosynthesis and Root Exudation of Citric and Malic Acids in Phosphate-starved Rape Plants. New Phytologist. 122: 675-680.

Hogh-Jensen H, Pedersen MB (2003) Morphological Plasticity by Crop Plants and Their Potassium Use Efficiency. J of Plant Nut 26: 969-984.

Holford ICR (1997) Soil Phosphorus: Its Measurement, and Its Uptake by Plants. Aus J of Soil Res 35: 227-39.

Horst WJ, Behrens T, Heuberger H, Kamh M, Reidenbach G, Wiesler F (2003) Genotypic Differences in Nitrogen Use Efficiency in Crop Plants. In: Lynch J.M., Schepers J.S., Unver I. (ed.): Innovative Soil Plant Systems for Sustainable Agricultural Production, pp. 75-92.

Houman F, Peter BE, Vetty M, Vessey JK (2013) ^{13}C and ^{15}N Partitioning Among Shoots, Roots, and Soil in *Brassica napus* Genotypes Varying in Seed Oil Content Potential, Biocatalysis and Agric Biotechno, http://dx.doi.org/10.1016/j.bcab.2013.02.001

Jagadeeswaran R, Murugappan V, Govindaswamy M (2005) Effect of Slow Release NPK Fertilizer Sources on the Nutrient Use Efficiency in Turmeric (*Curcuma longa* L.). World J of Agric Sci 1: 65-69.

Jan A, Khan N, Khan N, Khan IA, Khattak B (2002) Chemical Composition of Canola as Affected by Nitrogen and Sulphur. Asian J Pl Sci 1: 519-21.

Janssen BH (1999) Basics of Budgets, Buffers and Balances of Nutrients in Relation to Sustainability of Agroecosystems. pp. 27-56. In E.M.A. Smaling *et al.* (eds.) Nutrient Disequilibria in Agroecosystems: Concepts and Case Studies. CABI Publishing, Wallingford, UK.

Janzen HH, Bettany JR (1984) Sulfur Nutrition of Rapeseed: I. Influence of Fertilizer Nitrogen and Sulfur Rates. Soil Sci Soc Am J 48: 100-107.

Jungk A (2001) Root Hairs and the Acquisition of Plant Nutrients from Soil. J Plant Nutr Soil Sci 164: 121-129.

Jungk A, Claassen N (1997) Ion Diffusion in the Soil-root System. Advances in Agron 61: 53-110.

Karley AJ, Leigh RA, Sanders D (2000) Differential Ion Accumulation and Ion Fluxes in the Mesophyll and Epidermis of Barley. Plant Physiol 122: 835-844.

Khan HR, McDonald GK, Rengel Z (2003) Zn Fertilization Improves Water Use Efficiency, Grain Yield and Seed Zn Content in Chickpea. Plant Soil 249: 389-400.

Khan MA, Hussain I, Baloch MS (2000) Wheat Yield Potential Current Status and Future Strategies. Pakistan J of Biological Sci 3: 82-86.

Kirkby EA, Johnston AE (2008) Soil and Fertilizer Phosphorus in Relation to Crop Nutrition. In 'The Ecophysiology of Plant–Phosphorus Interactions'. Vol. 7. (ed.) PJ White, JP Hammond, pp. 177-223. Springer, Dordrecht, Netherlands.

Leigh RA (2001) Potassium Homeostasis and Membrane Transport. J Plant Nutr Soil Sci 164: 193-198.

Li BY, Zhou DM, Cang L, Zhang HL, Fan XH, Qin SW (2007) Soil Micronutrient Availability to Crops as Affected by Long Term Inorganic and Organic Fertilizer Applications. Soil Till Res 96: 166-173.

Ligaba A, Shen H, Shibata K, Yamamoto Y, Tanakamaru S, Matsumoto H (2004) The Role of Phosphorus in Aluminium-induced Citrate and Malate Exudation from Rape (*Brassica napus*). Physiologia Plantarum 120: 575-584.

Lipton GS, Blanchar RW, Blevins DG (1987) Citrate, Malate and Succinate Concentrations in Exudates from P Sufficient and P-stressed *Medicago sativa* L. Seedlings. Plant Physiology 85: 315-317.

Liu GD, Li YC, Alva AK (2007) Moisture Quotients for Ammonia Volatilization from Four Soils in Potato Production Regions. Water, Air, and Soil Pollution 183: 115-127.

Liu GD, Li YC, Alva AK (2007a) High Water Regime can Reduce Ammonia Volatilization from Soils. Comm in Soil Sci and Plant Analysis 38: 1203-1220.

Lynch JP (2007) Roots of the Second Green Revolution. Aus J Bot 55: 1-20.

Malakouti MJ (2008) The Effect of Micronutrients in Ensuring Efficient Use of Macronutrients. Tur J Agric For 32: 215-220.

Malhi SS (2001) Improving Canola Yields with Balanced and Efficient Nutrition. Final Report Prepared for Canola Council of Canada [Online] available: http://www.saskcanola.com/quadrant/System/research/reports/report-Malhi-balancednutrition-long.pdf [January 29, 2012].

Malhi SS, Gan Y, Raney JP (2007) Yield, Seed Quality, and Sulfur Uptake of *Brassica* Oilseed Crops in Response to Sulfur Fertilization. Agron J 99: 570-577.

Malhi SS, Schoenau JJ, Grant CA (2005) A Review of Sulfur Fertilizer Management for Optimum Yield and Quality of Canola in the Canadian Great Plains. Can J Plant Sci 85: 297-307.

Marschner A (1986) Mineral Nutrition of Higher Plants, p. 356. Academic Press Inc., London, UK.

Marschner H (1995) Mineral Nutrition of Higher Plants, Second Edition. Academic Press Inc., London, UK.

Mason MG, Brennan RF (1998) Comparison of Growth Response and Nitrogen Uptake by Canola and Wheat Following Application of Nitrogen Fertilizer. J of Plant Nutr 21: 1483-1499.

McGrath SP, Zhao FJ (1996) Sulphur Uptake, Yield Responses and the Interactions Between Nitrogen and Sulphur in Winter Oilseed Rape (*Brassica napus*). J Agric Sci 126: 53-62.

McIvor JG, Guppy C, Probert ME (2011) Phosphorus Requirements of Tropical Grazing Systems: The Northern Australian Experience. Plant Soil 349: 55-67.

McLaughlin MJ, Alston AM (1986) The Relative Contribution of Plant Residues and Fertilizer to the Phosphorus Nutrition of Wheat in a Pasture/Cereal System. Aus J of Soil Res 24: 517-526.

McLaughlin MJ, Alston AM, Martin JK (1988) Phosphorus Cycling in Wheat Pasture Rotations. I. The Source of Phosphorus taken up by Wheat. Aus J of Soil Res 26: 323-331.

McLaughlin MJ, Alston AM, Martin JK (1988b) Phosphorus Cycling in Wheat-pasture Rotations. III. Organic Phosphorus Turnover and Phosphorus Cycling. Aus J of Soil Res 26: 343-353.

Mensink RP, Katan MB (1993) Trans Monounsaturated Fatty Acids in Nutrition and Their Impact on Serum Lipoprotein Level in Man. Prog. Lipid Res 32: 111-122.

Miller RW, Donahue RL (1990) Soils: An Introduction to Soils and Plant Growth: Prentice-Hall International Inc 250-263, 289-294.

Moll RH, Kamprath EJ, Jackson WA (1982) Analysis and Interpretation of Factors which Contribute to Efficiency of Nitrogen Utilization. Agron J 74: 562-564.

Mortvedt JJ, Cox FR, Shuman LM, Welch RM (1991) In Micronutrients in Agriculture, 2nd Ed Soil Sci Soc Am Madison WI.

Nadian H, Najarzadegan R, Saeid KA, Gharineh M, Siadat A (2010) Effects of Boron and Sulfur Application on Yield and Yield Components of *Brassica napus* L. in a Calcareous Soil. World Applied Sciences J. 11(1): 89-95.

Pandey N, Pathak GC, Sharma CP (2006) Zinc is Critically Required for Pollen Function and Fertilization in Lentil. J Trace Elem Med Bio 20: 89-96.

Pastor J, Aber JD, McClaugherty CA (1984) Above Ground Production and N and P Cycling Along a Nitrogen Mineralization Gradient on Blackhawk Island, Wisconsin. Ecology 65: 256-268.

Pearse S, Veneklaas E, Cawthray G, Bolland M, Lambers H (2006) Carboxylate Release of Wheat, Canola and 11 Grain Legume Species as Affected by Phosphorus Status. Plant and Soil 288: 127-139.

Peng S, Garcia FV, Laza RC, Sanico AL, Visperas RM, Cassman KG (1996) Increased N-use Efficiency Using a Chlorophyll Meter on High Yielding Irrigated Rice. Field Crops Res 47: 243-252.

Pleines S, Friedt W (1988) Breeding for Improved C18-fatty Acid Composition in Rapeseed (*Brassica napus* L.). Fat Sci Technol 90: 167-171.

Porter P (1993) Canola Response to Boron and Nitrogen Grown on the Southeastern Coastal Plain. J of Plant Nutrition 16(12): 2371-2381.

Power JF, Prasad R (2010) Soil Fertility Management for Sustainable Agriculture: CRC press 118-161, 230-239, 283-289.

Rakow G, Stringam GR, McGregor DI (1987) Breeding (*Brassica napus* L.) Canola with Improved Fatty Acid Composition, High Oil Content and High Seed Yield. Proc. 7th Int. Rapeseed Congr, Poznan, Poland, Vol. 2, pp. 27-32.

Rathke GW, Behrens T, Diepenbrock W (2006) Integrated Management Strategies to Improve Seed Yield; Oil Content and Nitrogen Efficiency of Winter Oilseed Rape (*Brassica napus* L.): A Review. Agriculture Ecosystems and Environment 117: 80-108.

Rathke GW, Christen O, Diepenbrock W (2005) Effects of Nitrogen Sources and Rate on Productivity and Quality of Winter Oilseed Rape (*Brassica napus* L.) grown in Different Crop Rotation. Field Crops Res 94: 103-113.

Raun WR, Johnson GV (1999) Improving Nitrogen Use Efficiency for Cereal Production. Agron J 91: 357-363.

Rengel Z (1993) Mechanistic Simulation Models of Nutrient Uptake: A Review. Plant Soil 152: 161-173.

Rengel Z, Marschner P (2005) Nutrient Availability and Management in the Rhizosphere: Exploiting Genotypic Differences. New Phytol 168: 305-312.

Roy RN, Pederson OS (1992) International Rice Communication Newsletter 41: 118-125.

Ryan MH, Derrick JW, Dann PR (2004) Grain Mineral Concentrations and Yield of Wheat Grown Under Organic and Conventional Management. J Sci Food Agric 84: 207-216.

Sander DH, Penas EJ, Eghball B (1990) Residual Effects of Various Phosphorus Application Methods on Winter Wheat and Grain Sorghum. Soil Sci Soc of America J 54: 1473-1478.

Sander DH, Penas EJ, Walters DT (1991) Winter Wheat Phosphorus Fertilization as Influenced by Glacial Till and Loess Soils. Soil Sci Soc of America J 55: 1474-1479.

Sarkar D, Mandal B, Kundu MC (2007) Increasing Use Efficiency of Boron Fertilisers by Rescheduling the Time and Methods of Application for Crops in India. Plant Soil 301: 77-85.

Sattelmacher B, Horst WJ, Becker HC (1994) Factors that Contribute to Genetic Variation for Nutrient Efficiency of Crop Plants. Z Pflanzenernahr Bodenkd 157: 215-224.

Schlesinger WH, Hartley AE (1992) A Global Budget for Atmospheric NH_3. Biogeochemistry 15: 191-211.

Schnug E, Haneklaus S, Murphy S (1993) Impact of Sulphur Supply on the Baking Quality of Wheat. Aspects Appl Biol 36: 337-345.

Sharma AR, Mitra BN (1990) Complementary Effect of Organic, Bio and Mineral Fertilizer in Rice Based Cropping System. Fertilizer News 35: 43-51.

Shaver GR, Melillo JM (1984) Nutrient Budgets of Marsh Plants: Efficiency Concepts and Relation to Availability. Ecology 65: 1491-1510.

Shengri AH, Gharineh MH, Bakhshandeh A, Fathi G, Karmollachaab A (2012) Effect of Terminal Heat Stress and Nitrogen on Morphophysiological Characteristics, ANUE and Yield of Canola (*Brassica napus* L.). Intern J of Agric and Crop Sci 4: 284-288.

Shorrocks VM (1997) The Occurrence and Correction of Boron Deficiency. In: Bell RW, Rerkasem B, Eds. Boron in Soils and Plants. Dordrecht: Kluwer 121-148.

Shuman LM (1991) Chemical Forms of Micronutrients in Soils. In: Mortvedt JJ, Cox FR, Shuman LM, Welch RM (eds) Micronutrients in Agriculture, 2nd Edn, Soil Science Society of America, Madison, pp. 113-144.

Simpson RJ, Oberson A, Culvenor RA, Ryan MH, Veneklaas EJ, Lambers H, Lynch JP, Ryan PR, Delhaize E, Smith FA, Smith SE, Harvey PR, Richardson AE (2011) Strategies and Agronomic Interventions to Improve the Phosphorus-use Efficiency of Farming Systems. Plant Soil 349: 89-120.

Smil V (2001) Enriching the Earth: Fritz Haber, Carl Bosch, and the Transformation of World Food Production. The MIT Press, Cambridge, MA, USA.

Snapp S, Borden H, Rohrbach D (2002) Improving Nitrogen Efficiency: Lessons from Malawi and Michigan. In: Optimizing Nitrogen Management in Food and Energy Production and Environmental Protection, 2nd International Nitrogen Conference. A.A. Balkema Publishers, Lisse, Potomac, pp. 42-48.

Stewart WM, Dibb DW, Johnston AE, Smyth TJ (2005) The Contribution of Commercial Fertilizer Nutrients to Food Production. Agron J 97: 1-6.

Stevenson FJ, Cole MA (1999) Cycles of Soils: Carbon, Nitrogen, Phosphorus, Sulfur, Micronutrients: Wiley.com

Sultana N, Ikeda T, Kashem MA (2001) Effect of Foliar Spray of Nutrient Solutions on Photosynthesis, Dry Matter Accumulation and Yield in Seawater-stressed Rice. Environ Exp Bot 46: 129-140.

Syers JK, Johnston AE, Curtin D (2008) Efficiency of Soil and Fertilizer Phosphorus Use. Reconciling Changing Concepts of Soil Phosphorus Behaviour with Agronomic Information. FAO Fertilizer and Plant Nutrition Bulletin No. 18. Rome, Italy: FAO.

Sylvester-Bradley R, Kindred DR (2009) Analyzing Nitrogen Responses of Cereals to Prioritize Routes to the Improvement of Nitrogen Use Efficiency. J of Exp Bot 60: 1939-1951.

Tandon HLS (1995) Micronutrients in Soils, Crops and Fertilizers. Fertilizer Development and Consultation Organization: New Delhi, India.

Tiessen H (2008) Phosphorus in the Global Environment. In: Hammond JP, White PJ, (eds) The Ecophysiology of Plant-phosphorus Interactions. Dordrecht, Netherlands: Springer, 1-7.

Tilman D, Cassman KG, Matson PA, Naylor R, Polasky S (2002) Agricultural Sustainability and Intensive Production Practices. Nature 418: 671-677.

Trautwein EA (1997) Food Quality of Rapeseed Oil Aspects from a Nutritional Point of View. GCIRC Bull. 14: 123-128.

Trehan SP, Sharma RC (2002) Potassium Uptake Efficiency of Young Plants of Three Potato Cultivars as Related to Root and Shoot Parameters. Comm in Soil Sci and Plant Anal 33: 1813-1823.

Troeh FR, Thompson LM (2005) Soils and Soil Fertility: Blackwell Ames 211-231, 269-305.

Umar AS, Iqbal M (2007) Nitrate Accumulation in Plants, Factors Affecting the Process, and Human Health Implications. A Review Agron Sustain Dev 27: 45-57.

Vance CP, Uhde-Stone C, Allan DL (2003) Phosphorus Acquisition and Use: Critical Adaptations by Plants for Securing a Non-renewable Resource. New Phytologist 157: 423-447.

Vu DT, Armstrong RD, Sale PWG, Tang CX (2010) Phosphorus Availability for Three Crop Species as a Function of Soil Type and Fertilizer History. Plant and Soil 337: 497-510.

Watanabe T, Broadley MR, Jansen S (2007) Evolutionary Control of Leaf Element Composition in Plants. New Phytologist 174: 516-523.

Welch RM, Allaway WH, House WA, Kubota J (1991) Geographic Distribution of Trace Element Problems. In: Mortvedt JJ, Cox FR, Shuman LM, Welch RM (eds) Micronutrients in Agriculture, 2nd Edn. Soil Science Society of America Inc., Madison, WI, pp. 31-57.

White PJ, Hammond JP, eds. 2008. The Ecophysiology of Plant–Phosphorus Interactions. Dordrecht, the Netherlands: Springer.

Wiesler F, Behrens T, Horst WJ (2001) The Role of Nitrogen-efficient Cultivars in Sustainable Agriculture. In: Optimizing Nitrogen Management in Food and Energy Production and Environmental Protection: Proceedings of the 2nd International Nitrogen Conference on Science and Policy, The Scientific World.

Wissuwa M, Ismail AM, Graham RD (2008) Rice Grain Zinc Concentrations as Affected by Genotype, Native Soil Zinc Availability, and Zinc Fertilization. Plant Soil 306: 37-48.

Woodend JJ, Glass ADM, Person CO (1987) Genetic Variation in Uptake and Utilization of Potassium in Wheat (*Triticum aestivum*) Varieties Grown Under Potassium Stress. In W.H. Gabelman and B.C. Loughman (eds.) Genetic Aspects of Plant Mineral Nutrition. Nijhoff, Dordrecht, Netherlands. pp. 383-391.

Xu FS, Wang YH, Ying WH, Meng JL (2002) Inheritance of Boron Nutrition Efficiency in *Brassica napus*. J of Plant Nutrition 25: 901-912.

Xue JM, Yang YA (1994) Genotypic Variation in Response of Rape (*Brassica napus*) to Boron Deficiency. J of Zhejiang Agricultural University 20: 422-426.

Xue JM, Yang YA, Ye ZQ (1995) Effect of Boron on the Growth, Yield and Quality of Different Rape Cultivars. J of Zhejiang Agricultural University 21: 66-70.

Yadav RL, Prasad K, Gangwar KS, Dwibedi BS (1998) Cropping Systems and Resource Use Efficiency. Indian J Agric Sci 68: 548-558.

Yau SK, Thurling N (1987) Variation in Nitrogen Response Among Spring Rape (*Brassica napus*) Cultivars and its Relationship Between Nitrogen Uptake and Utilization. Field Crops Res 16: 139-155.

Yu M, Chu HY, Wu LS, Wang YH (1999) Study on Boron Uptake, Distribution in Different Rape (*Brassica napus*) Genotypes. Chinese J of Oil Crop Sci 21: 49-52.

Zhang FS, Ma J, Cao YP (1997) Phosphorus Deficiency Enhances Root Exudation of Low-molecular Weight organic Acids and Utilization of Sparingly Soluble Inorganic Phosphates by Radish (*Raghanus sativus* L.) and Rape (*Brassica napus* L.) Plants. Plant and Soil 196: 261-264.

Zhang SX, Wang XB, Jin K (2001) Effect of Different N and P Levels on Availability of Zinc, Cooper, Manganese and Iron Under Arid Conditions. Plant Nutr Fert Sci 7: 391-396.

Zhao FJ, Evans EJ, Bilsborrow P, Syers JK (1993) Influence of Sulphur and Nitrogen on Seed Yield and Quality of Low Glucosinolate Oilseed Rape (*Brassica napus* L.) J Sci Food Agric 63: 29-37.

Zhao FJ, Withers PJA, Evans EJ, Monaghan J, Salmon SE, Shewry PR, McGrath SP (1997) Sulphur Nutrition: An Important Factor for the Quality of Wheat and Rapeseed. *In*: Ando, T., K. Fujita, T. Mac, H. Matsumoto, S. Mozi, J. Sekiya (eds.), Plant Nutrition for Sustainable Food Production and Environment. pp. 917-22. Kluwer.

Pages: 108-125

BIOTECHNOLOGY, AGRO-ECOLOGY AND ENVIRONMENT
Edited by: **Dr. Avnish Chauhan; Dr. Pawan Kumar 'Bharti'**
ISBN: 978-93-5056-757-9
Edition: **2015**
Published by: **Discovery Publishing House Pvt. Ltd., New Delhi (India)**

5

Production of Poly β-hydroxybutyrate (PHB) *A Biodegradable Polymer for its Industrial Applications*

Prakhar Rathore

INTRODUCTION

The Plastics are of wide range of synthetic or semi-synthetic organic compounds. They are used in almost all aspects of daily life. They play a very important and vital role in transport, telecommunications, clothing, packaging materials footwear and some environmental applications (Poirier *et al.*, 1995). These important applications are not only due to their specific mechanical & thermal properties but also due to their stability and durability (Rivard*et al.,* 1995). Petroleum is considered as principal source of the most chemical industrial products including polymers and plastics. About $24 billion (US) worth of hydrocarbon feed stocks are used annually in chemical industry (Gavrilescu and Chisti 2005).

Almost 140 million ton plastics are consumed every year in the whole world. Simultaneously the exponential growth of human population has led to the accumulation of large amount of non-degradable wastes across the planet. The living conditions in our environment are changing dramatically because the presence of non-biodegradable wastes is affecting the potential

Department of Biotechnology, Delhi Technological University (Formerly Delhi College of Engineering) Shahbad Daulatpur, Main Bawana Road, Delhi - 110 042, (India).

survival of huge amount of species. Bio-plastics are very good & feasible alternative in that they do not utilize the fossil resources and can easily be biodegraded. So the production of eco-friendly biodegradable plastics is expanding in order to trimdown the reliance on synthetic and hazardous plastics. But in the current scenario, main limitations are high production and recovery costs of bio-plastic (Byrom*et al.,* 1987).

Poly β-hydroxybutyrates (PHB) are thermoplastic, biodegradable and biocompatible (Hocking *et al.,* 1994) which can be obtained from renewable carbon sources. It is insoluble in water and resistant to hydrolytic degradation. PHB has good oxygen permeability. PHB has good UV-resistance but has poor resistance to acids and bases. It is soluble in chloroform and other hydrocarbons. PHB is suitable for the medical applications as bone plates, nails, screws (Azehar*et al.,* 2003), patch materials, stents, drug delivery systems and scaffolds for tissue engineering and in the treatment of osteomyelitis (Fusun*et al.,* 2000).

The molecular weight of polymers are in the range of 2×10^5 to 3×10^6 Dalton, depend on the type of microorganism and its growth condition (Byron, 1994). The melting point of PHB is 175 °C and the glass transition temperature is 15°C. It is nontoxic as well as it sinks in H_2O, while polypropylene floats. But the sinking of PHB facilitates its anaerobic degradation in the sediments.PHB is used in the production of following products: Shampoo bottle, Food container, Suitable dishwasher due to good impact and temperature resistance of material, Disposable razor, Disposable utensils, Fishing net, Composite glial growth factor, Drug carrier, PHB coated paper, Golf tees, etc.

REVIEW OF LITERATURE

In a research the important study has done on the screening, isolation and molecular characterization of PHB producing *Staphylococcus spp.* (S.Srilakshmi*et al.,* 2012). Based on the PHB assays, the unknown bacteria were identified by partial 16S rRNA sequencing which indicated the predominant presence of gram-positive species, specifically *Staphylococcus spp.* In addition, although, the genome of *Staphylococcus* does contain the genes involved in PHB metabolism.

Microalgae are used as bioreactors for the PHB bioplastic production introducing the bacterial PHB pathway of *Ralstoniaeutropha* H16 into the diatom *Phaeodactylumtricornutum,* thereby demonstrating for the first time that PHB production is feasible in a microalgal System (Uwe G Maier et al., 2011). Purification of polyhydroxybutyrate produced by *Burkholderiacepacia* IPT64 through a chemical and enzymatic route (Daniel V. Suzuki et al., 2008)

The production of PHB and its biodegradation is studied by *Pseudomonas Lemoignei*and *Aspergillus niger* (R.Hema et al., 2010). Bacterial as well as fungal isolates were isolated from the local industrial ecosystem. All these isolates were tested for the degradation of the above polymers in assay agar medium as well in liquid cultures. The culture biomass and the clear zone around the colonies were measured to evaluate the activity of these isolates. In all, the fungal isolates were found to degrade these polymers more rapidly when compared to bacteria, due to their versatile depolymerase activities.

$$\left(-O-\underset{\displaystyle |}{\overset{\displaystyle CH_3}{}}\!\!\!\!\!\!\!\!\!\!\!\!CH-CH_2-CO- \right)_n$$

Fig. 5.1: General Structure of PHB

Methods and Materials

There are various sources for the PHB bioplastic production like: Glycerol, Carbon dioxide,Soya waste, malt waste, Castor oil, coconut oil, mustard oil, cottonseed oil, groundnut oil, olive oil, sesame oil, Bagasse. (Ashby RD 2005) (Madden LA *et al.*, 1999) (Braunegg G *et al.*, 1998) (Poirier Y *et al.*, 1992) (Sudesh K *et al.*, 2002)

Biosynthetic Pathway of PHB

Polyhydroxybutyrates are the polyesters of hydroxybutyrates (HBs) with the general structural formula as shown in Figure 5.1 (Steinbüchel, 1991; Lee, Ojumu *et al.*, 1996). It was discovered in 1926 as a constituent of the bacteria *Bacillus megaterium* (Lemoigne, 1926). Many bacteria synthesize & accumulate the PHB as carbon as energy storage materials or as the sink for redundant reducing power under the specific condition of limiting nutrients in the presence of excess carbon source (Steinbüchel, 1991; Byron, 1994; Yu, 2001; Du and Yu, 2002b). The stored PHA can be degraded by the intracellular depolymerises and metabolized as carbon and energy source as the supply of the limiting nutrient is restored. (Byrom, 1994).

The PHB is more osmotic neutral reservoir of the carbon and energy and is synthesized when more carbon sources are available than can be consumed by the bacteria (Keiichi *et al.*, 2007). In the absence of a suitable exogenous carbon source, bacteria reutilize these PHB to enhance their survival. PHB is synthesized from acetyl-coA using three enzymatic steps. The 3 enzymes involved in PHB biosynthesis are acetyl-coA acyltransferase, acetoacetyl-coA reductase and PHB synthase.

Bacterial Strains

The production of various PHB using natural and recombinant bacteria from renewable carbon sources is presented in Table 5.1. Among the more than 250 various natural PHB producers, only a few bacteria have been employed for the biosynthetic production of PHB. These bacteria include *Alcaligeneslatus*, *B. megaterium*, *C. necator* and *P. oleovorans* etc., which are having capacity of utilizing different carbon sources including plant oils or wastes to produce the PHB. *C. necator*has been mostly studied and commonly used bacterium for the PHA production. In the 1980s, a glucose utilizing mutant of the *C. necator* was employed by Imperial Chemical Industries (UK) for the industry level production of PHB-co-3HV, which was sold under the trade name of BiopolTM(Luzier WD *et al.*, 1992). However some limitations are there which are associated with use of natural PHB producers. Natural PHB producing bacteria usually has native machinery for the polymer degradation and are often hard for lysing, making therecovery of PHB difficult (Luzier WD *et al.*, 1992). For the industrial production of PHB, it is needed to develop strains that can reach high final cell density in a comparatively short period of time as well as produce high PHB content from the simple & inexpensive substrates (Khanna S *et al.*, 2005). So genetic engineering serves as a powerful tool in the development of strains that can produce the PHB from inexpens0ive renewable energy resources efficiently. Genetically engineered bacteria like recombinant strains of E. coli, which produce PHB containing 3HB, 3HHx & 3HO monomers from soybean oil and a recombinant strain of the *C. necator* harboring the Aeromonascaviae PHB synthase gene, which produces P(3HB-co-3HHx) from palm oil have been developed (Fonseca GG *et al.*, 2006) (Loo CY*et al.*, 2005).

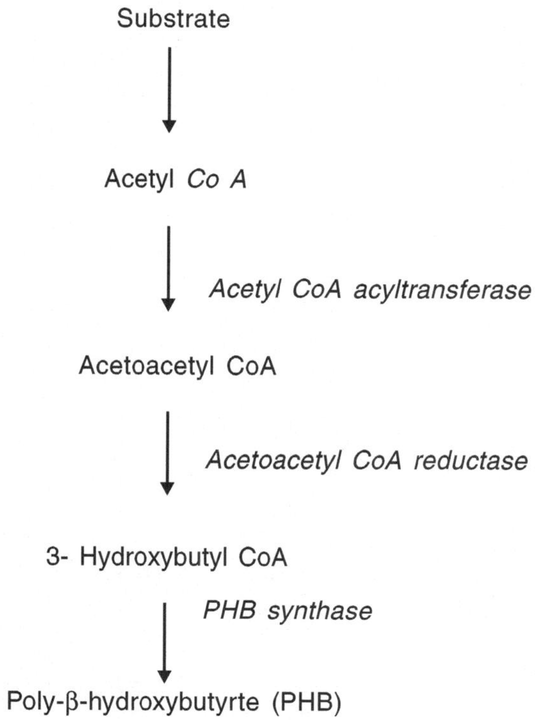

Fig. 5.2: General Biosynthesis of PHB (Lee, Ojumu *et al.*, 1996)

Table 5.1: Bacteria Used for PHB Production from Plant Oils and Wastes

Strains	PHA type	Substrates	References
Alcaligeneslatus DSM 1124	P(3HB)	Soya waste, malt waste	(Yu P *et al.*, 1999)
Bacillus megaterium	P(3HB)	Beet molasses, date syrup	(Omar S *et al.*, 2001)
Burkholderia sp. USM (JCM 15050)	P(3HB)	Palm oil derivatives, fatty acids,	(Chee JY *et al.*, 2010)
Comamonas testosterone	MCL-PHA	Castor oil, coconut oil, mustard oil, cottonseed oil, groundnut oil, olive oil, sesame oil	(Thakor n *et al.*, 2005)
Cupriavidusnecator	P(3HB)	Bagasse hydrolysates	(Yu J *et al.*, 2008)
Cupriavidusnecator H16	P(3HB-*c*- 3HV)	Crude palm kernel oil, olive oil, sunflower oil, palm kernel oil, cooking oil, palm olein, crude palm oil, coconut oil, sodium propionate	(lee WH *et al.*, 2008)
Cupriavidusnecator DSM 545	P(3HB)	Waste glycerol	(Cavalheiro JMBT *et al.*, 2008)
Recombinant *Cupriavidusnecator*	P(3HB-*co*-3HHx)	Palm kernel oil, palm olein, crude palm oil, palm acid oil	(Loo CY *et al.*, 2005)
Recombinant *Escherichia coli*	P(3HB-*co*-3HHx-*co*-3HO)	Soybean oil	(Fonseca GG*et al.*, 2006)

MCL-PHA: medium-chain-length polyhydroxyalkanoate; P (3HB): poly (3-hydroxybutyrate); P(3HB-*co*-3HV): poly(3-hydroxybutyrate-*co*-3-hydroxyvalerate); P(3HB-*co*-3HHx): poly(3-hydroxybutyrate-*co*-3-hydroxyhexanoate); P(3HV-*co*-3HHp-*co*-3HN-*co*-3HU): poly(3-hydroxyvalerate-*co*-3-hydroxyheptanoate-*co*-3-hydroxynonanoate-*co*-3-hydroxyundecanoate)

Fermentation Processes

Depending on the culture conditions that favour PHB accumulation, bacteria that are used for the production of PHB can be classified into 2 groups. The first group of the bacteria needs limitation of essential nutrients like nitrogen, oxygen & the presence of excess carbon source for the efficient synthesis of PHB. The bacteria belonging to this group include *C. necator, Protomonasextorquens* and *Protomonasoleovorans*. While, the second group of bacteria does not need any nutrient limitation for PHBsynthesis and can accumulate PHB during the exponential growth phase. Some of the bacteria included in the group are *Alcaligeneslatus*, a mutant strain of *Azotobacter vinelandii* and recombinant *E. Coli* harboring PHB biosynthetic operon of *C. Necato r* (Khanna S *et al.*, 2005) (Lee SY*et al.*, 1996).

The specific culture conditions needed for the PHB biosynthesis are important criteria to be taken into consideration for the development ofcultivation techniques used in large scale synthesis of PHB. Batch & fed-batch fermentations are mainly used in the industry level fermentation processes. Fed-batch cultivation is better than batch cultivation in terms of achieving high amount of product and cell concentration because the media composition can be controlled by the substrate inhibition. So, high initial concentration of the substrates fed should be avoided. The limitations of fed-batch are long downtime between 2 batches, which results in high operation costs (Yu J *et al.*, 2007). Fed-batch culture is very suitable for the bacteria belonging to the first group. A two-stage method of cultivation is mostly employed, which was initially adopted by the ICI for the industrial production of PHB-co-3HV and the technique has not been changed much since then (Byrom D *et al.*, 1987). In the very first stage, the bacterial cells are grown until a pre-determined cell concentration is reached without any nutrient limitation. Then cells are transferred to second stage medium with some limiting nutrients and carbon substratesfed, are utilized by the cells to synthesize the PHB. The high production cost of PHB has been a main drawback in the replacement of petrochemical plastics (Byrom D *et al.*, 1987) (Choi JI *et al.*, 1997). Taking consideration the price of the most commodity plastics derived from petroleum, such as polyethylene and polypropylene are below US$1 kg-1(Lee SY *et al.*, 1996), PHB cannot currently compete with the bulk synthesis of petrochemical plastics. So efforts have been devoted to reduce production cost through the development of efficient bacterial strains, fermentation as well as the recovery processes (Grothe E *et al.*, 1999) (Lee SY *et al.*, 1996). The major cost in the PHB production is the highcost of the substrate (Yamane T *et al.*, 1993).

So, the selection of suitable carbon substrate is a critical factor that determines the overall performance of the bacterial fermentation and the cost of the final product. The simplest approach is to choose renewable, inexpensive & most available carbon substrates that could support the microbial growth and PHB production. Microorganisms that are capable of producing PHB from various carbon sources ranging from inexpensive, complex waste effluents to the plant oils(Fukui T *et al.*, 1998), fatty acids (Eggink G *et al.*, 1992), alkanes (Lageveen RG *et al.*, 1988) and as well as simple carbohydrates. Every year, large amount of waste materials are discharged from agricultural and food processing industries and the wastes represent a potential renewable feedstock for PHA production. Utilizing the waste materials as carbon source for PHB production not only reduces substrate cost, but also saves the cost of waste disposal (Yu J *et al.*, 2007).

In another method of the PHB production by *Bacillus spp*. from the intestines of different fishes (Pinar Kaynar*et al.*, 2009), the bacteria content of the digestive tracts of samples of fresh fish, were studied. Samples (1 g) of the digestive tract were suspended in 9 ml sterile distilled water & shaken vigorously for 2 min. These samples were heated at 60°C for 60 min in water bath for elimination of bacteria except Bacillus. The liquid was serially diluted with the sterile distilled water, with the dilutions from 10-1 to 10-6 were plated on the nutrient agar. Theplates were incubated at the temperature of 37°C for 24-48 h (Chilcott CN *et al.*, 1993).

30 strains belonging to genus Bacillus were isolated & classified, with the Bergey'smanual (Sneath 1986). By using the criteria of: Gram reaction, spores, growth temperature range (5, 30, 40, 50, 55, 65°C), growth in different pH medium (5.7, 6.8), salt tolerance (2, 5, 7, 10 g NaCl/100 ml), activity of catalase, lecitinase activity, production of gas from the glucose & sugar fermentation (D-glucose, mannitol, lactose, sucrose, melebiose, D-xylose, L-arabinose, maltose and salicin, 1 g/100 ml), reduction of the nitrate, and hydrolysis of gelatine& starch. The strains were finally cultivated in nutrient broth(NB) which contained 1 g lab-lemco powder, 2 g yeast extract, and 5 g peptone, & 5 g NaCl. ThepH was then adjusted to 6.8 with 0.01 M HCl or 0.01 M KOH. Fermentations were carried out in 250-ml flasks containing 100 ml of culture medium. The temperature was finally maintained at 37°C for 48 h, and agitation wasadjusted at 100 rev/min. The cultures were inoculated with 2% (v/v) inocula.

Enhancement of PHB Production

The effect of different C and N sources on production of PHB Two strains of Bacillus spp. (*B. pasteurii P2* and *B. lentus P18*) with the maximum PHB production in nutrient broth medium were examined for the further PHB production in different carbon and nitrogen sources. Carbon sources (such as glucose, lactose, mannitol, sucrose, or sodium acetate) were added to the nutrient broth medium. Peptone in nutrient broth was taken out, and nitrogen sources (tryptophan, L-cysteine, L-glycine, protease peptone, or tryptone) were added. Nitrogen and carbon sources were sterilized by passing through a 0.45-lm pore size Millipore filter. The carbon and nitrogen sources leading to the maximum PHB production by *B. pasteurii* P2 and *B. lentus* P18 which were chosen and medium containing these C & N sources in combination were prepared. PHB production by *B. pasteurii* P2 was determined in the nutrient broth medium having lactose and L-glycine. PHB production by *B. lentus* P18 was further examined in themedium with glucose and tryptophan.

A study has discovered that microalgae like the diatom *P. tricornutum* have a good potential not only as biosynthetic factory for the recombinant proteins but also as fuelled bioreactors photosynthetically (Uwe G Maier *et al.*, 2011) for synthesizing biotechnologically very important polymers like PHB. Even though less enzyme engineering, no adaptations to *P. tricornutum*specific codon-usage as well as no large-scale screening have been applied in these analyses, relatively high PHB levels of up to 10.6% of algal dry weight have been taken out.

Detection of PHB Production

Thin Layer Chromatography (TLC) was carried out on a glass plate (20×10 cm^2) coated with silica gel. The 5 overnight grown bacterial cultures were treated with propanolysis solution (50% dichloroethane, 10% HCL + 40% 1-propanol). 50µl of propanolysed organic phase of the samples were placed on the TLC plate. Then the plate was placed in presaturated chromatographic chamber having the solvent system of the ethyl acetate & benzene (1:1) mixture for 40 min. Then 50ml iodine solution was vaporized in water bath at 80-100°C. TLC plate was placed over the beaker containing iodine solution for 5-10min in order to get saturated with iodine vapour. After 10min spots indicated the presence of PHB. Then Rf (Retardation factor) value was measured andcompared it with the standard (Rawate T *et al.*, 2002).

Gas Chromatography is also used for the analyses of PHB production where cultures were grown in $NH4^+$ containing medium, then washed in nitrogen-free medium and transferred to $NO3^-$ containing medium for 7 days. The Cells were harvested (1500 × g, 10 min), washed with phosphate buffered saline (PBS) and lyophilized for 24 hours. The PHB contents of cells were determined upon methanolysis of 5-10 mg lyophilized cells in the presence of 2 ml methanol/sulphuric acid (85:15, v/v) and 2 ml chloroform. The resulting methyl esters of 3-hydroxybutyrate were analysed by gas chromatography using an Agilent 6850 GC (Agilent Technologies, Waldbronn, Germany) as described previously (Brandl H *et al.*, 1988) (Timm A *et al.*, 1990).

PHB Extraction and Quantification

It was done by using the dispersion method of sodium hypochlorite and chloroform (Chang Y*et al.*, 2007) (Law JH *et al.*, 1961) with some minor modifications. The overnight grown culture was put into an eppendorf tube andcentrifuged at 15,000rpm for 10min at normal room temperature followed by washing in phosphate buffered saline (PBS). The cell pellet was then air dried for 20min at room temperature and weight of pellet was determined. Chloroform and 6% sodium hypochlorite were put to the cell pellets according to the following ratio-12.5µl chloroform to 12.5µl of 6% (v/v) sodium hypochlorite per mg of the pellet weight. Then tubes were incubated at 30°C for overnight. After that the sample was centrifuged at 8,000rpm for 10min at room temperature finally resulted in a three phase solution with bottom phase of chloroform containing the PHB bioplastic. The chloroform phase solution was carefully transferred to fresh tube and its volume was measured. 5X volume of methanol & water (7:3 v/v) mixture was added to that chloroformsolution. The solution was centrifuged at 15,000rpm for 10min at normal room temperature and 0.1ml of the concentrated sulphuric acid was added to the pellet. Then contents were transferred to the glass tubes. The mixture was boiled for 20min at 100°C and cooled. The PHB content in this mixture was quantified by measuring the absorbance at 235nm with UV Visible spectrophotometer. PHB concentration was then normalized over cell pellet weights. The standard curve for PHB was made using poly-3-hydroxybutyric acid from Sigma as standard to determine the PHB content. Stock solution of standard was 200µg of PHB/ml of the chloroform.Statistical analysis was performed by use of SPSS (Version 10.0). The correlation between bacterial dry cell (g/l) weight and PHB production (g/l) of the bacteria was determined by use of Spearman's q correlation coefficient test (Conover WJ 1971).

CHARACTERIZATION

FT-IR analysis revealed the presence of C–H & carbonyl stretching band in extracted PHB and compared with standard PHB. The presence of absorption bands at 1726 cm^{-1} and 1280 cm^{-1} were the characteristic feature of C–O andC–O stretching groups and were identical to those reported for PHB (Khardenavis *et al.*, 2007), there by confirming the presenceof biopolymer. NMR spectrum visualized three groups of signals corresponding to the characteristic of PHB polymer. One doublet at 1.30 ppm represented the CH3 group coupled to one proton while one doublet of quadruplet at 2.57 ppm resulted from the methylene group (CH2) adjacent to an asymmetric carbon atom bearing a single proton. The third signalwas a multiplet at 5.27 ppm which attributed to themethyne group (CH). The methyl esters showed a sharp signal around3.50 ppm, corresponding to the CH3–O group of the esters. These results suggest the polymer to be poly-3-hydroxybutyrate (PHB).Staining images captured at different time intervals showed similar pattern of polymer granulation inside the cell irrespective of the substrate used. Higher amount of polymer granules were observed at 24 h followed by 48-72 h.

PHB is the most common type of PHA produced by the bacteria. The PHB homopolymeris a highly crystalline, stiff, relatively brittle, material. PHB shows high tensile strength (43 MPa), and low elongation to break (5%). The copolymer PHB-co-20 mol%-3-hydroxyvalerate (PHB-co-20 mol% HV) shows lesser crystallinity, less stiffness (20 MPa), but very higher elasticity and flexibility (50% elongation to break) compared to homopolymer PHB. Incorporation of the various monomeric subunits, like 4-hydroxybutyrate (4HB), 3-hydroxyhexanoate (HHx) and other mclhydroxyalkanoates (for e.g. 3-hydroxyoctanoate [3HO], 3-hydroxydecanoate [3HD], 3-hydroxydo-decanoate [3HDD]), with 3HB results in copolymers with varying the aterialproperties to govern the numerous applications in medical and engineering fields. Compared to commercially available polylactic acid (PLA) which is also renewable as well as biodegradable, different combinations of PHA monomeric units are superior to the PLA, which only consists of one single monomer-lactic acid.

Molecular Approach

Molecular Characterization of Isolate by Amplification and Sequencing 16s rRNA Gene

The Genomic DNA was isolated from overnight grown bacterial culture was amplified with the universal bacterial primers.25µl of the reaction mixture contains, 15µl of master mix (NEB, USA) (10x assay buffer, dntp's, Taqpolymerase and $MgCl_2$), 1µl of the forward primer (5'G G C G A A C G G G T G A G T A A3'), 1µl of the reverse primer (5'A C T G C T G C C T C C C G T A G3'), 2µl of the template DNA and 6µl of distilled water by using the Thermal cycler (Corbett Research, Australia).Then PCR was carried out by the thermal cycler under following conditions- An initialization step at 94°C for 4-5min followed by 30 cycles of 94°C for 1min, 52°C for 1min, 72°C for 1.15min followed by final extension at 72°C for 7min and holding temperature at 10°C for 5min. These amplified DNA fragments were observedby agarose gel electrophoresis in 2% agarose gel and then sequenced. The unknown bacterium was identified by using the GenBank database. Partial 16S rRNA sequences obtained from isolates were joined in a contig using thephred/Phrap/CONSED programme (Godon *et al.*, 1997) (Ewing *et al.*, 1998). 16S rRNA gene sequences determined were aligned with sequences of the type strains obtained from the GeneBank using the CLUSTAL X programme version 1.82 (Thomson J D et al., 1997). Distance matrices for aligned sequences were calculated by the two-parameter method (Kimura M *et al.*, 1980). A phylogenetic tree was constructed by neighborjoining method (Saitou N *et al.*, 1987) with the programme PHYLIP version 3.64.Confidence values of individual branches in the phylogenetic tree were determined by the bootstrap analysis based on 1000 samplings Felsentein (Felsenstin J *et al.*, 1985).

Table 5.2: Comparison of Physicochemical and Mechanical Properties of Selected PHB Polymers and Petroleum-derived Plastics

Polymers	Crystallinity[a](%)	Tm[b](°C)	Tg[b](°C)	Tensile Strength (MPa)	Elongation to Break (%)
PHB	60	177	4	43	5
PHB-*co*-20%HV	56	145	1	20	50
PHB *co* 16%4HB	45	150	7	26	444
PHB *co* 10%HHx	34	127	1	21	400
Polypropylene	5070	176	10	38	400
Polyethylene (LDPE)d	2050	130	36	10	620

(a) degree of crystallinity, (b) melting temperature, (c) glass transition temperature, (d) LDPE: low density polyethylene. (Lee 1996) (Poirier *et al.*, 1995).

In another experiment to study the PHB production in a molecular approach, it was focused to measure the phbC gene expression (Fernanda Laroza Paganelli *et al.*, 2011). This gene was selected, instead of phbA and phbB genes, because this is the main step to have PHB accumulation. This was done for the primer designing. While on the other steps, the monomers could be diverted for the several other pathways. By following this approach, the sequences used for the quantification of the phbC gene (PHB polymerase) were obtained from NCBI database. The sequences of phbC genes of Sinorhizobirummeliloti and Rhizobium etli were selected. These sequences were aligned by ClutalX 1.5b programme (Thompson *et al.* 1997) and visualizedby Bioedit programme (Hall 1999), which displayed a consensus sequence. On the basis of thisconsensus sequence, it was selected one 97 bp region that included two conserved regions, in which 19 bp are in the beginning & 16 bp are at the end. These sequences were used for the primer designing with the Primer Express programme (Primer Express Software, Applied Biosystems 7500 version). The endogenous internal control gene used was 16S rRNA gene. Different 16S rRNA gene sequences for a group of rhizobia were obtained from the NCBI and the process was same for the phbC gene. Then for the quantification of phbC gene, the relative intensity of gene expression was estimated byquantitative real-time PCR.

Applications

PHB has a wide range of potential applications because of its desired features such as biocompatibility, biodegradabilityand negligible cytotoxicity to the cells. Hence, the potential application of PHB as replacement for petrochemical basedpolymers is gaining popularity in various fields involving packaging, medical and coating materials.

The basic application areas (Holmes, 1985) in whichit features meet some market needs are:

Packaging: PHB-HV is used for the films, blow moldedbottles and as a creating on paper.

Medical: PHB-HV biocompatibility coupled with itsslow hydrolytic degradation lead to the potential inreconstructive surgery. According to Lee (1996) thedegradation product of PHB, has been detected in relatively large amount inhuman blood plasma. So, it is highly plausiblethat implanting PHB in the mammalian tissues would notbe toxic.

Disposable personal hygiene: P (HB-HV) could beused as the sole structural materials, it could also be used as part of degradable composites. For examplePHAs could be substituted for polypropylene/polyethyleneas matrix material in some compositematerial to achieve desirable properties comparableto these of petro-chemical origin.

Wastewater Treatment during PHB Synthesis

COD removal treatment efficiency was also considered to be crucial alongwith PHB and biohydrogen production. COD, VFA and pH were evaluated at the regular time intervals during the process.COD removal was noticed in all the experimental cases during PHB production irrespective of the substrate used suggesting the effective function of the system towards carbon removal. Substrate degradation efficiency varied with the function of substrate used. PHB has been manufactured for non-woven materials, polymer films, sutures, & pharmaceutical products used insurgery, transplantology, tissue engineering, & pharmacology. In the tissue engineering, the cells are grown in vitroon biodegradable polymers to manufacture tissue for implantation purposes. A high level of biocompatibility isusually needed before foreign materials can be incorporated into human body. Shape, surface porosity, chemistry of thematerials and the tissue environment play very important roles in biocompatibility.PHB has a distinct advantagein the medical field over silicone, a traditionally used polymer, which is believed to have lots of maligned effects andcontribute to cancer cell growth. Although PHB can serve as a substitute biomaterials for silicone, five key elements required to be fulfilled for successful application of PHB in tissue engineering, i.e. biocompatibility, support cell growth and cell adhesion, guide & organize the cells, allow in growth of cells and allow passage of nutrients as well as the wasteproducts, and finally biodegradable without producing any harmful compounds.

METHODOLOGY

Polyhydroxyalkanoates (PHAs) are a group of biodegradable plastics that are produced by a wide variety of microorganisms, mainly as a storage intermediate for energy and carbon. Polyhydroxybutyrate (PHB) is a short-chain-length PHA with interesting chemical and physical properties.

Large scale production of PHB is not wide-spread mainly due to some problems.

The main problem which I came to know through the literature study is the high cost of downstream processing of bacterial cultures to extract the PHB. Moreover another problem is also associated with PHB that is its poor resistance to acids and bases.

To resolve these problems I have several ideas in my mind as follows:

1. Secretion of PHB from a specific gene of engineered *Escherichia coli* could reduce downstream processing costs. PHB are non-proteinaceous polymers, hence cannot be directly targeted for secretion. So we need to find out a particular gene whose gene product will help in reducing PHB granule size so that it can be easily extracted.

2. In another way we can identify a new strain of bacteria based on 16 S rDNA. PHB production conditions can be optimized with different carbon and nitrogen sources. The highest PHB production may be observed with mannitol, sucrose and ammonium sulphate. Ammonium sulphate is the best nitrogen source. C/N ratio is also a good factor that affects the production of PHB. The ratio of C/N that reaches to a certain level, can give best ratio to produce the highest production of PHB.

Schematic Representation

Sample collection

↓

Isolation & Screening of PHB producing bacteria via viable colony staining

↓

Identification of bacteria by physiological, morphological and molecular approach

↓

PHB production and extraction

↓

Estimation of cell dry weight

↓

Determination of PHB using analytical techniques

↓

PHB spectrophotometer assay

↓

PHB analysis using SEM

CONCLUSION

Development of PHB as a potential substitute material to different conventional plastics has drawn very much attention due to thebiodegradable and biocompatible properties of the PHB. The potential applications of the PHB in various industries as well as in the medical fields are encouraging. Although the production cost of PHB has been a major drawback. Simultaneously, scientists have shown much progress in searching for new bacterial strains, creating new types of recombinant strains and producing various kinds of PHB to reduce the cost of production. The ongoing commercialization activities in the several countries are expected to make PHB available for the applications in various areas soon.

FUTURE PERSPECTIVE

In the final discussion we can say that by researchers have used several approaches in the production of PHB bioplastic as well as to reduce the cost of high production, but still there is very less cost reduction in the PHB production due to its costly downstream processing.So we should discover some new approaches in doing so.

The plastics market is worth more than $400 billion and it has grown at an average of 3.5% per year over last two decades. But the contribution made by the PB bioplastics is lesser. The main reason for the minor contribution is its high cost. The next challenge for the group is to do appropriate scale-up experiments, to enable the manufacture of bioplastics on an industrial level. Thegood news is that significant R&D investments are made into the bioplastics by manycompanies especially in Europe, and these efforts are likely to result in significantcost reductions. Such cost reductions for bioplastics in general are expected to makealgae-based bioplastics more viable as well.

In the future, there will be focus on various targets for enhancing PHB biosynthesis in P. tricornutum. Other sub-cellular compartments such as plastids might yet be interesting sites for PHB production. Diatoms are naturally rich in lipids and silicate and already have the wide applications in biotechnology. So, inserting and altering the various biochemical pathways in diatoms in order to produce the complex molecules, biologically active substances, and raw materials may have a number of applications in for e.g. the nanotechnology industry and the production of renewable biofuels.

REFERENCES

1. Ashby RD. Synthesis of Short-medium-chain-length poly(hydroxyalkanoate) Blends by Mixed Culture Fermentation of Glycerol. *Biomacromolecules* 2005; 6: 2106-2112.
2. Ben Rebah F, Prévost D, Tyagi RD, Belbahri L. Poly-beta-hydroxybutyrate Production by Fast-growing Rhizobia Cultivated in Sludge and in Industrial Wastewater. Appl Biochem Biotechnol. 2009 Jul; 158(1): 155-63. doi: 10.1007/s12010-008-8358-1.
3. Brandl H, Gross RA, Lenz RW, Fuller RC: Pseudomonas Oleovorans as a Source of Poly(beta-Hydroxyalkanoates) for Potential Applications as Biodegradable Polyesters. Appl Environ Microbiol 1988, 54(8): 1977-1982.
4. Braunegg G, Lefebvre G, Genser KF. Polyhydroxyalkanoates, Biopolyesters from Renewable Resources: Physiological and Engineering Aspects. *Journal of Biotechnology* 1998; 65: 127-161.
5. Byrom D. Polyhydroxyalkanoates, In: Mobley DP (ed) Plastic from Microbes: Microbial Synthesis of Polymers and Polymer Precursors. Hanser Munich, (1994) pp. 5-33.
6. Cavalheiro JMBT, de Almeida MCMD, Grandfils C, da Fonseca MMR. Poly (3-hydroxybutyrate) Production by *Cupriavidusnecator* Using Waste Glycerol. *Process Biochemistry* 2009; 44: 509-515.
7. Chang Y, Hahn S, Kim B, Chang H. Optimization of Microbial Poly (3- hydroxybutyrate) Recovery. Using Dispersions of Sodium Hypochlorite Solution and Chloroform. *BiotechnolBioeng.*(2007); 44(2): 256 261.

8. Chee JY, Tan Y, Samian MR, Sudesh K. Isolation and Characterization of a *Burkholderia*sp. USM (JCM15050) Capable of Producing Polyhydroxyalkanoate (PHA) from Triglycerides, Fatty Acids and Glycerols. *Journal of Polymer and the Environment* 2010; in Press, doi: 10.1007/s10924-010-0204-1.

9. Chilcott CN, Wigley PJ. Isolation and Toxicity of Bacillus Thuringiensis from Soil and Insect Habitats in New Zealand. *InvertebrPathol*(1993); 61: 244-247.

10. Choi JI, Lee SY. Process Analysis and Economic Evaluation for Poly (3-hydroxybutyrate) Production by Fermentation. *Bioprocess Engineering* 1997; 17: 335-342.

11. Conover WJ Practical Nonparametric Statistics. Wiley, New York. 1971; ISBN: 0471168521.

12. Du G, Yu J. Green Technology for Conversion of Food Scraps to Biodegradable Thermoplastic Polyhydroxyalkanoates. *Environ. Sci. Technol.* (2002b); 36: 5511-5516.

13. Eggink G, van der Wal H, Huijberts GNM, de Waard P. Oleic Acid as a Substrate for poly-3-hydroxyalkanoate Formation in Alcaligeneseutrophus and Pseudomonas putida. *Industrial Crops and Products* 1992; 1: 157-163.

14. Ewing, B., Hillier, L., Wendl, M., Green, P. Basecalling of Automated Sequencer Traces Using Phred. I. Accuracy Assessment. *Genome Research* 8, 175-185 (1998).

15. Felsenstin J, Confidence Limits on Phylogenesis: An Approach Using the Bootstrap*, Evolution*, 39, 783791 (1985).

16. Fernanda Laroza Paganelli, Eliana Gertrudes de MacedoLemos, Lu´cia Maria Carareto Alves Polyhydroxybutyrate in Rhizobium and Bradyrhizobium: Quantification and phbC Gene Expression. J Microbiol Biotechnol (2011) 27: 773-778.

17. Fonseca GG, Antonio RV. Polyhydroxyalkanoates Production by Recombinant *Escherichia coli* Harboring the Structural Genes of the Polyhydroxyalkanoate Synthases of *Ralstoniaeutropha* and *Pseudomonas aeruginosa* Using Low Cost Substrate. *Journal of Applied Sciences* 2006; 6: 1745-1750.

18. Fukui T, Doi Y. Efficient Production of Polyhydroxyalkanoates from Plant Oils by Alcaligeneseutrophus and its Recombinant Strain. *Applied Microbiology and Biotechnology* 1998; 49: 333-336.

19. Gavrilescu M, ChistiY. Biotechnology: A Sustainable Alternative for Chemical Industry. *BiotechnolAdv* (2005); 23: 471-499.

20. Godon, J.J., Zumstein, E., Dabert, P., Habouzit, F., Moletta, R., Molecular Microbial Diversity of an Anaerobic Digester as Determined by Small-subunit rDN Asequence Analysis. *Applied and Environmental Microbiology* 63, 2802 2813 (1997).

21. Grothe E, Moo-Young M, Chisti Y. Fermentation Optimization for the Production of Poly(beta-hydroxybutyric Acid) Microbial Thermoplastic. *Enzyme and Microbial Technology* 1999; 25: 132-141.

22. Hall TA BioEdit: A User-friendly Biological Sequence Alignment Editor and Analysis Programme for Windows 95/98NT. Nucl Ac SympSer (1999); 41: 95-98. doi: 10.1111/j.1469-8137.2009.02874.x

23. Hocking PJ, Marchessault RH In: Chemistry and Technology of Biodegradable Polymers. *Griffin GJL (eds) Blackie Academic.* New York, (1994) pp. 48-96.

24. Keiichi Uchino, Terumi Saito, Birgit Gebauer, and Dieter Jendrossek Isolated Poly(3-Hydroxybutyrate) (PHB) Granules are Complex Bacterial Organelles Catalyzing Formation of PHB from Acetyl Coenzyme A (CoA) and Degradation of PHB to Acetyl-CoA. *J Bacteriol.* ; 189(22): 8250 8256 (2007 November).

25. Khardenavis, A.A., Kumar, M.S., Mudliar, S.N., Chakrabarti, T., Biotechnological Conversion of Agro-industrial Wastewaters into Biodegradable Plastic Poly Hydroxybutyrate. *Biores. Technol.* 2007; 98, 3579-3584.

26. Khanna S, Srivastava AK. Recent Advances in Microbial Polyhydroxyalkanoates. *Process Biochemistry* 2005; 40: 607-619.

27. Kimura M, A Simple Method for Estimating Evolutionary Rates of Base Substitution Through Comparative Studies of Nucleotide Sequences, *J Mol Evol*, 2, 111 120 (1980).
28. Lageveen RG, Huisman GW, Preusting H, Ketelaar P, Eggink G, Witholt B. Formation of Polyesters by Pseudomonas Oleovorans: Effect of Substrates on Formation and Composition of Poly-(R)-3-hydroxyalkanoates and poly-(R)-3-hydroxyalkenoates. *Applied and Environmental Microbiology* 1988; 54: 2924-2932.
29. Law JH, Slepecky RA. Assay of Poly-β- Hydroxybutyric Acid. *J.Bacteriol.* (1961); 82: 33-36.
30. Lee SY. Bacterial Polyhydroxyalkanoates. Biotechnol. Bioeng.(1996); 49: 1-14.
31. Lee WH, Loo CY, Nomura CT, Sudesh K. Biosynthesis of Polyhydroxyalkanoate Copolymers from Mixtures of Plant Oils and 3-hydroxyvalerate Precursors. *Bioresource Technology* 2008; 99: 6844-6851.
32. Lemoigne M. Produit de déshydratationet de polymérisation de l'acide β-oxybutyrique. Bull. Soc. *Chim. Biol.* 8: (1926); 770-782.
33. Loo CY, Lee WH, Tsuge T, Doi Y, Sudesh K. Biosynthesis and Characterization of Poly (3-hydroxybutyrate-*co*-3-hydroxyhexanoate) from Palm Oil Products in a *Wautersiaeutropha* mutant. *Biotechnology Letters* 2005; 27: 1405-1410.
34. Luzier WD. Materials Derived from Biomass Biodegradable Materials. *Proceedings of the National Academy of Sciences of the United States of America* 1992; 89: 839-842.
35. Madden LA, Anderson AJ, Shah DT, Asrar J. Chain Termination in Polyhydroxyalkanoate Synthesis: Involvement of Exogenous Hydroxy-compounds as Chain Transfer Agents. *International Journal of Biological Macromolecules* 1999; 25: 43-53.
36. Omar S, Rayes A, Eqaab A, Voβ I, Steinbuchel A. Optimization of Cell Growth and Poly (3-hydroxybutyrate) Accumulation on Date Syrup by a *Bacillus megaterium* strain. *Biotechnology Letters* 2001; 23: 1119-1123.
37. Pinar Kaynar,YavuzBeyatli. Determination of Poly-b-hydroxybutyrate Production by Bacillus spp. Isolated from the Intestines of Various Fishes. Fish Sci (2009) 75: 439-443.
38. Poirier Y, Dennis D, Klomparens K, Nawrath C, Sommerville C. Perspectives on the Production of Polyhydroxyalkanoates in Plants. *FEMS Microbiology Reviews* 1992; 103: 237-246.
39. Poirier Y, Nawrath C, Somerville C. Production of Polyhydroxyalkanoates, a Family of Biodegradable Plastics and Elastomers, in Bacterial and Plant. *Biotechnol.* (1995); 13: 142-150.
40. Rawate T & Mavinkurve S, Chacterization of Polyhydroxyalkonates-Biodegradable Plastics from Marine Bacteria, *currsci,* 83, 562 564 (2002).
41. Rivard C, Moens L, Roberts K, Brigham J, Kelley S. Starch esters as Biodegradable Plastics: Effects of ester Group Chain Length and Degree of Substitution on Anaerobic Biodegradation. *Enzyme and Microbial Tech.* (1995); 17: 848-852.
42. Saitou N &Nei M, The Neighbour-joining Method: A New Method for Reconstructing Phylogenetic Trees, *Mol Boil Evol*, 4, 406-425 (1987).
43. SneathPHA Endospore-forming Gram-positive Rods and cocci. In: Sneath PHA, Mair NS, Sharpe ME, Holt JG (eds) Bergey's Manual of Systematic Bacteriology, Vol. 2. *Williams.*
44. Steinbüchel A, Fuchtenbusch B. Bacteria and Other Biological Systems for Polyester Production. *TIBTECH*, (1998)16: 419-427.
45. Steinbüchel A. Polyhydroxyalkanoic Acids. In: Byrom D (ed) *Biomaterials: Novel Materials from Biological Sources. Stockton,* New York, (1991) pp. 124-213.
46. Sudesh K, Taguchi K, Doi Y. Effect of Increased PHA Synthase Activity on Polyhydroxyalkanoates Biosynthesis in *Synechocystis* sp. PCC6803. *International Journal of Biological Macromolecules* 2002; 30: 97-104.
47. S. Srilakshmi, C.S.V. Ramachandra Rao. Studies on Screening, Isolation and Molecular Characterization of PHB Producing *Staphylococcus Spp. International Journal of Integrative Sciences, Innovation and Technology* 2012 eISSN 2278-1145.

48. Thakor N, Trivedi U, Patel KC. Biosynthesis of Medium Chain Length Poly (3-hydroxyalkanoates) (mcl-PHAs) by *Comamonastestosteroni* during Cultivation on Vegetable Oils. *Bioresource Technology* 2005; 96: 1843-1850.

49. Thomson J D, Gibbon T J, Plewonick F, Jeanmougin F & Higgins D G, the CLUSTAL X Windows Interface: Flexible Strategies for Multiple Sequence Alignment Aided by Quality Analysis Tools, *Nucleic Acids res*, 25, 4876 4882 (1997).

50. Timm A, Steinbüchel A: Formation of Polyesters Consisting of Mediumchain-length 3-hydroxyalkanoic Acids from Gluconate by Pseudomonas Aeruginosa and Other Fluorescent Pseudomonads. *Appl Environ Microbiol* 1990, 56(11): 3360-3367.

51. Uwe G Maier, FranziskaHempel, Andrew S Bozarth, Nicole Lindenkamp, Andreas Klingl, Stefan Zauner, Uwe Linne, Alexander Steinbüchel. Microalgae as Bioreactors for Bioplastic Production. *Microbial Cell Factories* 2011, 10: 81.

52. Yamane T. Yield of poly-D (—)-3-hydroxybutyrate from Various Carbon Sources: A Theoretical Study. *Biotechnology and Bioengineering* 1993; 41: 165-170.

53. Yu Jn. Production of PHA from Starch Wastewater via Organic Acids. *J. Biotechnol* 2001 86: 105-112.

54. Yu J. Microbial Production of Bioplastics from Renewable Resources. In: S. T. Yang Editor. *Bioprocessing for Value-added Products from Renewable Resources*; 2007.

55. Yu J, Stahl H. Microbial Utilization and Biopolyester Synthesis of Bagasse Hydrolysates. *Bioresource Technology* 2008; 99: 8042-8048.

56. Yu P, Chua H, Huang AL, Ho KP. Conversion of Industrial Food Wastes by *Alcaligeneslatus* into Polyhydroxyalkanoates. *Applied Biochemistry and Biotechnology* 1999; 78: 445-454.

Pages: 126-138

BIOTECHNOLOGY, AGRO-ECOLOGY AND ENVIRONMENT

Edited by: **Dr. Avnish Chauhan; Dr. Pawan Kumar 'Bharti'**

ISBN: 978-93-5056-757-9

Edition: **2015**

Published by: **Discovery Publishing House Pvt. Ltd., New Delhi (India)**

6

Chitosan as a Substitute of Fungicides for Controlling Plant Diseases

Farid Abd-El-Kareen and Wafaa M. Haggag

ABSTRACT

Chitosan is naturally-occurring compound that have potential in agriculture with regard to controlling plant diseases. These molecules were shown to display toxicity and inhibit fungal growth and development. Chitosan exhibits a variety of antimicrobial activities against several plant pathogens which depend on the type of chitosan (native or modified), its degree of polymerization, the host, the chemical and/or nutrient composition of the substrates, and environmental conditions. In some studies, oligomeric chitosans have been reported to exhibit a better antifungal activity than larger units. The mechanism by which chitosan affects the growth of several pathogenic fungi has not been fully elucidated, but several hypotheses have been postulated, first: its polycationic nature, it is believed that chitosan interferes with negatively charged residues of macromolecules exposed on the fungal cell surface. This interaction leads to the leakage of intracellular electrolytes and proteinaceous constituents. Second the interaction of diffused hydrolysis products with microbial DNA, which leads to the inhibition of mRNA and protein synthesis, third the chelating of metals, spore elements and essential nutrients. Forth:

Plant Pathology Department, National Research Centre, Dokki, Giza, 12662, Egypt.

the interaction of chitosan with fungal DNA and RNA. Five: Malformation of fungal mycelial. On the other hand, chitosan had different properties *i.e.* had inhibitory effect against pathogenic fungi and had ability to be potent elicitors of plant defense resistance.

Chitosan induce host defense responses in both monocotyledons and dicotyledons. These responses include lignification, cytoplasmic acidification, membrane depolarization and protein phosphorylation, chitinase and glucanase activation, phytoalexin biosynthesis, generation of reactive oxygen species), biosynthesis of jasmonic acid and the expression of unique early responsive and defense-related genes. In addition to, chitosan was reported to induce callose formation and proteinase inhibitors. Applications of chitosan for controlling plant diseases included seed coating, foliar treatment, soil amendment and fruit coating.

Key words: Chitosan, Fungicidal activity, Plant defenses, Induced Resistance, Combination, Plant Diseases.

INTRODUCTION

Chitosan, deacetylated chitin, is currently obtained from the outer shell of crustaceans such as crabs, krills and shrimps (Sandford and Hutchings, 1987; Sandford, 1989 and El Hadrami, *et al.*, 2009 & 2010). Chitin and chitosan are polysaccharides, chemically similar to cellulose differing only by the presence or absence of nitrogen. Chitosan exhibits a variety of antimicrobial activities against several plant pathogens (El-Badawy, *et al.*, 2003; Abd-El-Kareem *et al.*, 2002, 2006 ; El-Mohamedy *et al.*, 2014 and Abd-El-Kareem and Haggag, 2014) which depend on the type of chitosan (native or modified), its degree of polymerization, the host, the chemical and/or nutrient composition of the substrates, and environmental conditions. In some studies, oligomeric chitosans have been reported to exhibit a better antifungal activity than larger units (Badawy, *et al.*, 2003; El Hadrami, *et al.*, 2010 and Abd-El-Kareem and Haggag, 2014),. In others, the antimicrobial activity increased with the increase in chitosan molecular weight (Kulikov *et al.*, 2006), and seems to be faster on fungi and algae than on bacteria.

FUNGICIDAL ACTIVITY OF CHITOSAN AGAINST FUNGI AND OOMYCETES

Fungicidal activity of chitosan has been documented against various species of fungi and oomycetes (Muzzarelli, *et al.*, 1990 and Vasyukova, *et al.*, 2005). Rabea, *et al.* (2005), reported on the fungicidal activity of 24 new derivatives of chitosan (*i.e.*, *N*-alkyl, *N*-benzylchitosans) and showed, using a radial hyphal growth bioassay of *B. cinerea* and *P. grisea*, that all derivatives have a higher fungicidal action than the native chitosan. *N*-dodecylchitosan, *N*-(*p*-isopropylbenzyl) chitosan and *N*-(2,6-dichlorobenzyl) chitosan were the most active against *B. cinerea*, with EC_{50} values of 0.57, 0.57 and 0.52 $g.L^{-1}$, respectively. Against *P. grisea*, *N*-(*m*-nitrobenzyl)chitosan was the most active, with 77% inhibition at 5 $g.L^{-1}$.

O-(decanoyl) chitosan at mol ratio of 1:2 (chitosan to decanoic acid) was the most active compound against *B. cinerea* (EC_{50} = 1.02 g.L^{-1}) and *O*-(hexanoyl)chitosan displayed the highest activity against *P. grisea* (EC_{50} = 1.11 g.L^{-1}). Some of the derivatives also repressed spore formation at rather high concentrations (1.0, 2.0 and 5.0 g.L^{-1}) (Badawy, *et al.*, 2005). Recently, Palma-Guerrero, *et al.* (2009) demonstrated that chitosan is able to permeabilize the plasma membrane of *Neurospora crassa* and kills the cells in an energy-dependent manner. In general, chitosan, applied at a rate of 1 mg/mL, is able to reduce the *in vitro* growth of a number of fungi and oomycetes except Zygomycetes, which have chitosan as a component of their cell walls [Allan, *et al.*, 1979]. Another category of fungi that seems to be resilient to the antifungal effect of chitosan, the nemato-/entomo-pathogenic fungi that possess extracellular chitosanolytic activity (Abd-El-Kareem, *et al.*, 2006 ; Palma-Guerrero, *et al.*, 2008 ; and El-Mohamedy, *et al.*, 2013 & 2014).

Mechanisms of Chitosan as Antimicrobial Activities

Chitosan exhibits a variety of antimicrobial activities (Badawy, *et al.*, 2005 ; Abd-El-Kareem, *et al.*, 2006; El-Mohamedy, *et al.*, 2013 and Abd-El-Kareem and Haggag, 2014), which depend on the type of chitosan (native or modified), its degree of polymerization, the host, the chemical and/or nutrient composition of the substrates, and environmental conditions. Kulikov *et al.*, (2006) reported that the antimicrobial activity increased with the increase in chitosan molecular weight and seems to be faster on fungi and algae than on bacteria. Fungicidal activity of chitosan has been documented against various species of fungi and oomycetes (Vasyukova, *et al.*, 2005 and El-Mohamedy, *et al.*, 2013). The minimal growth-inhibiting concentrations varied between 10 and 5,000 ppm (Rabea, *et al.* 2005). Some of the derivatives also repressed spore formation at rather high concentrations (Badawy, *et al.*, 2005). Recently, Palma-Guerrero, *et al.* (2009) demonstrated that chitosan is able to permeabilize the plasma membrane of *Neurospora crassa* and kills the cells. In general, chitosan is able to reduce the *In Vitro* growth of a number of fungi and oomycetes (Palma-Guerrero, *et al.*, 2008). For instance, chitosan was reported to exert an inhibitory action on the hyphal growth of numerous pathogenic fungi, including root and necrotrophic pathogens, such as *Fusarium oxysporum*, *Botrytis cinerea*, *Monilina laxa*, *Alternaria alternata* and *Pythium aphanidermatum* (El Hassni, *et al.*, 2004).

The mechanism by which chitosan affects the growth of several pathogenic fungi has not been fully elucidated, but several hypotheses have been postulated, first: its polycationic nature, it is believed that chitosan interferes with negatively charged residues of macromolecules exposed on the fungal cell surface. This interaction leads to the leakage of intracellular electrolytes and proteinaceous constituents (El Hassni, *et al.*,2004). Second the interaction of diffused hydrolysis products with microbial DNA, which leads to the inhibition of mRNA and protein synthesis (Vasyukova, *et al.*, 2005), third the chelating of metals, spore elements and essential nutrients (Rabea, *et al.* 2005). Forth: the interaction of chitosan with fungal DNA and RNA (Palma-Guerrero, *et al.*, 2008). Five: Malformation of fungal mycelial. Chitosan is not only effective in inhibition the growth of the pathogen fungi, but also induces marked morphological changes, structural alterations and molecular disorganization of fungal cells (El Ghaouth *et al.*, 2002 and Ait Barka *et al.*, 2004). Moreover, El Hassni *et al.*, (2004) reported that, chitosan caused morphological changes such as large vesicles or empty cells devoid of cytoplasm in the mycelium of *B. cinerea*. Furthermore, Banos *et al.*, (2006) revealed that by microscopic observation of fungi treated with chitosan, it can affect the morphology of the hyphae.

In this regard part of the effect observed by chitosan on the reduction of soil-borne pathogens comes from the fact that it enhances plant defense responses. The other part is linked to the fact that this biopolymer is composed of polysaccharides that stimulate the activity of beneficial microorganisms in the soil such as *Bacillus*, fluorescent *Pseudomonas*, actinomycetes, mycorrhiza and rhizobacteria. This microbial equilibrium in the rhizosphere disadvantaging plant pathogens. Beneficial organisms, on the other hand, are able to outcompete them through mechanisms such as parasitism, antibiosis, and induced resistance (Uppal, *et al.*, 2008 Elwagia and Algam, 2014 and Mishra, *et al.*, (2014).

APPLICATIONS OF CHITOSAN FOR CONTROLLING PLANT DISEASES

Chitosan used to control plant pathogens has been extensively explored with more or less success depending on the pathosystem, the used derivatives, concentration, degree of deacylation, viscosity, and the applied formulation (*i.e.*, soil amendment (Abdel-Latif, Faten and Wafaa, 2002, Haggag. Abd-El-Kareem, *et al.*, 2006 ; Palma-Guerrero, *et al.*, 2008; and El-Mohamedy, *et al.*, 2013 & 2014) or foliar application (Abd-El-Kareem, *et al.*, 2002 and Abd-El-Kareem and Haggag, 2014). Substratum amendment with chitosan was reported to enhance plant growth and suppress some of the notorious soil-borne diseases. For example, in soilless tomato, root rot caused by *Fusarium oxysporum* f. sp. *radicis-lycopersici* was suppressed using chitosan amendments (Abd-El-Kareem, *et al.*, 2006; El-Mohamedy, *et al.*, 2013 & 2014).

Applied Chitosan as Seed Coating

Guan *et al.* (2009) examined the use of chitosan to prime maize seeds. Although chitosan had no significant effect on germination under low temperatures, it enhanced germination index, reduced the mean germination time, and increased shoot height, root length, and shoot and root dry weights in two tested maize lines. In both tested lines, chitosan induced a decline in malonyldialdehyde content, altered the relative permeability of the plasma membrane and increased the concentrations of soluble sugars and proline, and of peroxidase and catalase activities. In other studies, seed priming with chitosan improved the vigor of maize seedlings (Shao, *et al.*, 2005). It was also reported to increase wheat seed resistance to certain diseases and improve their quality and/or their ability to germinate (Reddy, et al, 1999). Similarly, peanut seeds soaked in chitosan were reported to exhibit an increased rate of germination and energy, lipase activity, and gibberellic acid and indole acetic acid levels (Zhou, *et al.*, 2002). Ruan and Xue (2002) showed that rice seed coating with chitosan may accelerate their germination and improve their tolerance to stress conditions. In carrot, seed coating helps restrain further development of Sclerotinia rot (Cheah and Page 1997). Chitosan has also been extensively utilized as a seed treatment to control *F. oxysporum* in many host species (Badawy, *et al.*, 2003).

Applied Chitosan as Foliar Treatment

Foliar application of chitosan has been reported in many systems and for several purposes. Treated potato plants with chitosan induced resistance against late blight disease and reduced infection. Moreover, Abd-El-Kareem *et.al.* (2001) reported that, treated potato plants with chitosan induced resistance against late blight disease and increased tuber yield under field conditions. Chitosan has also been extensively utilized as a foliar treatment to control the growth, spread and development of many diseases involving viruses, bacteria, fungi and pests (Badawy, *et al.*, 2003). It has also been used to increase yield and tuber quality of micropropagated greenhouse-grown potatoes. Faoro, *et al.* (2008) showed that the use of chitosan applied as a foliar spray on barley reduced locally and systemically the infection by powdery mildew pathogen *Blumeria graminis* f. sp. *hordei*. Moreover, Abd-El-Kareem and Haggag, (2014) reported that spraying potato plants with chitosan resulted in reducing early blight disease and increasing tuber yield.

Applied Chitosan as Soil Amendment

Chitosan utilized as a soil amendment was shown to control *Fusarium* wilts in many plant species (Badawy, *et al.*, 2003 and Mahdy *et al.*, 2014). Applied at an optimal concentration, this biomaterial is able to induce a delay in disease development, leading to a reduced plant wilting (Benhamou, *et al.*, 1994; Abd-El-Kareem, *et al.*, 2006; El-Mohamedy, *et al.*, 2013 & 2014). These infections were dramatically reduced upon the use of chitosan as soil amendment. *Aspergillus flavus* was also completely inhibited in field-grown corn and peanut after soil treatment with chitosan (El Ghaouth, *et al.*, 1992). Part of the effect observed by chitosan on the reduction of soilborne pathogens comes from the fact that it enhances plant defense responses. The other part is linked to the fact that this biopolymer is composed of polysaccharides that stimulate the activity of beneficial microorganisms in the soil such as *Bacillus*, fluorescent *Pseudomonas*, actinomycetes, mycorrhiza and rhizobacteria (Murphy, *et al.*, 2000). This alters the microbial equilibrium in the rhizosphere disadvantaging plant pathogens. Beneficial organisms, on the other hand, are able to outcompete them through mechanisms such as parasitism, antibiosis, and induced resistance (Uppal, *et al.*, 2008 and El Hadrami, *et al.*, 2009).

Applied Chitosan as Fruit Coating

Coating fruits with chitosan decreased postharvest diseases of tomato, strawberry and lime fruits (El- Ghaouth *et al.*, 1992; Morsy *et al.* 1999 and Abd El- Kareem *et al.*, 2002). Coating fruits with chitosan reduced the respiration rate, ethylene production, interval O_2 levels and increased the interval CO_2 of peach and pear fruits (Du *et. al.* 1997).They added that coated fruits were markedly firmer and less mature of the end of storage.

Allan and Hadwiger, (1979) reported that chitosan films appear to extend the shelf life of fruit and vegetable by modifying the internal atmosphere and improving the retention of moisture during storage.

El Ghaouth (1994) reported that chitosan, a cationic polysaccharide [Polyglucosamine, $(Glc\ NH_2)_n$] produced commercially from Crab and shrimp shells has been advocated as an active packaging material with antimicrobial and physiologically useful properties. Chitosan-treated fruits such as apples, kiwfruit, pears and others significant reduction of storage rots (Bautista Banos *et al.*, 2004; Due *et al*; 1997; Ben-shalom *et al.*, 2003 and Rommanazzi *et al.*, 2003). Furthermore, Abd-El-Latif, (2010) reported that coating lime fruits with combined treatments between citral at 4.0 or 5.0 ml/l and chitosan at 6.0 or 8.0 g/l reduced the disease incidence and rotted part tissue more than 89.5 and 93.5% respectively.

COMBINATION BETWEEN CHITOSAN AND OTHER TREATMENTS FOR CONTROLLING PLANT DISEASES

El-Mohamedy, *et al.*, (2014) reported that effect of individual or combined application of *Trichoderma harzianum* and chitosan against *Fusarium oxysporum* f. sp. *radicis-lycopersici* (Forl), was assessed in vitro and in vivo. *T. harzianum* had significantly reduced the mycelia growth of the five Forl tested isolates. Chitosan applied at different concentrations (from 0.5 to 4 g/l) had also significantly decreased the mycelial growth of the pathogen and a total inhibition was obtained at the concentration 4 g/l. Under greenhouse conditions, application of *T. harzianum* and chitosan (1g/l) as root dipping treatment combined with chitosan (0.5 g/l) as foliar spray has reduced disease incidence and severity by 66.6 and 47.6%, respectively. Treatments based on *T. harzianum* alone or in combination with chitosan led to an increase in the total phenols and to an enhancement of chitinase and b,1-3-glucanase activities in leaves of treated tomato plants compared with the untreated ones.

Also, Abd-El-Kareem and Haggag, (2014) reported that Chitosan or Citral alone or in combinations were tested to study their effect against early blight disease of potato plants under field conditions. Different concentrations of chitosan and Citral were tested to study their inhibitory effect on linear growth of *Alternaria solani* in vitro. Both treatments significantly reduced the linear growth of *Alternaria solani*. Complete inhibition was obtained with chitosan at 5.0 g/L and Citral at 5.0 mL/L. The highest reduction was achieved with chitosan at 4.0 g/L and Citral at 4.0 mL/L. which reduced the linear growth by 93.3 and 95.6 % respectively. Moreover, under field conditions results indicated that chitosan and Citral alone or in combination significantly reduced the disease incidence. The highest reduction was obtained combined treatments between chitosan at 2.0 g/L. and Citral at 4.0 or 5.0 ml/L which reduced the early blight incidence more than 76.6 and 83.3 % respectively during two growing seasons as compared with untreated plants. As for tuber yield the highest increase was obtained with combined treatments between chitosan at 2.0 g/L. and Citral at 4.0 or 5.0 ml/L which increased the tuber yield more than 88.6 and 80.0% during two growing seasons respectively as compared with untreated plants. These treatments also increased chitinase activity which increased the activity by 124.2 and 127.3% respectively as compared with untreated plants. In the other hand Abd-El-Kareem, and Abd-Alla, (2002) investigated that combination between citral and different carriers varied in their protective effect of coated navel orange fruits against decay caused by green and blue mould diseases. It was observed that, fruits coated with citral 2% + chitosan at 6g/L showed the highest protective effect against disease incidence it reduced disease incidence by 89.8 and 88.0% for green and blue mould, respectively.

Percentage of rotted tissue parts of infected navel orange fruits showed the same trend. Moreover, Abd-El-Latif, (2010) stated that he promising concentrations of citral *i.e* 4.0 & 5.0 ml/L and chitosan at 6.0 & 8.0 g/L were applied as single or in combination against sour rot disease. Fresh lime fruits were artificially wounded using sterilized scalpel and inoculated with spore suspension (10^6 spores/ml) of *G. candidum* then treated with citral and /or chitosan.Results indicate that the most effective treatments are combined treatments between citral at 4.0 or 5.0 ml/l and chitosan at 6.0 or 8.0 g/l which reduced the disease incidence and rotted part tissue more than 89.5 and 93.5% respectively.While single treatments of each concentration of citral and chitosan reduced the sour rot incidence and rotted part tissue more than 81.5 and 84.5%. respectively.

MECHANISMS OF ACTION OF CHITOSAN IN REDUCING PLANT DISEASES

Although the exact mechanisms of action of chitosan in reducing plant disease are currently not fully understood, there is growing evidence showing its action through direct toxicity or chelation of nutrients and minerals from pathogens. Because of its biopolymer properties, this compound can also form physical barriers around the penetration sites of pathogens, preventing them from spreading to healthy tissues. This and bioactive derivatives can activate H^+-ATPases, depolarizing biological membranes and inducing other series of events. Chitosan is known to induce reactions locally and systemically that involve signaling cascades, and the activation and accumulation of defenses-related antimicrobial compounds and proteins (El Hadrami, *et al.*, 2010).

Direct activity Against Pathogens

Against, bacteria, fungi, oomycetes and other pests, it seems that chitosan is likely to operate indirectly *via* other means such as the enhancement of host resistance. However, a number of studies have shown that chitosan, at defined concentrations, presents antimicrobial properties (Sudarshan, et al., 1992).

Physical Barrier Around Pathogen Penetration Sites

Chitosan, when applied to plant tissues, often agglutinate around the penetration sites and has two major effects. The first one is the isolation of the penetration site through the formation of a physical barrier preventing the pathogen from spreading and invading other healthy tissues. This phenomenon resembles the abscission zones often observed on leaves preventing several necrotrophic pathogens from spreading further. It is widely observed on potato tubers for example (El Hadrami *et al.*, 2009). Around the isolated zones, often an elicitation of a hypersensitive response occur with the accumulation of H_2O_2 that helps in cells wall fortification and serve as an alert signal for other healthy parts of the plant. The second effect is due to the chitosan' ability to bind various materials and initiate fast the wound healing process El Hadrami *et al.*, 2010).

Chelation of Nutrients and Minerals

Chitosan is well used in the fresh and salt water purification process as chelators for minerals and metals. These abilities are also explored when chitosan is applied to plants to prevent diseases because it can chelate nutrients and minerals (*i.e.*, Fe, Cu), preventing pathogens from accessing them. These polysaccharide molecules were also reported to bind mycotoxins (Bornet, *et al.*, 2007), which may reduce damage to the host tissues due to toxins. In the beverage industry, for example, chitosan and derivatives are often used for their antimicrobial properties linked to their chelating abilities of nutrient and minerals, thus reducing fungal spoilage.

Effect on H^+-ATPase and Depolarization of Biological Membranes

Amborabé *et al.* (2008) reported on the early events that occur during the elicitation of plant defenses using chitosan. They showed that this molecule was able to trigger, in a dose-dependent manner, a quick and transient depolarization of *Mimosa pudica* motor cell membranes. These modifications were also accompanied by a transient rise in pH. Using plasma membrane vesicles, the authors determined the site of action of this polysaccharide to be the plasma membrane H^+-ATPase due to the inhibitory effect observed on the proton pumping and the catalytic activity of the enzyme. Chitosan was also shown to alter many other H^+-mediated processes (Amborabé *et al.* 2008). For example, the uptake of certain carbohydrate and amino-acids was altered because of their dependence on co-transporters involving an exchange with H^+. Similarly, the light-induced H^+/K^+-mediated turgor reaction was shown to be inhibited in *M. pudica* motor cells in response to the treatment with chitosan.

Modulation of Plant Responses and Signaling

Chitosan and derivatives are known to act as potent inducers, enhancing a battery of plant responses both locally around the infection sites and systemically to alert healthy parts of the plant. These include early signaling events as well as the accumulation of defense-related metabolites and proteins such as phytoalexins and PR-proteins (Reddy, et al., 1999 and El Hadrami, *et al.*, 2009). Modulation of plant responses using chitosan has been reported in many pathosystems involving various plant species and a diverse range of pathogens, including virus and viroids, bacteria, fungi, nematodes and other pests. This biopolymer was shown to be an effective inducer of phytoalexins synthesis and accumulation in various host cells and triggers callose formation, lignification responses, and the production of proteinase inhibitors (Pena-Cortes *et al.*, 1988; El Hadrami, *et al.*, 2010).

Effect on Nuclear Distortion and Cell Death

Chitosan induces programmed-cell death (PCD) and hypersensitive-associated responses in plants (Vasil, *et al.*, 2009). It induced chromatin condensation and marginalization followed by a destruction of the nuclei and subsequent inter-nucleosomal DNA fragmentation. It did not affect stomatal guard cells but affected epidermal cells. Anaerobic conditions prevented the chitosan-induced destruction of epidermal cells' nuclei. The antioxidants nitroblue tetrazolium or mannitol suppressed the effects of chitosan, H_2O_2, or chitosan + H_2O_2 on epidermal cells. Using a series of inhibitor assays, the same authors demonstrated that chitosan-induced epidermal cell death involves reactive oxygen species generated by the NADPH oxidase of the plasma membrane. For example, the alternative oxidase inhibitors propyl gallate and salicylhydroxamate prevented chitosan-induced destruction of epidermal cells nuclei; and the plasma membrane NADPH oxidase inhibitors diphenylene iodonium and quinacrine abolished chitosan-induced destruction of epidermal cells nuclei. The mitochondrial protein synthesis inhibitor lincomycin removed the destructive effect of chitosan on epidermal cells.

Activated Oxygen Species -Scavenging and Antioxidant Activity

In recent years, a growing attention has been directed towards the antioxidant activity of chitosan Xie, *et al.*, 2001 and Chen, *et al.*, 2009). Water-soluble chitosan was shown to be an excellent scavenger of hydroxyl radicals, H_2O_2 and anion superoxide. The 50% inhibition concentrations (IC_{50}) values ranged from 246 to 498 mg/mL (Xie, *et al.*, 2001) and most of the activity was attributed to the chitosan contents of hydroxylated amino- and other substituting groups. The scavenging rate increased with the applied concentrations of chitosan Xie, *et al.*, 2001. Sun *et al.* (2006) tested the antioxidant activity of several chitosan oligomers with various molecular weights and determined the IC_{50} of their scavenging ability against superoxide anion and hydroxyl radicals. The lowest scavenging abilities against superoxide anion and hydroxyl radicals were recorded with the oligomer having the highest tested molecular weight. Meanwhile, chitosan oligomers with lower molecular weight exhibited a better antioxidant activity. Chen *et al.* (2009) reported on the improvement of the antioxidant activity of chitosan for medical uses through grafting of essential oil component eugenol and carvacrol to the chitosan nanoparticles.

Wound-healing Accelerators

Because of their ability to adhere to biological membranes and other biomolecules and their positive changes, chitosan and derivatives are excellent supports for healing wounds produced upon mechanical injuries or pathogen attacks. Application of dressings made of chitin derivatives on injured tree-barks resulted in a faster wound healing (Hirano, *et al,* 1999). As a general elicitor, chitosan is also reported to activate the synthesis and accumulation of a series of PR-proteins and defense-related proteins among which phenylalanine ammonia-lyase and peroxidase. Given the involvement of these two enzymes in the synthesis and assembly of lignin matrix and in the formation of tylloses, chitosan seems to accelerate the process of wound healing.

CONCLUSION

Chitosan products can be used in a numbers of ways to reduce disease levels and prevent the development and spread of pathogen, thus preserving yield and quality. Interesting theoretical and applied findings were gathered in recent years and more are needed to examine the mechanisms governing the mode of action of these compounds by pathosystem, when applied at large scales. Chitosan exhibits a variety of antimicrobial activities against several plant pathogens which depend on the type of chitosan (native or modified), its degree of polymerization, the host, the chemical and/or nutrient composition of the substrates, and environmental conditions. The mechanism by which chitosan affects the growth of several pathogenic fungi has not been fully elucidated, but several hypotheses have been postulated. On the other hand, chitosan had different properties *i.e.* had inhibitory effect against pathogenic fungi and had ability to be potent elicitors of plant defense resistance.

Chitosan induce host defense responses in both monocotyledons and dicotyledons. These responses include lignification, cytoplasmic acidification, membrane depolarization and protein phosphorylation, chitinase and glucanase activation, phytoalexin biosynthesis, generation of reactive oxygen species), biosynthesis of jasmonic acid and the expression of unique early responsive and defense-related genes. Applications of chitosan for controlling plant diseases included seed coating, foliar treatment, soil amendment and fruit coating.

REFERENCES

Abd-El-Kareem, F. Abd-Alla, M.A., and El-Mohamedy R.S.R 2001. Induced Resistance in Potato Plants for Controlling Late Blight Disease Under Field Conditions. *Egypt. J. Phytopathol.* 29: (2) 29-41.

Abd-El-Kareem, F.; Abd-Alla, M.A. and El-Mohamedy R.S. 2002. Effect of Chitson on Postharvest Diseases of Lime Fruits. *Egypt.J. Phytopathol.* 30: 51-63.

Abd-El-Kareem, F. and Abd-Alla, M.A. 2002. Citral for Controllng Postharvest Diseases of Navel Orange Fruits. *Egypt. J. App.Sci.* 17: 238-256.

Abd-El-Kareem, F.; El-Mougy, Nehal, S.; El-Gamal, Nadia, G. and Fotouh,Y.O. 2006. Use of Chitin and Chitosan Against Tomato Root Rot Disease Under Greenhouse Conditions. *Research J. of Agricultural and Biological Science.* 2 (4) 164-169.

Abd-El-Kareem, F. and Haggag, W.M. 2014. Chitosan and Citral Alone or in Combination for Controlling Early Blight Disease of Potato Plants Under Field Conditions. Research Journal of Pharmaceutical, Biological and Chemical Sciences (Under Press).

Abd-El- Latif, F.M. 2010. Combination Between Citral and Chitosan for Controlling sour rot Disease of Lime Fruits. Research Journal of Agriculture and Biological Sciences, 6(6): 744-749.

Abdel-Latif, M. Faten and Haggag, Wafaa, M. (2002). Evaluation of Four Vasicular Arbuscular Mycorrhizae Fungi on Controlling Fusarium Root-Rot and Wilt Diseases of Some Legume" Egypt. J. Appl. Sci. 17(10): 524-543.

Ait Barka, A.; Eullaffroy, P.; Clément, C.; Vernet, G. 2004. Chitosan Improves Development, and Protects *Vitis vinifera* L. Against *Botrytis cinerea.* Plant Cell Rep., 22 pp. 608-614.

Allan, C.R. and Hadwiger, L.A. The Fungicidal Effect on Fungi of Varying Cell Wall Composition. Expt. Mycol., 3 (1979), pp. 285-287.

Amborabé, B.E.; Bonmort, J.; Fleurat-Lessard, P. and Roblin, G. 2008. Early Events Induced by Chitosan on Plant Cells. J Exp Bot. 59: 2317-2324.

Badawy, M.T.; Rabea, M.T.; Rogge, T.M.; Stevens, C.V. and Smagghe, G. 2003. Fungicidal and Insecticidal Activity of Chitosan Derivatives. *Polymer Bull.* 2005; 54: 279-289.

Badawy, M.T.; Rogge, T.M.; Stevens, C.V.; Höfte, M.; Steurbaut, W. and Smagghe, G. 2005. Insecticidal and Fungicidal Activity of New Synthesized Chitosan Derivatives. *Pest Manag Sci.* 2005; 61: 951-960.

Bautista-Baños, S.L.; Molina, M. and Luna, B. 2004. Evaluación del quitosano en el desarrollo de la pudrición blanda del tomate durante el almacenamiento Rev. Iberoamer. Tecnol. Postcosecha, 1: 63-67(c.f. El Hadrami, *et al.,* 2009)

Benhamou, B.; Lafontaine, P.G. and Nicole, M. 1994. Induction of Systemic Resistance to Fusarium Crown and Root Rot in Tomato Plants by Seed Treatment with Chitosan. Phytopathology, 84: 1432-1444.

Benhamou, N. and Thériault, G. 1992. Treatment with Chitosan Enhances Resistance of Tomato Plants to the Crown and Root Rot Pathogen *Fusarium oxysporum* f. sp. *radicis-lycopersici.* Physiol. Mol. Plant Pathol. 41: 33-52.

Ben-Shalom, N.; Ardi, R.; Pinto, R. and Fallik, F. 2003. Controlling Gray Mould Caused by *Botrytis cinerea* in Cucumber Plants by Means of Chitosan.Crop Prot., 22: 285-290.

Bornet, A. and Teissedre, P.L. 2007. Chitosan, Chitin-glucan and Chitin Effects on Minerals (Iron, Lead, Cadmium) and Organic (Ochratoxin A) Contaminants in Wines. Eur Food Res Technol. 226: 681-689.

Cheah, L.H. and Page, R.S. 1997. Chitosan Coating for Inhibition of Sclerotina Carrots. Crop Hort. Sci., 25: 89-92.

Chen, W.G.; Liu, X. and Chen, H.X. 2009. Preparation of Modified Chitosan with Quaternary Ammonium Salt. Textile Bioeng Infor Symp Proc. 1: 226-230.

Du, J.; Gemma, H and Iwahori, S. 1997. Effects of Chitosan Coating on the Storage of Peach, Japanese Pear and Kiwifruit. J. Jpn. Hort. Sci., 66: 15-22.

El Hadrami, A.; El Hadrami, I. and Daayf, F. 2009. Suppression of Induced Plant Defense Responses by Fungal Pathogens. In: Bouarab K, Brisson N, Daayf F, Editors. Molecular-Plant Microbe Interactions. Chapter 10. CABI; Wallingford, UK: 2009. pp. 231-268.

El Hadrami, A.; Adams, L.R.; El Hadrami, I. and Daayf, F. 2010. Chitosan in Plant Protection. *Mar. Drugs*, 8, 968-987; doi:10.3390/md8040968

El Ghaouth, A.; Arul, J.; Asselin, A. and Benhamou, N. 1992. Antifungal Activity of Chitosan on Post-harvest Pathogens: Induction of Morphological and Cytological Alterations in *Rhizopus stolonifer.* Mycol Res. 1992; 96: 769-779.

El Ghaouth, A.; Smilanick,. JL., and Wilson, C.L., 2000. Enhancement of the Performance of Candida Saitoana by the Addition of Glycolchitosan for the Control of Postharvest Decay of Apple and Citrus Fruit. Postharvest Biol Technol. 2000; 19: 103-110.

El- Ghaouth, A.; Arul, J.; Asselin, A.and Benhamou. N. 2002. Antifungal Activity of Chitosan on Post-harvest Pathogens: Induction of Morphological and Cytological Alterations in *Rhizopus stolonifer. Mycol Res.* 1992; 96: 769-779.

El-Mohamedy, R.S.; Abdel-Kader, M.M.; Abd-El-Kareem, F. and El-Mougym N.S. 2013. Inhibitory Effect of Antagonistic Bio-agents and Chitosan on the Growth of Tomato Root Rot Pathogens *In vitro. Journal of Agricultural Technology,* 9: 1521-1533.

El-Mohamedy, R. S,R. Abd-El-Kareem, F.; Khiareddine, H.J. and Daami-Remadi, M. 2014. Chitosan and *Trichoderma harzianum* as Fungicide Alternatives for Controlling Fusarium Crown and Root Rot of Romato. Tunisian Journal of Plant Protection 9: 31-43.

Elwagia, M.E.F. and Algam, S. 2014. Evaluation of Chitosan Efficacy on Tomato Growth and Control of Early Blight Disease. *Third Conference of Pests Management in Sudan February* 3-4, 2014, CPRC-ARC, Wad Medani (Sudan) Page 10.

Faoro, F.; Maffi, D.; Cantu, D. and Iriti, M. 2008. Chemical-induced Resistance Against Powdery Mildew in Barley: The Effects of Chitosan and Benzothiadiazole. Bio Control. 53: 387-401.

Guan, Y.J.; Hu, J.; Wang, X.J. and Shao, C.X. 2009. Seed Priming with Chitosan Improves Maize Germination and Seedling Growth in Relation to Physiological Changes Under Low Temperature Stress. J Zhejiang Univ Sci B. 2009; 10: 427-433.

Hirano, S.; Nakahira, T.; Nakagawa, M. and Kim, S.K. 1999. The Preparation and Applications of Functional Fibres from Crab Shell Chitin. J Biotechnol. 1999; 70: 373-377.

Kulikov, S.N.; Chirkov, S.N.; Lopatin, S. and Varlamov V.P. 2006. Effect of the Molecular Weight of Chitosan on its Antiviral Activity in Plants. *Prik Biokhim Mikrobiol.*; 42(2): 224-228.

Mahdy, A.M.M.; Abd-El-Mageed, M.H.; Abd-El-Latif, F.M.; Diab, M.M.M. and Saied, N.M. 2014. Induction of Resistance in Watermelon Plants Against Fusarium Wilt Disease Using Chemical Inducers Under Greenhouse Conditions. *Egypt. J.of Phytopathol.* (Under Press)

Mishra, S.; Jagadeesh, K.S.; Krishnaraj, P.U. and Prem, S. 2014. Biocontrol of Tomato Leaf Curl Virus in Tomato with Chitosan Supplemented Formulations of *Pseudomonas* sp. Under Field Conditions. *Australian Journal of Crop Science*, 8: 347-355.

Morsy, A.A; Abd-Alla,.M.A. and Abd-El-Kareem, F. 1999. Evaluation of Chitosean as Substitute of Fungicides for Postharvest Disease Control: Strawberry Decay. *Egypt J. Phytopathol:* 27: 109-116.

Muzarelli, R.A.A. 1990. Amphoteric Derivatives of Chitosan and Their Biological Significance In S.-B. Gudmund, A. Thorleif, S. Paul (Eds.), Chitin and Chitosan. Sources, Chemistry, Biochemistry. Physical Properties and Applications, Elsevier Applied Science, London and New York (1990), pp. 87-99.

Murphy, J.G.; Rafferty, S.M. and Cassells, A.C. 2000. Stimulation of Wild Strawberry (*Fragaria vesca*) Arbuscular Mycorrhizas by Addition of Shellfish Waste to the Growth Substrate: Interaction Between Mycorrhization, Substrate Amendment and Susceptibility to Red Core (*Phytophthora fragariae*) Appl Soil Ecol. 2000; 15: 153-158.

Palma-Guerrero, J.; Huang, I.C.; Jansson, H.B.; Salinas, J. ; Lopez, L.V. and Read, N.D. 2008. Effect of Chitosan on Hyphal Growth and Spore Germination of Plant Pathogenic and Biocontrol Fungi. *J. Appl Microbiol.* 104: 541-553.

Palma-Guerrero, J.; Huang, I.C.; Jansson, H.B.; Salinas, J. ; Lopez, L.V. and Read, N.D. 2009. Chitosan Permeabilizes the Plasma Membrane and Kills Cells of *Neurospora crassa* in an Energy Dependent Manner. Fungal Gen Biol. 46: 585-594.

Pena-Cortes, H.; Sanchez-Serrano, J. ; Rocha-Sosa, M. and Willmitzer, L.1988. Systemic Induction of Proteinase-inhibitor-II Gene Expression in Potato Plants by Wounding. Planta. 174: 84-89.

Rabea, M.T.; Rogge, T.M.; Stevens, C.V. and Smagghe, G.2005. Insecticidal and Fungicidal Activity of New Synthesized Chitosan Derivatives. *Pest Manag Sci.* 61: 951-960.

Reddy, M.V.; Arul, J.; Angers, P. and Couture, L.1999. Chitosan Treatment of Wheat Seeds Induces Resistance to *Fusarium graminearun* and Improves Seed Quality. J Agric Food Chem.47: 1208-1216.

Romanazzi, G.; Nigro, F. and Ippolito, A. 2003. Short Hypobaric Treatments Potentiate the Effect of Chitosan in Reducing Storage Decay of Sweet Cherries Postharvest Biol. Technol., 29: 73-80.

Ruan, S.L. and Xue, Q.Z. 2002. Effects of Chitosan Coating on Seed Germination and Salt-tolerance of Seedlings in Hybrid Rice (*Oryza sativa* L.) *Acta Agron Sinica.* 28: 803-808.

Sandford, P.1989. Chitosan: Commercial Uses and Potential Applications. In: G. Skjak-Braek, T. Anthosen, P. Standford (Eds.), Chitin and Chitosan. Sources, Chemistry, Biochemistry. Physical Properties and Applications, Elsevier Applied Science, London and New York (1989), pp. 51-69.

Sandford, P.A. and Hutchings, G.P. 1987. Chitosan—a Natural, Cationic Biopolymer: Commercial Applications. In: M. Yapalma (Ed.), Industrial Polysaccharides Genetic Engineering, Structure/ Property Relations and Applications, Elsevier Science Publishers B.V., Amsterdam, The Netherlands (1987), pp. 363-376.

Shao, C.X.; Hu, J.; Song, W.J. and Hu, W.M. 2005. Effects of Seed Priming with Chitosan Solutions of Different Acidity on Seed Germination and Physiological Characteristics of Maize Seedling. *J. Zhejiang Univ Agric Life Sci.* 1: 705-708.

Sudarshan, N.R.; Hoover, D.G. and Knorr, D.1992. Antibacterial Action of Chitosan. Food Biotechnol. 6: 257-272.

Sun, T.; Zhou, D.; Xie, J. and Mao, F. 2006. Preparation of Chitosan Oligomers and Their Antioxidant Activity. Chem Mater Sci.; 225: 3-4. 451-456.

Uppal, A.K.; El Hadrami, A.; Adam, L.R.; Tenuta, M. and Daayf, F. 2008. Biological Control of Potato Verticillium Wilt Under Controlled and Field Conditions Using Selected Bacterial Antagonists and Plant Extracts. *Biol Control.* 44: 90-100.

Vasil, L.A.; Dzyubinskaya, E.V.; Zinovkin, R.A.; Kiselevsky, D.B.; Lobysheva, N.V. and Samuilov, V.D. 2009. Chitosan-induced Programmed Cell Death in Plants. Biochem-Moscow. 74: 1035-1043.

Vasyukova, N.I.; Chalenko, G.I.; Gerasimova, N.G.; Perekhod, E.A.; Ozeretskovskaya, O.L. and Albulov, A.I. 2005 Chitin and Chitosan Derivatives as Elicitors of Potato Resistance to Late Blight. *Appl Biochem Microbiol.* 36: 372-376.

Xie, W.; Xu, P. and Liu, Q. 2001. Antioxidant Activity of Water-soluble Chitosan Derivatives. Bioorg Med Chem Lett. 11: 1699-1701.

Zhou, Y.G.; Yang, Y.D.; Zhang, Z.M.; Wang,X.J. and Hu, X.J. 2002. Effects of Chitosan on Some Physiological Activity in Germinating Seed of Peanut. *J Peanut Sci.* 31: 22-25.

Pages: 139-171

BIOTECHNOLOGY, AGRO-ECOLOGY AND ENVIRONMENT

Edited by: Dr. Avnish Chauhan; Dr. Pawan Kumar 'Bharti'

ISBN: 978-93-5056-757-9

Edition: 2015

Published by: Discovery Publishing House Pvt. Ltd., New Delhi (India)

7

Polytene Chromosome Analysis of *Lucilia Sericata Meigen* (Diptera: Calliphoridae)

Resham Bhalla

ABSTRACT

A polytene chromosome map is an invaluable tool for the genetic analysis and manipulation of any species because it allows the integration of physical and genetic maps. A complete polytene chromosome map of *Lucilia sericata Meigen* has been constructed. *Lucilia sericata Meigen* has a diploid number of 12 chromosomes ($2n = 12$): five pairs of autosomes and one pair of sex chromosomes (XX/XY), which do not polytenize. Pupal trichogen cells, which have chromosomes with a high degree of polytenization, were used to study the polytene chromosome map. The entire complement of these chromosomes has been divided into 48 zones, and zones are further sub-divided into regions, which are designated as A, B, C etc. A distinguished landmark represented by a swelling or a typical band is present at the beginning and end of each zone. Chromocentre is reported to be absent in the present species. Frequent asynaptic regions have been observed in various chromosomal arms. A few puffs have been observed in regions 14B, 15A and 16A of IIIR and 27C and 28B of VL chromosomal arm. These arms show puffing activity more than the

Department of Zoology, L.V.H. Arts, Science and Commerce College, Nashik - 422 003 (MS), India.

other arms. Various weak spots have been observed in arms VR, VIL and VIR in zones 31, 39, 40, 45 and 48 respectively. They act as additional landmarks for the identification of these arms.

Key words: Polytene Chromosomes, Mitotic Chromosomes, *Lucilia sericata Meigen* Diptera, Calliphoridae.

INTRODUCTION

A cytogenetic map is an invaluable tool for the genetic analysis and manipulation of any species, as it allows the integration of physical and genetic maps. The polytene chromosomes of Diptera have proved to be an especially favourable material because they allow for the identification of hundreds of bands in a single chromosome. Painter (1933) was the first to use them for preparing maps of *Drosophila* chromosomes using the squashing technique. In 1935, Bridges set up a system to assemble polytene chromosome maps. He divided the five main chromosome arms of *Drosophila melanogaster* into 100 divisions and two extra divisions for the small dot fourth chromosome. After successive revisions, he was able to distinguish a total of 2650 bands (Bridges, 1935, 1942; Zhimulev, 1996). Much of the work has already been done on the salivary gland chromosomes of Drosophila and mosquitoes. But, only little attention has been attributed to the dipteran flies.

The banding patterns of the salivary/polytene chromosomes of the Calliphorid flies have been rather poorly studied. These have been observed in the members like *Calliphora erythrocephala* (Bier, 1960 and Ribbert, 1967); *Calliphora stygia* (Thomson and Gunson, 1970); *Lucilia cuprina dorsalis* (Childress, 1969 and Foster et al., 1980); *Lucilia cuprina* (Sharma et al., 1976 and Kaur and Zope, 1983) and *Chrysomyia megacephala* (Handa et al., 1981). The above mentioned available literature reveals that the banding pattern of the polytene/salivary chromosomes of the flies of the family calliphoridae is very meager. Thus, the aim to deal with the present work on *Lucilia sericata* was a) To prepare a detailed standard map of the polytene chromosomes. b) To note the chromosomal homologies with other Calliphorid species viz., *L. Cuprina* R.D., *Chrysomyia megacephala* and *L. Cuprina dorsalis* R.D. This map has also been compared with the Polytene chromosome map of Musca domestica (family Muscidae).

MATERIAL AND METHODS

A metallic green fly, *Lucilia sericata Meigen* belonging to the tribe Luciliini of the subfamily Calliphoridae has been chosen for the present work. *Lucilia sericata* is a medium sized greenish to greenish bronze fly and measures 6 to 8 mm in size. The fly shows complete metamorphosis. The flies were reared under the laboratory conditions at temperature 27° C and a relative humidity of about 70-80%. Rearing was done as suggested by Kaur (1971 and 1975).

Method for Chromosomal Preparations: Pupal Thoracic Epidermal Chromosomes

Polytene chromosomal preparations were made from the trichogen cells associated with the macrochaetae of thoracic epidermis of the well developed 4th day old pupae.The temporary preparations were made permanent by the method suggested by Melander and Wingstrand (1953) and Bhaduri and Gosh (1954) but with slight modifications.

Mapping Technique: A complete polytene map from the trichogen cells of pupal thoracic epidermis consisting of 48 zones was obtained. Each chromosomal arm has been divided into zones and each zone is further divided into A to D regions. The designation for banding pattern has been adopted after Le Caluez (1953) but with slight modifications.

Mitotic chromosomes: Testes of the newly emerged young male files were used for the study of mitotic chromosomes because of the active cell division in the younger forms. The morphological classification was done by the method suggested by Levan *et al.* (1964) and Relative length, Arm ratio and Centromeric indices were calculated, using the formulae (Levan *et al.*, 1964 and Brown 1972). *Lucilia sericata Meigen* possesses a diploid number of 12 chromosomes as is revealed by the study of spermatogonial metaphases and metaphase I plates. Chromosomes at this stage are at their maximum state of condensation and staining capacity. The heterochromatic sex chromosomes constituting the pair I in other species, assume the shape of a big dot at metaphase I in this species. The smallest autosomal pair is represented by pair II and the largest is depicted by pair VI. Except pair V, which is submetacentric, rest of the pairs are metacentric in nature. The homologues of bivalents show a tendency to be close together or are completely synapsed. The morphometric analysis of 3 metaphase I plates is being presented is Table 7.1.

Table 7.1: Morphometrical Data of the Chromosomal Complement of *Lucilia sericata Meigen* from the Metaphase I Chromosomes (measurements in µ)

Chromosome	Absolute Length in µ m	Relative Length	Arm Ratio	Chromosome Type
Short arm IIL	1.58			
Long arm IIR	2.05	161.69	1.29	M
Total	**3.63**			
Short arm IIIL	1.91			
Long arm IIIR	2.05	176.39	1.07	M
Total	**3.96**			

(Table Contd...)

Short arm IVL	1.94			
Long arm IVR	2.11	180.40	1.09	M
Total	**4.05**			
Short arm VL	1.61			
Long arm VR	2.79	195.99	1.72	Sm
Total	**4.40**			
Short arm VIL	2.94			
Long arm VIR	3.47	285.52	1.18	M
Total	**6.41**			
Total II+VI	**22.45**			

According to Levan et al. (1964)

Polytene Karyotypes: The giant nuclei of the macrochaetae of pupal thoracic epidermal cells of *Lucilia sericata Meigen* contains five long polytene elements or ten chromosomal arms and designated as chromosomes II to VI according to their length in an ascending order. The characteristic free and centromeric ends of each of these chromosomal arms have a typical shape and banding pattern. Each arm has been divided into right (longer) and left (smaller) using centromere as a differentiating marker as in Table 7.2.

Table 7.2: Distribution of Zones to the Five Polytene Chromosomes

Chromosome No.	Zones	Free End in Zone	Centromeric End in Zone
IIL	1-4	1	4
IIR	5-8	8	5
IIIL	9-11	9	11
IIIR	12-16	16	12
IVL	17-20	17	20
IVR	21-25	25	21
VL	26-28	26	28
VR	29-35	35	29
VIL	36-41	36	41
VIR	42-48	48	42

Though the chromosomes held together by their centromeric ends are not always clear due to clumping of the arms. A chromocentre, if present, becomes disintegrated under the slightest pressure during squashing resulting in the separation of all chromosomal arms. VR chromosomal arm has been the longest one and VL the shortest. Each arm has been arbitrarily divided into zones and regions. In all the ten arms have been divided into 48 zones and each zone is further subdivided into regions like A, B, C etc. The details of the biometrical measurements of arms and the distribution of various zones on the respective arms have been summarized in Table 7.3.

Table 7.3: Morphometrical Details of the Polytene Chromosomes and the Distribution of the Zones in the Chromosomal Arms *Lucilia sericata Meigen*

Chromosome	Absolute Length in μm	Relative Length	Arm Ratio	Chromosome Type	Distribution of Zones
Short arm IIL	44.54				1-4
Long arm IIR	50.90	138.32	1.14	M	5-8
Total	**95.44**				
Short arm IIIL	48.18				9-11
Long arm IIIR	68.18	168.64	1.41	M	12-16
Total	**116.36**				
Short arm IVL	51.81				17-22
Long arm IVR	72.72	180.49	1.40	M	23-29
Total	**124.53**				
Short arm VL	41.81				30-32
Long arm VR	110.00	220.03	2.63	Sm	33-39
Total	**151.81**				
Short arm VIL	94.54				40-43
Long arm VIR	107.27	292.49	1.13	M	44-48
Total	**201.81**				
Total II+VI	**689.95**				

According to Levan et al. (1964)

The heterochromatic sex chromosomes have not been observed as polytenized banded elements. They appear as under replicated, small, unattached loosely organized mass of granular hetrochromatin. Generally, the various polytenized chromosomal arms are closely synapsed but region IC and 2A of IIL and of zone 22 of IVR are characteristically being involved in asynapsis and sometimes asynapsis starts at zone 25 and goes upto the centromeric end in chromosomal arm IVR. Sequential puffing activity has not been traced during the present studies but a few puffs have been observed in the chromosomal arms IIIR and VL. Location wise they are situated in regions 14B, 15A, 16B and 28B of the above said arms.

The diagnostically marked bands and swellings are constant in all arms but the light banded regions do show slight to great variations. The bands have been graded according to their staining intensity as light, moderately light, moderate, moderately dark and dark etc. The detailed banding pattern, characteristic free/centromeric ends, typical swellings and diagnostic features of the various arms form the excellent landmarks for the identification of each chromosomal arm. These have been described below.

Chromosome II: Length 95.44 μ; Zones 1 to 8, Figs. 7.1-7.9, 7.11

Diagnostic features: The metacentric chromosome II has typical free and centromeric ends. A diagnostic swelling of zone 2; a doublet of dark bands in zones 3A, 3B, 4B, 4C, 5B and 7A; triplets of regions 5A, 6B, 7A and 8A and a light dotted swellings of regions 5C and 7C are some of the peculiar landmarks of this chromosomal arm.

Chromosomal arm IIL: Length 44.54 μ; zones 1-4; Figs. 7.1-7.9, 7.11

Zone 1: The semiflared free end is indicated by three moderately dark dotted bands. A dark and a moderately light band mark the end of region 1A. A swelling in region 1B has three moderately dark bands preceded and followed by two light bands. The region 1C has a characteristic swelling which begins with a thin light dotted band followed by two moderately dark dotted bands. At the end of this region there are present two dark bands separated by a moderate dotted band and preceded by two light bands.

Zone 2: The region 2A has two dark bands in the centre which mark the end of the swelling of region 1C. These are preceded and followed by three moderately light dotted bands. A diagnostic swelling present in regions 2BC begins with a dark and a dark curved band which are separated by moderate and light dotted bands. A doublet of moderately dark dotted bands is preceded by a light dotted and followed by two light dotted bands in region 2B. Two moderate dotted bands are separated by two light dotted bands in region 2C. A moderately dark curved dotted band marks the end of zone 2 in region 2C.

Zone 3: A dark band and a dark doublet are separated by two light dotted bands in the beginning of region 3A. A moderated dotted band and a moderate dotted doublet mark the end of the region 3A. Two dark doublets each followed by a dark band and separated by a light band mark the region 3B. Two light dotted bands are present in the beginning of region 3B whereas two moderately light dotted bands present in a small swelling mark the end of zone 3 in 3B.

Zone 4: A moderate band present in the beginning of region 4A is followed by a series of four doublets, of which the one which is present in the beginning is light. Moderately dark dotted, moderately dotted and the last one which is present at the end of region 4A is prominently dark dotted. A light dotted and moderate bands are followed by a light dotted and a moderately dotted band in region 4B. The end of this region is marked by a dark doublet which is followed by a moderate dotted doublet. The centromeric end of the chromosomal arm IIL lies in region 4C and is prominent in having a moderate dotted doublet and two dark doublets separated by a light dotted band towards the end of this region.

Chromosomal arm IIR: Length 50.90 μ; Zones 5-8; Figs. 7.1-7.9, 7.11

Zone 5: The typical centromeric end of this chromosomal arm lies in the zone 5. This is marked by the presence of three light bands in the beginning of the region 5A. Three moderately dark dotted bands are followed by a light dotted and a curved moderate band at the end of region 5A. Two light bands followed by a dark doublet mark the beginning of region 5B. Three moderately dark dotted bands are preceded by three very light bands in region 5B. Two dark doublets separated by a dotted band are preceded by a typical small swelling having three to four light dotted bands in region 5C.

Zone 6: A dark doublet preceded by two light dotted bands is followed by two light bands in region 6A. A series of three dark bands are present in the beginning of the region 6B. The swelling of this region begins with a doublet of moderately dark bands which is followed by a very light band. A moderately dark dotted band marks the end of this region. Region 6C begins with a doublet of moderately dark bands which actually constitute the end of the swelling of region 6B in 6C. In the centre of region 6C there is present a dark doublet which is preceded by a light band and followed by a moderately dark dotted band.

Zone 7: Region 7A begins and ends with the doublets of dark bands. Two moderately dark dotted bands are separated by a thin dark and a light band. Two moderate bands mark the beginning of the two swellings of regions 7B and 7C. In the first half of region 7B there is present a very light band which is followed by a curved moderately light dotted and a light dotted band. The centre is marked by a curved moderately dark band and a very thin curved light band. Two light dotted bands mark the end of region 7B. A thin light band separates the swellings of 7B and 7C. In region 7C a prominent moderately light dotted band present in the centre of the swelling is preceded by two slightly curved light dotted bands and is followed by a light dotted band. A broad moderately dark and a dark band, separated by a moderately light band, mark the end of region 7C.

Zone 8: Two doublets one of light bands and another of dark bands is preceded by a light dotted band and followed by a moderately dark dotted band in region 8A. The end of this region bears a moderate band. A swelling having three light dotted bands is present in region 8B. The end of this region is marked by a moderate band which is followed by a light dotted band. A series of three light bands are present at the beginning of region 8C. A doublet of dark bands present in the constriction is preceded by a light dotted band. The semiflared free end of chromosomal arm IIR is typical in having two moderately light bands.

Chromosome III R: Length 116.36 μ; Zones 9-16; Figs. 7.1-7.9

Diagnostic features: The metacentric chromosome III can be easily recognized by its typical semiflared free and centromeric ends. The two dark doublets in regions 9A, 10D, 11C, 14B and 15C; triplets of regions 9C and 12C; the swellings in regions 9C, 11A, 11D, 12B, 13B, 14A, 15A and 16A are very characteristic. A dark band in regions 10A, 15A, 15C, 16B and 16C; a dark doublet in regions 10C, 10D; an extensively broad dark doublet in regions 15B and 16C; two dark dotted bands in regions 10A, 10B, 12B, 15A and 16A; a series of three dark bands in regions 13C, 14A and 16B are very prominent identifying landmarks of this chromosome. Puffs have been observed in regions 14B, 15A and 16A.

Chromosomal arm III L: Length 48.18 μ; Zones 9-11; Figs. 7.1-7.9

Zone 9: The semiflared free end of the chromosomal arm IIIL in region 9A has two dark doublets which are preceded by two light dotted bands and separated by a light dotted band. A dark dotted band marks the end of region 9A. Region 9B bears a swelling of alternating light and moderate dark bands. A doublet of dark bands marks the end of the region 9B and in turn represents the beginning of the swelling of region 9C. In the centre of the swelling in region 9C there is present a dark doublet which is preceded by a very light dotted and a light band is followed by a moderately dark dotted band. The end of the swelling in region 9C possesses a moderate dark doublet and a dark doublet which are separated by a very thin light band and preceded by a thin moderate dotted band.

Zone 10: A conspicuous swelling in region 10A bears at the beginning a series of three light dotted bands. Two moderately dark dotted bands are typical of this swelling and are preceded by a moderately dark curved band and followed by a very thin light band. At the end there is present a moderate dark dotted band. The swelling in region 10B begins with a moderate band and ends with a light band. A curved doublet of dark bands and two dark dotted bands are present in the centre of the swelling of region 10B. Two thick dark bands are present in the constriction and represent the beginning of region 10C. Two dark moderate bands marking the end of region 10C are preceded by a thin light band and a moderately dark dotted band. In region 10D two dark doublets present towards the end are preceded by a thick moderate band.

Zone 11: A moderately dark dotted band followed by a slightly curved light band and a thin dark band mark the beginning of region 11A. A doublet of dark bands in the centre of the swelling is preceded and followed by a moderately dark dotted band. A light dotted band marks the end of region 11A. Two thick light bands followed by a moderately light band are present towards the end of the swelling of region 11A in region 11B. A light band preceded by two slightly curved light dotted bands marks the end of the region 11B. A moderately dark dotted band is present in the beginning of region 11C. Two dark doublets, separated by two dark dotted bands, are present in the region 11C. Region 11D marks the pot-like centromeric end of this chromosomal arm. A moderately dark dotted band is followed by a series of three light bands which form the substance of the characteristic swelling. A dark doublet is present in the constriction. A dark band present at the end of this region is preceded by a light band and followed by a moderately light dotted band.

Chromosomal arm IIIR: Length 68.18 μ; Zones 12-16; Figs. 7.1-7.9, 7.12

Zone 12: The typical semiflared centromeric end in region 12A has two thick dark dotted bands followed by two light dotted bands. Two dark bands present in the constriction mark the beginning of swelling of region 12B. The region 12A ends with a moderately dark dotted band. Two dark dotted bands lying in the centre of the swelling of region 12B are preceded by a light dotted and a light band. Two slightly curved light dotted bands mark the end of region 12B. A series of three dark bands present towards the end of the swelling of region 12B marks the beginning of region 12C. Two dark doublets separated by a dark dotted band mark the end of region 12C and the beginning of the swelling of region 13A.

Zone 13: On either side of the doublet of moderately light dotted bands there is present a light dotted band in region 13A. Two dark bands preceded by a light band mark the end of region 13A. A moderate dark band separates the two small swellings in region 13B. It is preceded and followed by two light dotted bands. In the centre of a small globular swelling there is present a prominent moderately dark dotted band which is followed by a light dotted band and marks the end of region 13B. In region 13C two dark doublets are separated by two moderately light bands and a dark band. The region 13D begins with a light doublet. A doublet of moderate bands and a light band marks the end of region 13D.

Zone 14: A dark doublet marks the beginning of region 14A. A small typical swelling of region 14A has two dark curved bands on either side which are separated by two light dotted bands in the centre. A light band marks the end of region 14A. Two dark doublets mark the beginning of a small swelling of region 14B. A doublet of light bands has a light dotted band on either side. A series of three moderately light bands followed by a light dotted band marks the end of region 14B.

Zone 15: The characteristic swelling of region 15A begins with two dark dotted bands. A very thick dark band is present in the centre of the prominent swelling. Two light bands are separated by a moderately dark dotted band at the end of region 15A. A extensively dark doublet present at the end of the swelling is the characteristic feature of the region 15B in this chromosomal arm. A moderately dark dotted band and a moderate dark band are preceded by two light dotted bands at the end of region 15B. A slightly curved light dotted band is followed by a light band are present in the beginning of the region 15C. A moderately dark dotted band and a light dotted band are separated by a dark band. The end of thin region bears two dark doublets.

Zone 16: A doublet of dark dotted bands has a light dotted band on either side in region 16A. The end of this region is characterized by two thin moderately dark dotted bands. The swelling in region 16B possesses a dark band followed by a light and a light dotted band. Three moderately dark bands in the centre are followed by a series of three light dotted bands present in a constriction. A dark band marks the end of the region 16B. The characteristic flared free end in region 16C has a doublet of thick dark bands which is preceded by two thin light bands and is followed by two moderately light dotted bands.

Chromosome IV: Length 124.53 μ; Zones 17-25; Figs. 7.1-7.10

Diagnostic features: Chromosome IV is metacentric. An excellent diagnostic region in this chromosome has a prominent broad dark doublet in region 18B and 24A. A typical light banded swelling is present in regions 17A, 17B. 19A, 19C, 20A, 22A, 23A and 24C. A broad dark band in region 17C; a dark doublet each in regions 18A, 18B, 19B, 19C, 20B, 20C, 21A, 21C, 22A and 24A are very characteristic. A triplet of moderately dark bands each in regions 19B, 21B and of light bands in 25A can be easily traced. A series of four moderately dark bands in regions 21C, 24B; two dark doublets in regions 18C, 21A, 23B, 24B and 25A are some of the major landmarks for the easy identification of this chromosome.

Choromosomal arm IVL: Length 51.81 μ; Zones 17-20; Figs. 7.1-7.10

Zone 17: The typical free end in region 17A has a series of four moderately dark dotted bands. A moderately dark doublet marks the end of region 17A. The region 17B has a rounded swelling which begins with a series of five light dotted bands. Two dark doublets separated by a light dotted band in the constriction mark the end of region 17B. A prominent dark thick band is present in the middle of a small swelling of region 17C which is preceded by two light dotted bands and followed by a light dotted band.

Zone 18: The region 18A begins with two dark bands. A moderately light dotted band separated by a moderate band marks the end of region 18A. The typical identifying mark of this arm has a doublet of thick dark bands, present in the centre of a swelling in region 18B. A dark dotted band is preceded by a light dotted and followed by a light band. A doublet of dark bands followed by a light and a dark band mark the end of this region. A light dotted band followed by a light band marks the beginning of region 18C. A series of four dark bands are present in a small swelling of region 18C.

Zone 19: A series of three moderately light dotted bands followed by a moderate and a dotted band marks the region 19A. A very prominent lightly staining swelling of this chromosomal arm lies in two regions 19B and C. A dark doublet is followed by a doublet of moderately dark bands in region 19B. A curved moderate band followed by a moderately dark thin dotted band marks the end of region 19B. The region 19C begins with two bands of moderately dark dotted nature which are followed by a light band. A series of three curved light dotted bands are followed by two moderately dark dotted bands. A doublet of dark bands marks the end of typical swelling. The end of this region is marked by a light dotted and a thin moderately dark band.

Zone 20: A small lightly staining swelling of region 20A precedes the centromeric end of chromosomal arm. It begins with a doublet of moderately dark bands which are followed by a doublet of light bands and a doublet of moderately dark dotted bands. The end of this region is represented by a light dotted and a light band. In region 20B two doublets, one of dark bands and other of moderately dark bands are followed by a light dotted band. The region 20C begins with a doublet of dark bands. A moderate band and a moderate dotted band precede the moderate doublet which is present at the end of the typical centromeric end of the chromosomal arm IVL.

Chromosomal arm IVR: Length 72.72 μ; Zones 21-25; Figs. 7.1-7.10, 7.13

Zone 21: Region 21A represents the centromeric end of this chromosomal arm and begins with a light band followed by a doublet of moderately dark dotted bands. Two dark doublets separated by a light dotted band mark the end of region 21A. The swelling in region 21B begins with a doublet of light dotted bands followed by a triplet of moderate bands. The end of this region is characterized by the presence of light band followed by a doublet of light dotted bands. A series of four moderate bands followed by a doublet of dark bands are characteristic of the region 21C.

Zone 22: A series of four light dotted bands are present in a small rounded swelling of region 22A. A doublet of dark bands is present at the end. A prominent swelling in region 22B begins with a doublet of light dotted bands followed by an interrupted moderate dark band. A series of four alternating moderately dark dotted and light dotted bands are present in the other half of the typical swelling of region 22B. Two moderate dark doublets separated by a dark dotted band and followed by a dark band mark the region 22C.

Zone 23 : A very thin light band is present in the beginning of a small swelling in region 23A. A prominent dark dotted band present in the centre of a small swelling has a light dotted band on either side in region 23A. Region 23B begins with a light band which is followed by a doublet of dark bands and a light dotted band. A doublet of dark dotted bands is present in the centre of a swelling is followed by a moderate dark and a light band. A doublet of dark bands is present at the end of the region 23B. A dark band is preceded by a moderate and a light band in region 23C. Two light dotted bands are present at the end of the region 23C.

Zone 24: Beginning of region 24A possesses a doublet of dark bands followed by a doublet of light bands. A doublet of very prominent dark bands is present in the centre of the swelling of region 24A and is followed by an interrupted light band and two light dotted bands. A thick moderately dark band is present in the beginning of region 24B and it is followed by a dark band and a light dotted band. A curved doublet of dark bands followed by two light dotted bands is present towards the beginning of this region. A series of four moderate bands mark the end of the region 24B. A dark doublet is found in the beginning of swelling in region 24C. A dark prominent dotted band lying in the centre of the lightly staining swelling has two light dotted bands on either side in region 24C.

Zone 25: A series of two dark doublets followed by a triplet of light bands and a dark band are the characteristic bands of the region 25A. A light dotted band marks the end of this region. Region 25B begins with a light band. A prominent dark dotted band is preceded by a dark band. A doublet of light bands is followed by a doublet of dark bands. The end of region 25B is represented by two dark dotted bands which are preceded by a light dotted band. A light dotted band is represented in the beginning of region 25C and is followed by a light band and a light dotted band. A moderate band present in the constriction is followed by a light band. The free end of this chromosomal arm is represented by the presence of a doublet of moderate bands followed by a very thin light band in region 25C.

Chromosome V: Length 151.81 μ; Zones 26-35; Figs. 7.1-7.9, 7.14

Diagnostic features: Submetacentric chromosome V is unique in the sense that the chromosomal arm VL is the smallest while VR is the longest one. A lightly stained typical free end of VL is present in region 26A. A prominent broad dark dotted band in region 29A forms the typical centromeric end of chromosome VR. A prominent dark dotted band each in regions 27B, 28B, 33A and 34C; a dark doublet each in regions 26B, 27B, 28C, 31A, 32A, 33C, 34A, 35C and D; two dark doublets in regions 26C and 33B are some of the diagnostic landmarks of this chromosome. A series of four moderate bands in the constriction in 27C and 32A; of five moderate dark bands in 30B; triplets of moderate and light bands in 28A and 34B respectively are characteristic features of this chromosome. Two dark dotted bands in regions 28A, 32B and 33C are the characteristic landmarks of the chromosome V. A weak spot present between the dividing line of zone 30 and 31 is another landmark for its identification. The typical free end followed by the dark doublets at intervals in zone 35 is the unique feature of this chromosome.

Chromosomal arm VL: Length 41.81 μ; Zones 26-28; Figs. 7.1-7.10

Zone 26: The lightly stained typical free end bears three light dotted bands followed by slightly curved dark band. Two slightly curved doublets of moderately light dotted bands present in the swelling mark the region 26A. Region 26B begins with a doublet of dark bands which is followed by a curved dark band. A small rounded swelling of this region contains a series of four light dotted bands. A curved dark band at the end of this region is preceded and followed by a light band. A curved dark doublet and a moderately dark doublet are separated by a dark dotted band mark the beginning of region 26C. At the end of this region there are present two light bands which are followed by a moderately dotted and a moderate band.

Zone 27: Two light bands mark the beginning of region 27A. Two moderate dotted bands, present in the centre of swelling are followed by a light band in region 27A. Region 27B begins with a moderately dark doublet and ends in a thick dark doublet. A prominent dark dotted and a light dotted band are present in the centre of this region. The swelling in region 27C possesses a curved light band which is followed by two moderate dotted bands. A series of four moderate bands are preceded by two dark dotted bands in region 27C.

Zone 28: A strikingly characteristic swelling of region 28A bears a series of three doublets of dark dotted, moderately dark dotted and of dark dotted bands. A set of three dark bands present in the constriction mark the end of this region. A prominently rounded swelling of region 28B contains light dotted, moderate dotted and dark dotted bands. A doublet of light bands is situated at the end of region 28B. The characteristic tubular centromeric end is easily recognized by the presence of a doublet of dark bands followed by a light dotted and a light band in region 28C. Two doublets, one of moderately dark and other of dark bands separated by a dark dotted and a light band characterize the typical end of the region 28C of this chromosomal arm.

Chromosomal arm VR: Length 110.00 μ; Zones 29-35; Figs. 7.1-7.10

Zone 29: The typical semiflared lightly stained centromeric end in region 29A is marked by the presence of a moderate dotted band. Two light bands are present on the either side of a moderate band. The end of this region bears a moderately light dotted band lying almost in the centre of a swelling which is followed by a light dotted band. A moderate doublet, each present in the constriction of a small swelling of region 29B are separated by light and dotted bands. Region 29C begins with a curved light and a thick light dotted band. Two moderately dark dotted bands mark the region of a rounded swelling. The end is recognized by a curved moderate band.

Zone 30: A dark doublet lying in the constriction is followed by a doublet of moderately dark bands and they are present in the beginning of region 30A. Two doublets, of thin moderately dotted bands and of thick moderately dark dotted bands are present in the centre of region 30A. A light curved band marks the end of region 30A. A series of five moderate bands in the constriction is followed by a light dotted band in region 30B. The centre of swelling in region 30C is marked by two moderately dark dotted bands followed by a series of three light dotted bands. The end of region 30C bears a doublet of light bands.

Zone 31: A conspicuous swelling is present in the region 31AB. It bears a dark doublet in the constriction which is followed by two light bands and a prominent dark curved band. A moderately dark dotted band followed by two light dotted bands marks the end of region 31A. The region 31B is marked by the presence of three moderately light bands. Two doublets of moderately dark bands separated by a light band mark the beginning of region 31C. Two dark bands, each preceded by a light dotted band mark the end of region 31C.

Zone 32: A characteristically rounded swelling is present in the region 32A which possesses two dark dotted bands and followed by a curved light band. The end of this swelling is marked by the doublet of dark bands which is followed by a series of four moderate bands. The region 32B has two moderate and two dark dotted bands. Its end is marked by a light dotted band. The beginning of region 32C has a doublet of light bands. Two moderate bands present in the constriction are separated by a doublet of dark bands. A light band marks the end of region 32C. Two prominent doublets formed by alternating moderately dark and dark band mark the beginning of region 32D. A moderately dark dotted band and a moderately dark band are separated by a light band in region 32D.

Zone 33: A dark curved band marks the beginning of region 33A. Three curved light dotted bands are followed by a prominent dark dotted band which is present in the middle of swelling. A light dotted band marks the end of region 33A. A curved moderately dark band is present in the beginning of the region 33B. Two dark doublets separated by a light band are followed by a moderately dark dotted band. The end of region 33B has a doublet of moderately light bands. Region 33C has a moderate band and a doublet of broad dark bands in the beginning. The middle of the swelling possesses a doublet of dark dotted bands. A light dotted and a dark dotted doublet mark the end of region 33C.

Zone 34: Region 34A begins with an interrupted light band followed by a doublet of dark bands. Two thin light bands are present at the end of region 34A. A light dotted band is preceded by a doublet of moderately dark bands and followed by a dark band. A triplet of light bands is present in the centre of a small swelling which is followed by a moderately dark band at the end of region 34B. Region 34C begins with a light dotted band which is followed by a moderately dark band and a moderate dotted band.

A prominent dark dotted band is preceded by a light dotted and followed by a moderately light and moderately dark dotted band. At the end of this region a doublet of moderately dark curved bands are present which is followed by a thin light band.

Zone 35: A moderately dark band is present at the beginning of the swelling in region 35A which is followed by a very thin light band. A doublet of moderately dark bands followed by a dark dotted and a moderately dark band are present in the centre of this region. The end of region 35A bears two light dotted bands. In the constriction two dark bands separated by a dark dotted band indicate the beginning of a small swelling of region 35B. These are followed by a curved doublet of light bands. The end of this region has a light dotted and a light band. In region 35C two dark doublets are separated by a doublet of light bands. The end of this region possesses a single light band. The typically flared free end of this chromosomal arm is peculiar in having a doublet of dark bands at the beginning of region 35D which is followed by a light dotted band. A doublet of moderately light bands is followed by the presence of three moderately dark dotted bands.

Chromosome VI: Length 201.81 μ; Zones 37-48; Figs. 7.1-7.6, 7.9, 7.15, 7.17

Diagnostic features: The metacentric chromosome VI has a large number of typical swellings showing characteristic banding patterns in zones 36, 39, 41, 42, 44 and 47. Two lightly stained diagnostic swellings are present in regions 38C and 38D. Very characteristic free and centromeric ends are present in this chromosome. Four prominent weak spots in this chromosome are situated in zones 39, 40, 45 and 48 have been marked by arrows in Figs. 7.1 and 7.2. Very prominent dark interrupted doublet in region 41A and extensively dark doublets in regions 45B and 47B are identifying landmarks of this chromosome. Excepting the ends the rest of the chromosomal arm VIL generally shows overstretching and deformed areas in the regions of the swellings.

Chromosomal arm VIL : Length 94.54 μ; Zones 36-41, Figs. 7.1-7.3, 7.9, 7.15, 7.17

Zone 36: The broad free end of the chromosomal arm VIL in region 36A consists of two dark dotted bands which are followed by two thin light dotted bands. The constriction is formed by a dark doublet. The end of region 36A has two light dotted bands. The beginning of region 36B has a dark doublet which is preceded by a thin light and a dark band and followed by a thick dark dotted band. Towards the end a moderately dark and a dark doublet are preceded by a thin light dotted band. The swelling in the region 36C possesses a curved dark doublet which is followed by a light dotted band and a doublet of light bands. Two doublets of dark dotted bands are present in the centre of the swelling. A doublet of light bands and moderate band mark the end of zone 36 in region 36C.

Zone 37: A strikingly light banded swelling of region 37A is one of the diagnostic swelling which helps in easy identification of this arm. Three bands of light dotted intensity are present on either side of a prominently dark dotted band. The end of region 37A has a series of three light bands which precede two dark dotted bands. Two dark doublets present at the beginning and end respectively are separated by a series of three light dotted bands in region 37B. A very light swelling of region 37C consists of four bands of light dotted nature. The end of this region is represented by a dark band.

Zone 38: In region 38A a small swelling is present which has four moderately dark dotted bands. A broad dark doublet is present at the end of region 38A. In regions 38B a doublet of dark bands is preceded by a moderate dotted band. A doublet of dark dotted bands is followed by three moderately light dotted bands towards the end of region 38B. Two conspicuous very light swellings are present in region 38CD. Three dark bands are present in the beginning of region 38C. A series of four light dotted bands are present in the substance of the swelling. The end of 38C has two curved light bands. Four bands of light dotted intensity are present in the rounded swelling of region 38D. The end is marked by a curved doublet of moderately dark bands and preceded by a curved moderately dark dotted band and followed by a broad dark dotted band.

Zone 39: The region 39A has a doublet of moderately light dotted bands. In the middle of the swelling a moderate light band is preceded by a moderately dark dotted band and followed by a moderate dark band. A moderate dark dotted band is present at the end of region 39A. Two dark doublets in the small swelling of region 39B are separated by a moderately dark dotted and a moderately light dotted band. At the end a thick dark band is present in the constriction. This also marks one of the weak spots where this arm generally shows a break. A prominent swelling in region 39C has a dark doublet at the beginning which is preceded by a moderately dark dotted band. The large swelling consists of a series of five curved light dotted bands. The end is marked by a dark band preceded by a doublet of curved dark dotted bands and followed by a light band.

Zone 40: Two moderately dark dotted bands mark the beginning of 40A. A set of four alternating moderate light and moderately dark bands are present in the centre of region 40A. Two bands of moderately light dotted nature, present in a small swelling, mark the end of the region 40A. Region 40B begins with a light band which is followed by a doublet of dark bands and a moderate dark dotted doublet. The end of region 40B consists of a moderate dotted band preceded by a moderate band. In the beginning of region 40C a moderate light dotted band is followed by a moderately dark dotted band, present in the centre of the swelling, is followed by a doublet of moderately light dotted bands. A broad dark band, present in the beginning of region 40D marks the place where the other weak spot is present. This is followed by a curved dark band and a doublet of light dotted bands. A dark doublet is followed by a doublet of moderately dark dotted bands and a thin dotted band in region 40D.

Zone 41: A doublet of dark bands marks the beginning of a swelling in region 41A. Two prominently thick dark interrupted bands are preceded by a moderately dark broad band. The end of region 41A possesses two dark dotted bands. The region 41B begins with a dark moderately band and two dark dotted bands. The other end of this swelling possesses a series of three very light bands. The end of region 41B is marked by the presence of a thin dark band which is preceded by a dark dotted band. The distinctive character of centromeric end of this arm is marked by the presence of two doublets, each of moderately dark intensity, which are separated by a moderately light band in region 41C. A series of three light dotted bands lie in the middle of the swelling. A doublet of interrupted dark bands preceded by a doublet of curved moderately dark bands mark the centromeric end of VIL in region 41C.

Chromosomal arm VIR: Length 107.27 μ; Zones 42-48; Figs. 7.1-7.6, 7.9, 7.15

Zone 42: The typical swelling at the centromeric end of this arm in region 42A is characterized by a triplet of dark bands followed by a light dotted band. The middle of the swelling consists of a moderately dark dotted and a prominently dark dotted band. The end of this region contains a broad dark band. A typical swelling is present in the region 42BC. A series of three moderately dark dotted bands is present at the beginning of region 42B which is followed by a doublet of light bands. Two doublets of light dotted bands are present in the swelling of regions 42BC. A prominent doublet of moderately dark curved dotted bands is present in region 42C. A dark band preceded by a moderately light band mark the end of region 42C.

Zone 43: Region 43A begins with a thin dark dotted band follow by two moderate dotted and two light bands. A doublet of moderate bands and a moderate light dotted band mark the end of swelling in region 43A. Three dark bands separated by two thin dark dotted bands constituting the beginning of region 43B. A light doublet preceded by a moderate band is followed by a curved dark band and a light band in region 43B. The region 43C begins with a curved dark doublet which is followed by a doublet of light dotted bands and a thin moderately dark dotted band. Two dark doublets separated by a thick dark dotted band mark the end of region 43C.

Zone 44: The region 44A contains a doublet of light bands and a light dotted band in the constriction present in the beginning of the region. A moderately dotted doublet is followed by a moderately light band. The region 44B possesses a dark doublet in the centre which is preceded by two light dotted bands. Two dark dotted bands separated by a moderate band are present in region 44B. The end of this region is represented by the presence of a dark band followed by a doublet of moderately light bands. Two light dotted bands are followed a thin, interrupted light band in region 44C. Two light dotted bands separated by a moderately dark band constitute the end of region 44C. The region 44DE is peculiar in banding pattern, and forms one of the identifying marks of this arm. In region 44D a doublet of dark dotted bands is present in the beginning. A series of three light dotted bands and successively a series of three dark dotted bands constitute the end of region 44D. The region 44E is peculiar in having two doublets of dark bands and a dark band, each one of these are followed by a light dotted band. This also marks the weak spot of this arm.

Zone 45: The region 45A is identified by the presence of a moderate dotted doublet which is followed by a moderate doublet. The region 45B begins with a light dotted band and is followed by a moderately light band. The two dark doublets separated by a doublet of light bands constituting the end of region 45B. Region 45C begins with a light doublet which is followed by a curved dark and a dark dotted band. The end of this region is marked by a doublet of dark bands which is preceded by a light dotted doublet.

Zone 46: The region 46A is tubular and has two light dotted bands in the beginning which are followed by two doublets of moderately light and a doublet of light dotted bands. A dark dotted doublet and a dotted band of moderate intensity are followed by a dark doublet, present in the constriction in region 46A. The region 46B has a globular swelling with a dark doublet in the beginning of region 46B. This is followed by a doublet of light bands and two moderately dark dotted bands. The end of this region possesses a thick dark band.

Zone 47: A very prominent swelling is present in zone 47. It begins with a thick light band which is followed by a doublet of moderately dark bands. Two dark dotted bands are present on either side of a dark doublet. The end of the region 47A is characterized by a light doublet. An extensively thick doublet of dark bands is preceded by a light dotted and a dark dotted band in region 47B. The region 47C has a triplet of dark bands preceded by a moderately dark dotted band and is followed by a very thin light dotted band. A dark band followed by a light dotted band mark the end of region 47C and also the other weak spot of this arm.

Zone 48: The region 48 has a series of three light dotted bands in the beginning which is followed by a doublet of moderately dark dotted bands. The two thick dark bands separating the region 48A from 48B are separated by a light dotted band. In region 48B, a dark band is preceded by a doublet of light bands. A series of moderately dark dotted, light dotted, a dark dotted and a light dotted band is present in the swelling of region 48B. The end of this region bears a doublet of dark bands. The region 48C has a moderately light band followed by a curved doublet of dark bands in the beginning of the small rounded swelling. A doublet of moderately dark dotted bands is followed by a series of three light dotted bands in region 48C. The region 48D is the typical free end of this arm and possesses a thin moderate band which is followed by a doublet of light dotted bands. The end is strikingly characterized by two moderated dark dotted bands preceded by a doublet of dark bands.

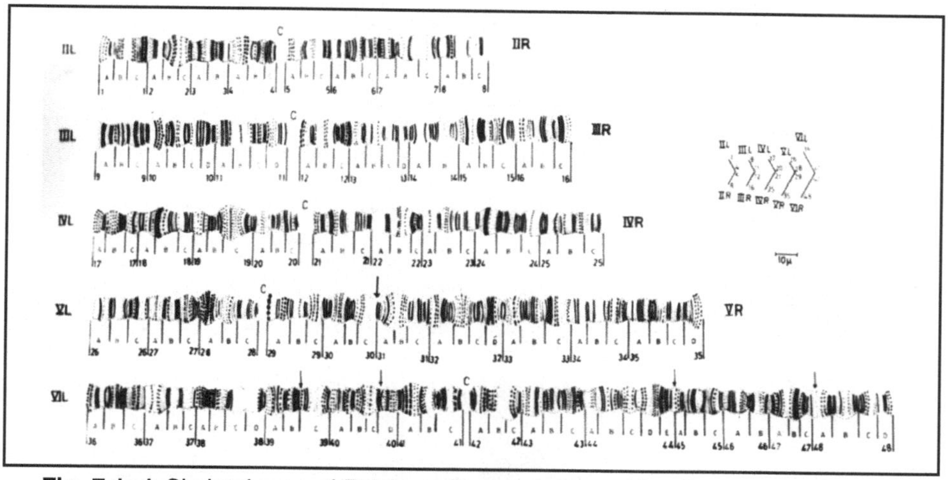

Fig. 7.1: A Skeletal map of Polytene Chromosomes of Lucilia sericata Meigen

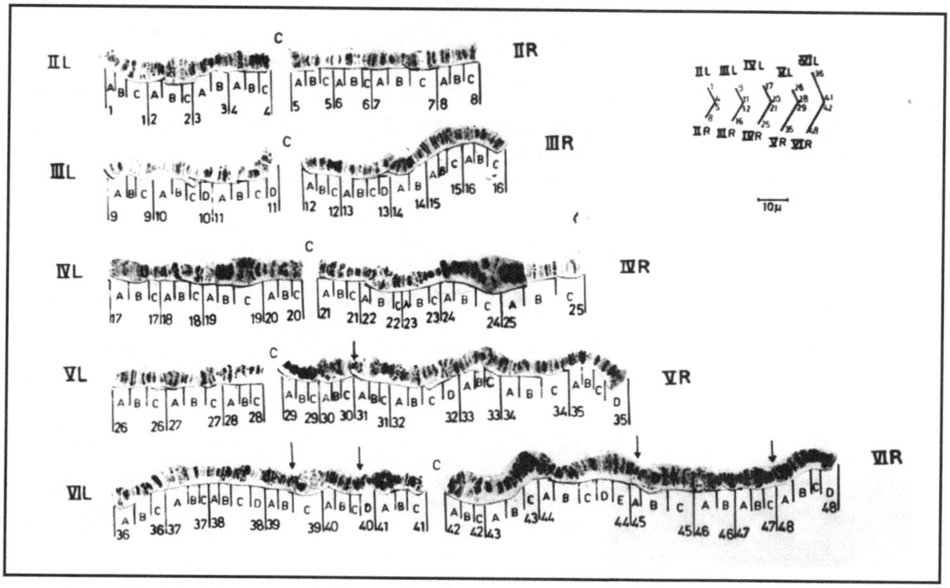

Fig. 7.2: A Photomap of Polytene Chromosomes of *Lucilia sericata Meigen*

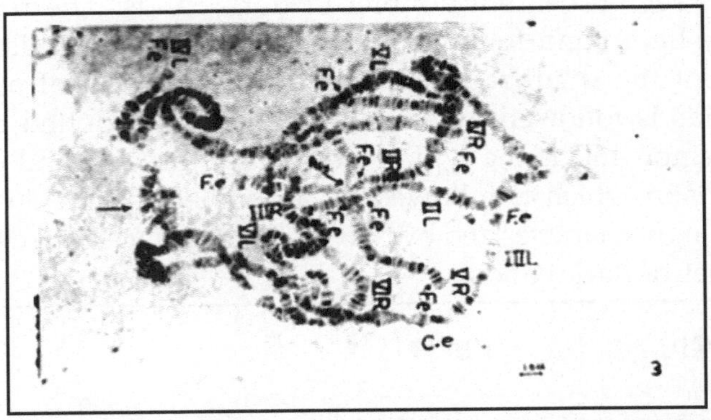

Fig. 7.3: Complete complement of the cell from the pupal thoracic epidermis of *Lucilia sericata Meigen* at 40 X. arrows represent the granular heterochromatic mass of sex chromosomes and asynapsis of chromosomal arm VR

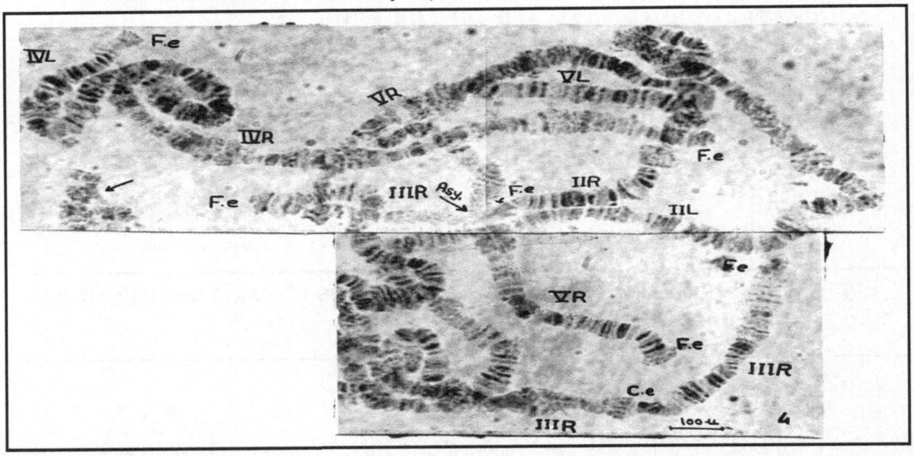

Fig 7.4: Same complement at Higher Magnification 100X. F.e. Free End, C.e. Centromeric end, L= Left arm; R= Right arm

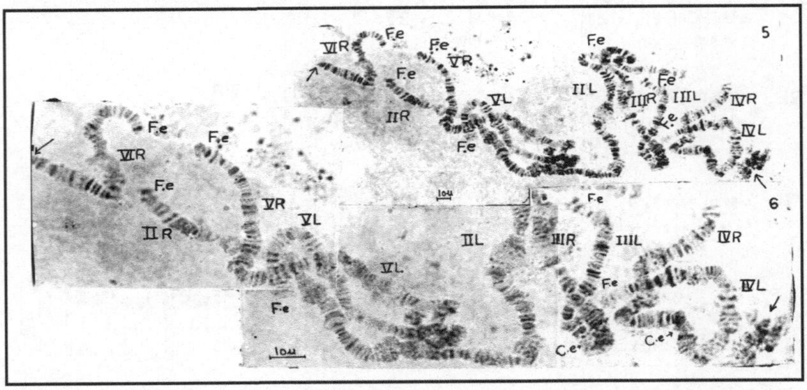

Fig. 7.5: Complete complement of the cell from the Pupal Thoracic epidermis of *Lucilia sericata Meigen.* Arrows represent the granular heterochromatic mass of sex chromosomes and weak spot of chromosomal arm VI R.

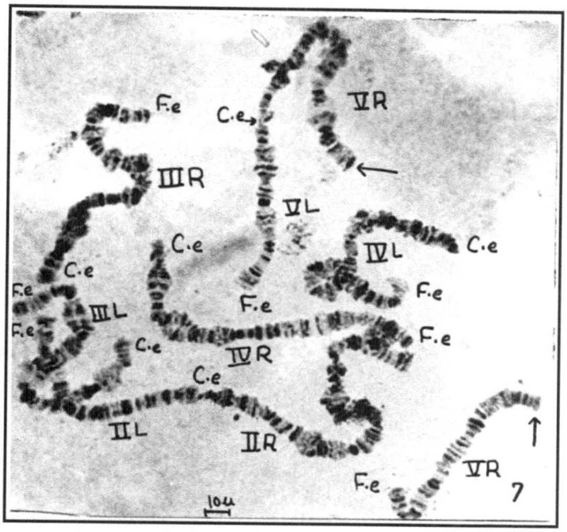

Fig. 7.6: Same complement at Higher Magnification 100X. F.e. Free End, C.e. Centromeric end, L= Left arm; R= Right arm

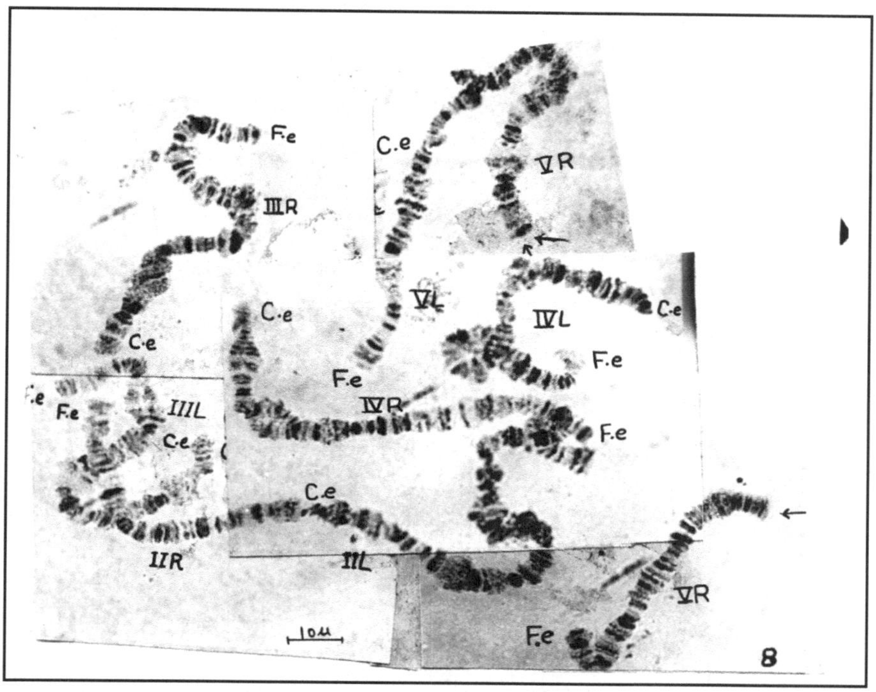

Fig. 7.7: Complete complement of the cell from the Pupal Thoracic epidermis of *Lucilia sericata Meigen.* Chromosomal arms III L and IV R show synapsis. Arrows indicate the broken ends of Chromosomal arm VR

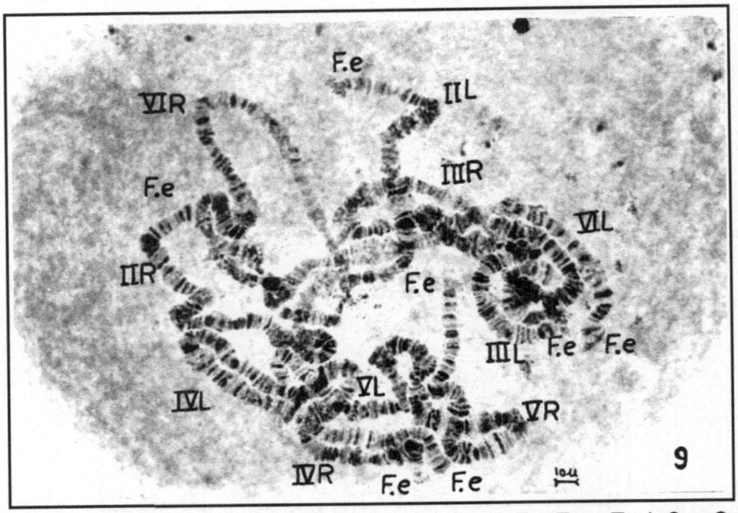

Fig. 7.8: Same complement at Higher Magnification 100X. F.e. Free End, C.e. Centromeric end, L= Left arm; R= Right arm.

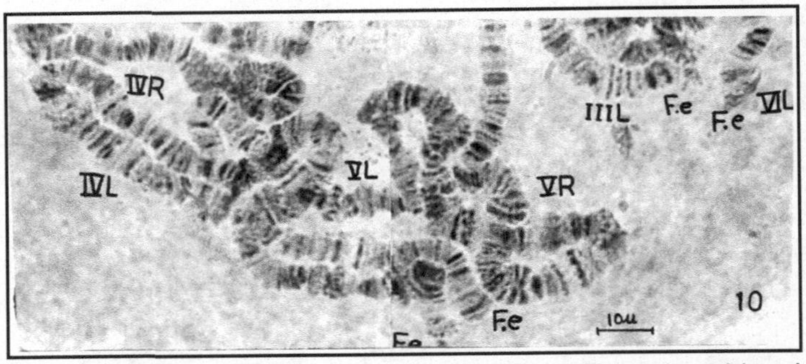

Fig. 7.9: Complete complement of the cell from the Pupal Thoracic epidermis of *Lucilia sericata Meigen*

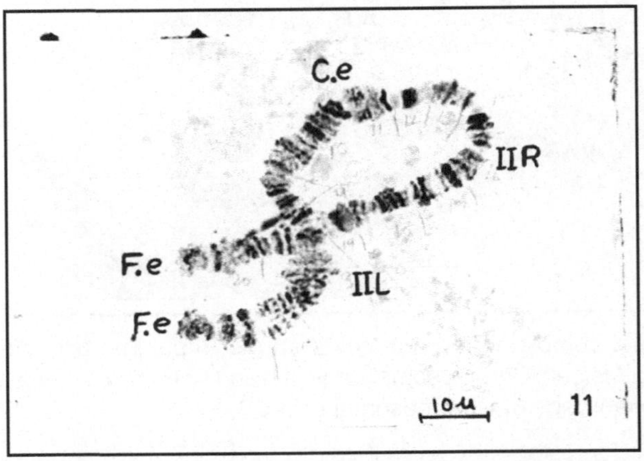

Fig. 7.10: Same complement at Higher Magnification 100X with Chrosomal arms IV L and IV R F.e. Free End, C.e. Centromeric end, L= Left arm; R= Right arm

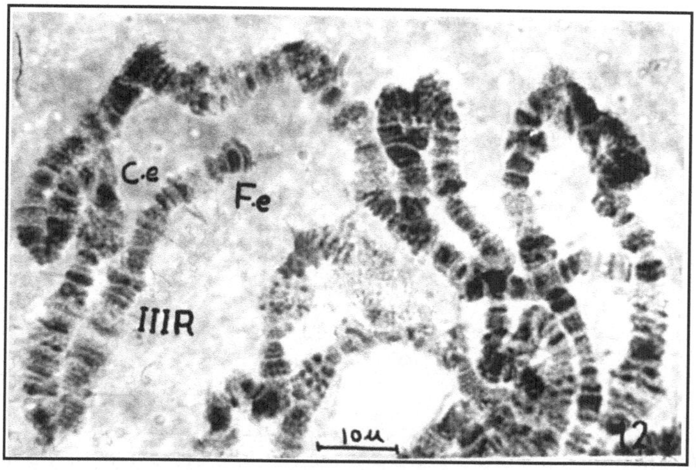

Fig. 7.11: Chromosomal arm II L and II R joined together at their centromere. Chromosomal arm II L show synapsis

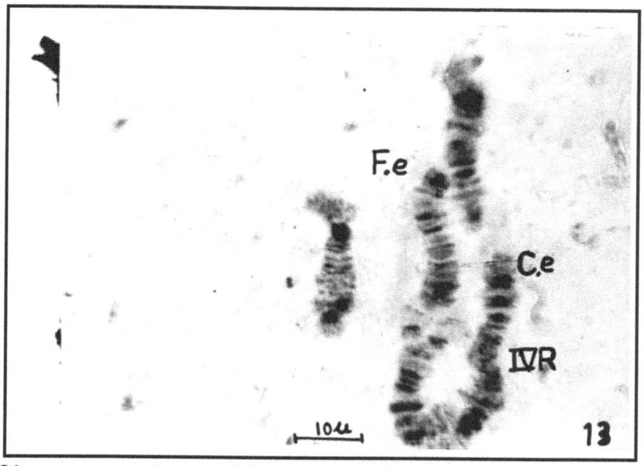

Fig. 7.12: Chromosomal arm IIR representing its free and centromeric ends

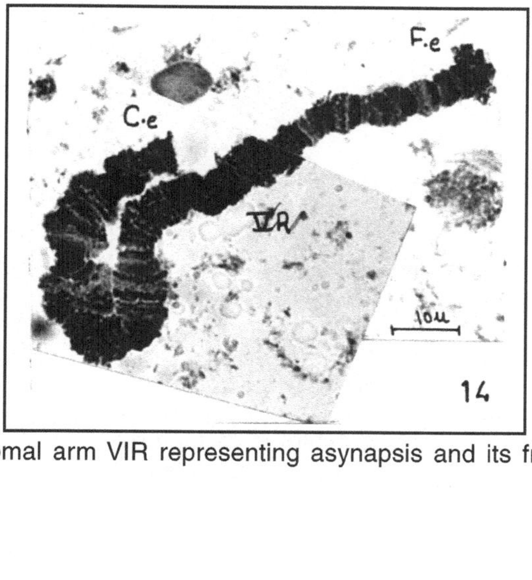

Fig. 7.13: Chromosomal arm VIR representing asynapsis and its free and centromeric ends

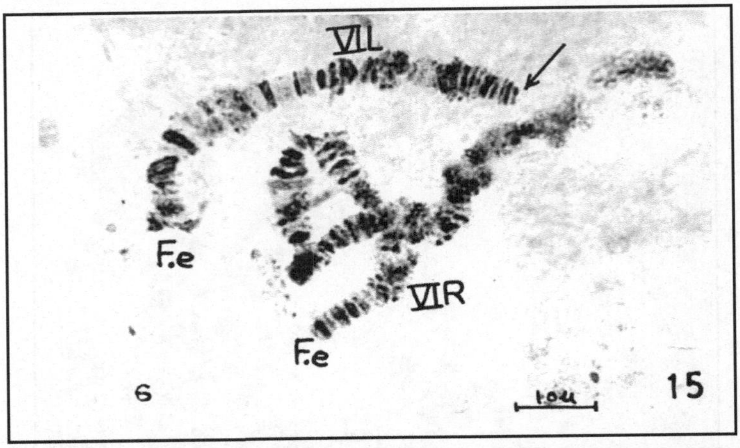

Fig. 7.14: Chromosomal arm VR with its typical flared free and centromeric ends

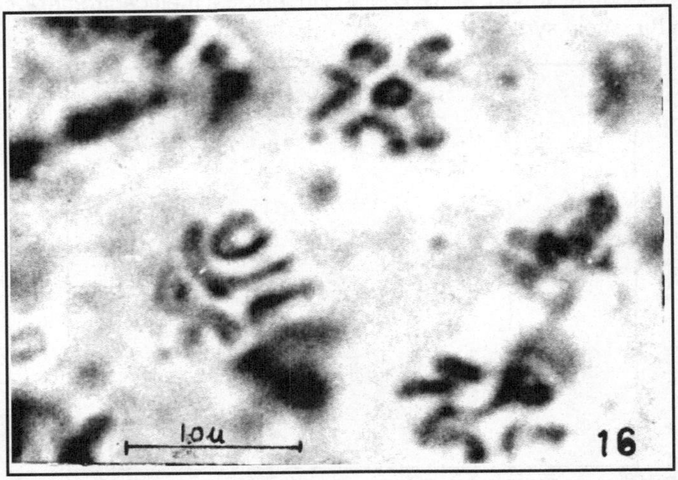

Fig. 7.15: Chromosomal arms VIL and VI R. Arrows indicate weak spots of VI L

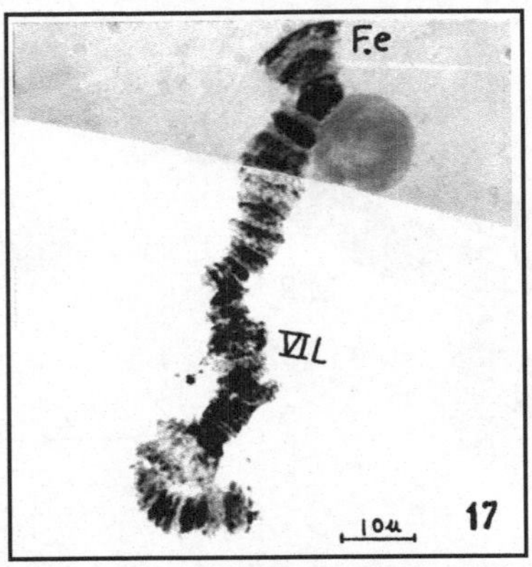

Fig. 7.16: Metaphase I : Dot in the centre of Metaphase I plate represent the granular heterochromatic mass of sex chromosomes

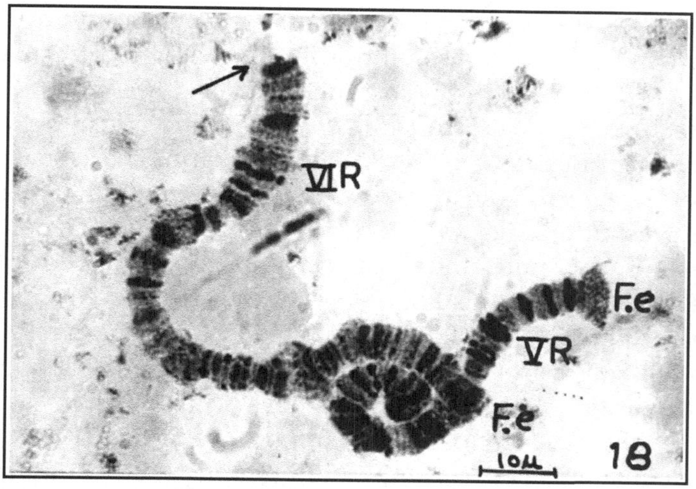

Fig. 7.17: Chromosomal arm VI L

DISCUSSION

The polytene chromosomes of *Lucilia sericata Meigen* consist of five pairs of polytenized euchromatic autosomes and unpolytenized heterochromatic sex chromosomes. The heterochromatin is a loosely organized mass. The centromeric ends of the chromosomal arms of the entire complement meet in the centre and form a chromocentre. A definite chromocentre has been observed in *Sarcophaga bullata* (Whitten, 1969b), *Anopheles stephensi* (Chaudhry, 1971 and 1972), *Lucilia cuprina* (Sharma *et al.*, 1976), *Sarcophaga barbata* (Trepte, 1976), *Parasarcophaga hirtipes* (Handa et al., 1980), *Chrysomyia megacephala* (Handa *et al.*, 1981), *Atherigona orientalis* (Kaur and Kaur, 1985) and *Chironomus striatipennis (kieffer)* (Bhaduri *et.al.*,2011). Chromocentre has been reported to be absent in *Parasarcophaga argyrostoma, P. ruficornis, P. misera, P. Knabi* (Kaul and Tewari, 1978) and *Musca domestica* (Sharma *et al.*, 1979).The chromocentre in the present species seems to be weak and fragile and gets disintegrated under the slightest pressure during squash preparations, resulting in the separation of all chromosomal arms as separate entities. Thus, the survival of the chromocentre in some of the above said species is just incidental. But the right and left arms of the same chromosome united at their centromeric ends have been observed very frequently.

Sex-chromosomes

Metaphase preparations of *Lucilia sericata* have the same diploid complement of chromosomes as described by Fish (1950) and Ullerich (1963), but the giant cells do not show any evidence of polytenized sex chromosomes during the present investigations. In fact, they appear as a loosely organized, granular mass in the giant cells as in the figures. (7.3, 7.4, 7.5, 7.6)

Asynapsis: Frequent asynaptic regions have been found at different places in the chromosomal arms in forms like Drosophila and Anopheles etc. Sharma *et al*. (1979) have reported the rare occurrence of asynaptic regions in the salivary chromosomes of *Musca domestica* but Kaur and Kaur (1982) observed asynapsis in almost every chromosomal arm. The asynaptic regions involved, however, vary from arm to arm and from individual to individual. During the present studies also it has been observed that generally the homologous chromosomes are consistently paired, but there were a few localized regions with identical banding patterns that occasionally showed asynapsis as in figures 7.3, 7.4, 7.7, 7.8, 7.11 and 7.13. These regions varied from cell to cell and from individual to individual. The distribution of these regions in the various chromosomal arms have been shown in Table 7.4. The perusal of the table 7.4 indicates that chromosomal arms IIIR and IVR show more asynaptic regions and zone 42 of VIR is more prone to asynapsis.

Table 7.4: Distribution of Asynaptic Regions in the Various Chromosomal Arms of *Lucilia sericata Meigen*

Sl. No.	Chromosomal Arm	Asynapsis		Fig. No.
		From	To	
1.	IIL	1B	2A	11
2.	IIL	3B	4C	11
3.	IIR	5A		3 & 4
4.	IIR	6B	7A	3 & 4
5.	IIIL	10B	11A	
6.	IIIR	13A		
7.	IIIR	12A	15C	
8.	IIIR	15C		
9.	IVL	17B		3 & 4
10.	IVL	20B		
11.	IVR	21C		
12.	IVR	22A	22B	7, 8 & 13
13.	IVR	24A	24C	
14.	IVR	25A		
15.	IVR	25B		
16.	VL	28A		
17.	VR	31A	31C	
18.	VR	33B	Centromeric end	3 & 4
19.	VIL	38C, D		15
20.	VIR	42B	43B	
21.	VIR	42A	44A	

Puff formation: Sharma *et. al.*, (1979) and Kaur and Kaur (1982) reported the frequent occurrence of puffs in the chromosomal arm IIIR of *Musca domestica*. But during the present investigations a few puffs have been observed in 14B, 15A and 16A regions of IIIR and 27C and 28B of VL chromosomal arms. It appears therefore, that chromosomal arms IIIR and VL show puffing activity more than the other arms.

Weak spots: Dev *et al.* (1985) and Ribbert (1967) have observed definite weak points along various chromosomal arms of *Cochliomyia hominivorax* and *Calliphora arythrocephala* respectively. These breakpoints act as additional landmarks for the identification of these chromosomal arms. During the present studies also prominent weak spots have been observed in chromosomal arms VR, VIL and VIR as in figures 7.1 and 7.2, in regions 31, 39, 40, 45 and 48. These regions have prominent banding patterns and in the beginning of studies, these were repeatedly confused for the free/ centromeric ends. But later on, when complete arms were observed, only then these were proved to represent the weak spots of these particular arms.

Polytene chromosome map:A detailed map of the five polytenized autosomes have been prepared from the macrochaetae of pupal thoracic epidermal cells of *Lucilia sericata Meigen*. The diploid chromosome complement of this fly is 2n = 12. Cytological evidences indicate that both X and Y chromosomes are largely hetero-chromatic, while all the autosomes are either metacentric or submetacentric. According to Childress (1969) in *Lucilia cuprina dorsalis* the sex chromosomes both in the polytene and mitotic preparations appear to be entirely heterochromatic and largely inert, the same results have been observed in the species under present investigations. The autosomal arms in the map have been arranged arbitrarily according to their relative length which corresponds to the mitotic chromosomal complement also. They have been marked from chromosome II to VI in an ascending order of their length. The chromosomal arm VL is the smallest and the chromosomal arm VR is the longest. Upon superficial examination the polytene chromosomes of all the species appear to be sufficiently similar and show a rough general agreement. The apparent homology and correspondence is summarized below.

Species	Chromosomes				
Lucilia sericata (present investigations)	II	III	IV	V	VI
Lucilia cuprina (Sharma et al., 1976)	I	V	II	III	IV
Lucilia cuprina (Kaur and Zope, 1983)	II	III	IV	V	VI
Chrysomyia megacephala (Handa et al., 1981)	II	III	IV	V	VI
Musca domestica (Sharma et al., 1979)	I	III	IV	II	V

A comparison in detail with the available maps of the polytene chromosomes of *Lucilia cuprina* (Sharma *et al.*, 1979 and Kaur and Zope, 1983), *Chrysomyia megacephala* (Handa *et al.*, 1981) and *Musca domestica* (Sharma *et al.*, 1979) with that of *Lucilia sericata,* the species under present study, reveals certain banding patterns showing striking resemblances and differences.

(A) Comparison with *Lucilia cuprina*: Points of similarities/differences in the polytene chromosomes of *Lucilia sericata* and salivary/polytene chromosomes of *Lucilia cuprina* (Sharma *et al.*, 1979; Kaur and Zope, 1983) have been tabulated below:

Table 7.5

Sl. No.	Chromosomal Arm	*L. sericata*	*L.cuprina*
1.	X and Y	Unpolytenized	Polytenized
2.	IIL	Banding pattern almost similar in the maps of two species	
3.	IIR	Banding pattern of zones 5 and 6 is almost similar to the banding pattern of zone 10.	
4.	IIIL	Excepting a few bands here and there the IIIL chromosomal arms are almost alike	
5.		Free end in region 9A	Free end in region 12A
6.	IIIL	Three dark doublets in 9C	Three dark doublets in 12B
7.		A dark band in 10A	A dark band in 13A
8.		Three moderately dark bands in 10CD	Three moderately dark bands in 13B
9.		Two dark doublets in 10D	A dark and a moderately light doublet in 13B
10.		Two dark bands in 11D	Two dark bands in 14E
11.	IIIR	IIIR in two species is almost similar	
12.		Centromeric end in 12A	Centromeric end in 15A
13.		A dark band and three dark doublets in 12C	A dark doublet and a series of three dark bands in 15D
14.		A prominent dark dotted band in 13B	A broad dark band in 15E
15.		A dark band in 15A	A dark band in 16C
16.		A broad dark doublet in 15B	A broad dark doublet in 16C
17.		A dark doublet in 16C constituting the free end	A dark doublet in 17 Constituting the free end
18.	IVL	Region 18B	Region 18B
19.	IVR	Region 23C upto region 24C	Region 24A to region 24C
20.		Zone 25	Zone 25
21.	VL	VL corresponds to VL and generally the banding pattern is same but of course with slight differences here and there	

(Table Contd...)

Sl. No.	Chromosomal Arm	*L. sericata*	*L.cuprina*
22.		Region 27C	Region 26D
23.	VR	From region 30B to 35A	From region 28A upto the middle of 30C
24.		A series of five moderate dark bands in 30B	A doublet and a series of four dark bands constituting the free end in region 28A
25.		A dark doublet in 31A	A dark doublet in 28B
26.		A dark doublet in 32A	A dark doublet in the beginning of 28E
27.		A series of four moderately light bands in 32A	A series of four dark bands in 28E
28.		Three dark bands and a moderate light band in 33B	For dark and a moderate light band in 28G
29.		Two dark dotted bands in 33C	Two moderately dark dotted bands in 29A
30.		Two dark bands in 34A	A dark doublet in 29C
31.		A prominent dark dotted in 34C	A dark band in 30C in a swelling
32.		A dark band in 35A	A dark band at the end of swelling in 30C
33.	VIL	Zone 36	Zone 32
34.	VIR	Region 42A to 44B constituting the centromeric end of VIR	Region 35A to 35E constituting the centromeric end of VIR
35.		Region 43C	Region 36C
36.		Region 43BC	Region 36B
37.		Two dark doublets in 47B	Two dark doublets in 38B
38.		A dark doublet in the constriction in 48D	A dark doublet in the constriction in 38D

(B) Comparison with *Chrysomyia megacephala:* Points of similarities/ differences in the polytene chromosomes of *Lucilia sericata* and *Chrysomyia megacephala* (Handa *et al.,* 1981) have been tabulated below:

Table 7.6

Sl. No.	Chromosomal Arm	*L. sericata*	*C. megacephala*
1.	II	IIL and IIR chromosomal arms are totally different from each other in the maps of two species.	
2.	III	Region 9C upto region 11A	Region 13C upto region 15B
3.		Three dark doublets in 9C	Three dark bands in 13C
4.		A series of dark and moderately dark bands in 10CD	A series of dark and moderately dark bands in 14C and 15A
5.		Dark bands in 11A	Dark bands in 15B
6.	IIIR	Banding pattern of region 13B	Banding pattern of region 18B
7.		Region 13D and 14A	Region 18C
8.		Region 14B	Region 19A
9.		Region 15AB	Region 19C
10.		Excepting the centromeric ends, the chromosomal arm IIIR of two species generally shows identical banding pattern	
11.	IVL	Region 17C upto 18B	Region 21BC
12.	IVR	Region 24AB	Region 25BC of IVR
13.		Excepting the free ends of IVL of the two species, the rest of the banding pattern is same upto the beginning of 19B of sericata and the rest of the region is absent in megacephala	
14.	VL	By and large the chromosomal arms VL of the two species show identical banding pattern.	
15.	VR	Similarly in VR we find that the major bands appear to be same in the two species upto 25C of *sericata* and 27B of *megacephala*.	
16.	VIL	Region 36B	Region 18C
17.		Region 37BC	Zone 40
18.		Region 39B	End of 42A and 42B
19.		A prominent dark dotted band in 40C	A dark dotted band in 42D
20.	VIR	Two dark doublets and a dark band in 44E	A series of dark bands in region 44AB
21.		A prominent dark doublet in 47B	A dark doublet in 47A
22.		A dark doublet in constriction in 48D constituting the free end of VIR	A dark doublet in constriction in 47C constituting the free end of VIR

It appears as if some internal rearrangements i.e. translocations etc. must have occurred in the chromosomes of *Chrysomyia* which have resulted in the formation of the chromosomes with slight modifications and hence the creation of a new genus i.e. *Lucilia.*

(A) Comparison with *Musca domestica:* Points of similarities/ differences in the polytene chromosome map of *Lucilia sericata* with the salivary chromosome map of *Musca domestica* (Sharma *et al.,* 1979) have been tabulated below.

Table 7.7

Sl. No.	Chromosomal Arm	*L. sericata*	*M. domestica*
1.	II	Chromosomal arms IIL and IIR of L.sericata correspond to the chromosomal arms IL and IR of M. domestica	
2.	IIL	A dark band at the end of region 3B	A dark band at the end of 3C in IL
3.		A doublet of dotted band of region 4A in IIL	A doublet of region 4A in IL
4.		A dark doublet at the end of 4B upto the end of 4C	A dark doublet at the same region in IL
5.		A dark band in region 7B	A dark band in 7C of IL
6.	III	A free end in region 9AB in IIIL correspond to the free end of IIIL in 18AB	
7.		A series of dark bands in 10CD	A series of dark bands in 19B
8.		Two doublets in region 11A	A dark doublet in region 20B
9.	IIIR	Shape of centromeric end of IIIR in 12A region correspond to the shape of centromeric end in 21A	
10.		A series of bands and swellings in region 12C upto 13A	A series of bands and swellings in 21C to 22A
11.		Free end of IIIR in 16B and C	Free end in 25A and B
12.	IV	Free end in 17A to 18B of IVL	Free end in 26 zone to the region 27B of IVL
13.		Region 20BC	Region 29D
14.	IVR	Banding pattern of the centromeric end in 21AB is identical to the centromeric end in 30AB	
15.		Two dark doublets and a dark band in region 25A	Three dark bands in 33AB
16.	V	A centromeric end in the region 28C of VL corresponds to the centromeric end in 12CD of IIL	

(Table Contd...)

Sl. No.	Chromosomal Arm	*L. sericata*	*M. domestica*
17.		Region 34BC	Region 16A upto 16C
18.		A free end in region 35CD	A free end in region 17D except the flared tip
19. 20.	VI	Region 40D to 41C of VIL Zone 43 of VIR	Zone 38 of VL Region 39C to 40B of VR
21.		Region 44E to 45C of VIR	Region 41D to 42A of VR

Thus, it appears that the five polytenized chromosomal arms behave as intact units, are relatively stable and have retained their identity. In spite of similarities, many differences like different shapes of free/centromeric ends, asynaptic regions and puffs have also been observed in the present species. The variations are due to species differences or may be of locality. The chromosomes in the two species *sericata* and *cuprina* of the genus *Lucilia* have remained largely conserved during evolution in the family calliphoridae.

SUMMARY

The present work was undertaken to prepare a complete polytene chromosome map from the pupal thoracic epidermal cells of *Lucilia sericata Meigen*. As against the diploid set of twelve chromosomes five pairs of polytenized autosomal chromosomes have been observed in this species.

REFERENCES

Bhaduri, P.N. and Gosh, P.N. 1954: Chromosome Squashes in Cereals. *Stain Technology*, 29: 269-270.

Bhaduri, S., Sarkar, P., Ghosh, C. and Midya, T. 2011: Response of the Chironomid Larvae to the Environmental Condition: A Study on the Polytene Chromosomes of *Chironomus striatipennis (kieffer) The Ecoscan* 5(1&2): 75-80, 2011.

Bier, K. 1960: Der karyotype von *Calliphora erythrocephala Meigen* unter besonderer Berucksichtigung der Nahrzellkern chromosome in gebundelten and gepaarten zustand, *Chromosoma* 11: 335-364.

Bridges, C.B. 1935: Salivary Chromosome Maps with a Key to the Banding of the Chromosomes of *Drosophila melanogaster. Journal of Heredity*, 26, 60-64.

Bridges, C.B. 1942: A New Map of the Salivary Gland 2L-chromosome of *Drosophila melanogaster. Journal of Heredity*, 33, 402.

Brown, W.V. 1972: Text Book of Cytogenetics. The C.V. Mosby Company, Saint Louis.

Chaudhry, S. 1971: Salivary Chromosomes of *Anopheles vogus* (Diptera: Culicidae). *J. Cytol. & Genet. Congr. Supply.* 174-177.

Chaudhry, S. 1972: Studies on the Chromosomes of Some Mosquitoes. Ph.D. Thesis Panjab University, Chandigarh.

Childress, D. 1969: Polytene Chromosomes and Linkage Group – Chromosome Correlations in the Australian Sheep Blow Fly. *Lucilia cuprina* (Diptera: Calliphoridae) *Chromosoma*, 26: 208-214.

Dev, V., LaChance, L.E. and Whitten, C.J. 1985: Polytene Chromosomes of the Screw-worm Fly, *Cochliomyia hominivorax*, *The Journal of Heredity*, 76: 132-133.

Fish, W.A. 1950: The Early Embryonic Development of *Lucilia sericata Meigen* (Diptera: Calliphoridae), Ohio State Univ. Doctoral Dissertation No. 57: 47-53, 1949. Biol. Abstr. No. 31383.

Foster, G.G., Whitten, M.J., Konovalov, C., Bedo, D.G., Maddern, R.H., and Boon, D.J. 1980: Cytogenetic Studies of *Lucilia cuprina dorsalis* R-D (Diptera: Calliphoridae) Polytene Chromosome Maps of the Autosomes and Cytogenetic Localization of Visible Genetic Markers, *Chromosoma,* 81: 151.

Handa, S.M., Kaur, P., Kaur, S. and Neelam Bala, 1980: Salivary Gland Chromosome Map of Parasarcophaga Hirtipes (Diptera Sarcophagidae), *Cytologia*, 46: 441-446.

Handa, S.M., Kaur, P., Kaur, S. and Kaur, H. 1981: Mapping of the Salivary Gland Chromosomes of *Chrysomyia megacephala* (Calliphoridae: Diptera). *Cytologia*, 46: 161-167.

Kaul, D. and Tewari, R.R. 1978: Polytene Chromosomes of the Flesh Fly *Parasarcophaga argyrostoma* (Sarcophagidae: Diptera) *Genetica,* 49: 189.

Kaur, P. 1971: Karyological Studies on Calyptrate Flies (Diptera) Ph.D. Thesis, Panjab University, Chandigarh.

Kaur, P. 1975: Chromosomes of Higher Diptera I. Studies on Chromosomes in Eight Species of Muscidae. *Genetica.*

Kaur, S. 1975: Salivary Gland Chromosomes of *Lucilia cuprina* (Diptera: Calliphoridae) M.Sc. Thesis, Panjab University, Chandigarh.

Kaur, P. 1984: A Cytological Note on the Possible Mode of Origin of *Atherigona orientalis Schin,* from *Musca domestica* L. *Current Science,* 53: 936-939.

Kaur, P. and Kaur, G. 1982: Polytene Chromosomes of *Musca domestica L.* (Muscidae: Diptera) *The Nucleus,* 25: 123-129.

Kaur, P. and Kaur, H. 1985: Salivary Chromosome map of *Atherigona orientalis schin.* (Phaoniinae: Muscidae). *The Nucleus,* 28: 222-228.

Kaur, P. and Zope, A.R. 1983: Studies on *Lucilia cuprina* – a Polytene Chromosome Map from Trichogen Cells. *The Nucleus*, 26: 118-123.

Levan, A. Fredga, K. and Sandberg, A.A. 1964: Nomenclature for Centromeric Positions on Chromosomes. *Hereditas*, 52: 201-221.

Melander, Y. and Wingstrand, K.G. 1953: Gomori's haematoxylin – a Chromosome Stain. Stain Techn. 28-217.

Painter, T.S. 1933: A New Method for the Study of Chromosome Rearrangements and the Plotting of Chromosome Maps. *Science*, 78, 585-586.

Ribbert, D. 1967: Die Polytanchromosomen der Borsten – Bildungszellen Von *Calliphora ervthrocephala. Chromosoma* 21: 296-344.

Ribbert, D. 1972: Relation of Puffing to Bristle and Foot pad Differentiation in Calliphora and Sarcophaga. Results Probl. *Cell Differ.* 4: 153-179.

Sharma, G.P., Handa, S.M., Kaur, P. and Kaur, S. 1976: Salivary Gland Chromosomes of *Lucilia cuprina* (Diptera: Calliphoridae) *Cytobios*, 17: 183-194.

Sharma, G.P., Handa, S.M., Kaur, P. and Chopra, K. 1979: Mapping of Salivary Gland Chromosomes of *Musca domestica* (Muscidae: Diptera). *Cytologia* (Japan), 44: 541-547.

Thomson, J.A., and Gunson, M.M. 1970: Developmental Changes in the Major Inclusion Bodies of Polytene Nuclei from Larval Tissues of Blow Fly, *Calliphora stvoia. Chromosoma*, 30(2): 193-291.

Trepte H.H. 1976: Patterns of Puffing Activity in the Bristle Apparatus Chromosomes of *Sarcophaga barbata. Chromosoma*, 55(2): 137-164.

Ullerich, F.H. 1963: Geschlechtschromosomen und Geschlechtsbestimmung bei einigen Calliphorinen (Calliphoridae, Diptera). *Chromosoma* (Berl.) 14: 45-110.

Ullerich, F.H. 1976: Chromosomen verhaltnisse, Konstitutines Heterochromatin und Geschlechtsbestimmung bei einigen Arten der Gattung *Chrysomyia* (Calliphoridae : Diptera). *Chromosoma* (Berl.), 58:113-136.

Whitten, J.M. 1969b: Co-ordinated Development in the Foot Pad of the Fly *Sarcophaga bullata* during Metamorphosis: Changing Puffing Patterns of the Chromosomes. *Chromosoma*, 26: 215-244.

Zhimulev, I.F. 1996: Morphology and Structure of Polytene Chromosomes. *Advances in Genetics*, 34, 1-490.

Index

P

R

S

T